Cirill.

The New American City
Faces Its Regional Future

The New American City Faces Its Regional Future

A Cleveland Perspective

Edited by

David C. Sweet,
Kathryn Wertheim Hexter,
and
David Beach

OHIO UNIVERSITY PRESS   ATHENS

Ohio University Press, Athens, Ohio 45701
© 1999 by David C. Sweet, Kathryn Wertheim Hexter, and David Beach
Printed in the United States of America
Ohio University Press books are printed on acid-free paper ⊚™

03 02 01 00 99   5 4 3 2 1

Library of Congress Cataloging-in-Publication Data

The new American city faces its regional future : a Cleveland perspective / edited by
    David C. Sweet, Kathryn Wetheim Hexter, and David Beach.
        p.   cm.
    Includes bibliographical references.
    ISBN 0-8214-1278-7 (acid-free paper)
    1. City planning—Ohio—Cleveland Metropolitan Area. 2. Regional planning—
Ohio—Cleveland Metropolitan Area. 3. Urban renewal—Ohio—Cleveland Metro-
politan Area. 4. Community development, Urban—Ohio—Cleveland Metropolitan
Area. 5. Cleveland Metropolitan Area (Ohio)—Social conditions. 6. Cleveland
Metropolitan Area (Ohio)—Economic conditions. I. Sweet, David C. II. Hexter,
Kathryn Wertheim. III. Beach, David, 1957- .

HT168.C54N48 1999

307.76'09771'32—dc21   98-54826

10-2062809

To Maxine Goodman Levin, whose love for the city, and belief in its vitality and viability, was expressed by her endowing a chair at the College in memory of her late husband Albert A. Levin in 1969 and whose subsequent gift to the College enabled it to grow in national stature and influence. Maxine shared the optimistic vision of our city's future and has dedicated her time, talents, and resources to the recovery of one of America's great cities and her neighborhoods.

And to Paul R. Porter, businessman, diplomat, federal official, labor leader, journalist, educator, and eternal optimist. In the 1970s after retirement, he undertook a study of cities and authored The Recovery of American Cities *(1976) and edited* Rebuilding American Cities: Roads to Recovery *(1984) and lifted the vision of Clevelanders of what our city might become.*

The City of Cleveland and The Seven-County Region

LAKE

GEAUGA

Cleveland

CUYAHOGA

LORAIN

MEDINA

SUMMIT

PORTAGE

Prepared by

Northern Ohio Data & Information Service (NODIS)
  a member of Ohio GIS-Net
The Urban Center
Maxine Goodman Levin College of Urban Affairs
Cleveland State University
February 1999 mjs

Contents

Part 3: Toward a Civic Dialogue

Preface

The Regeneration of Cities

David Beach

It is hard to appreciate the expanse of two hundred years—hard to hold in your mind the long, backbreaking process by which a city like Cleveland grew out of the North American wilderness, rode on the crests of American industrialization as the canals and railroads opened up the frontier, and eventually became home to masses of people from the far corners of the world.

My own ability to imagine this stretch of time was helped by a pleasant task I was asked to perform a few years ago for the Cleveland Bicentennial Commission. The commission was producing a book of photographs and short essays to evoke the spirit of the city. My assignment was to write a passage to complement a layout of photos of Moses Cleaveland trees— trees that had been alive two hundred years before when Gen. Moses Cleaveland led the first surveying party to Connecticut's Western Reserve. This is what I wrote:

> So the plaque says you're a Moses Cleaveland tree. A committee measured the diameter of your prodigious trunk (with a steel tape held chest high) and certified that you date from the time of Moses Cleaveland's first and only trip to the wilderness of the Western Reserve in 1796. You managed to survive 200 years

of European settlement, land speculation, agriculture, lumbering, commercialization, industrialization, and suburbanization.

How did you do it? Were you simply lucky enough to grow off the beaten path? Were you a warrior? Were you especially cunning? Did you work hard to cultivate friendly land owners over the years? And after you escaped the ax, what combination of good genes and favorable habitat allowed you to overcome all the other assaults—disease, drought, lightening, wind, insects, soil compaction, air pollution—that weaken trees and eventually kill them?

For, in the absence of a cataclysmic event, a tree dies like a city from a thousand small insults. A drought stresses it. Insects and disease attack more easily. One by one the branches drop. Leaves fall early. There are years of slow decline. Then the tree topples in the wind, and the stump rots away.

But you were stubborn. You rooted in this place and kept sowing your seeds. Two hundred years. A million seeds. A million hopes. Against all odds, you are going to regenerate the native forest.

Cleveland's bicentennial in 1996 offered many Greater Clevelanders a chance to take stock of their city. We pondered how Cleveland endured its first two hundred years. And we wondered how it will sustain itself in the twenty-first century.

It is a lot to wonder about. After all, nothing in civic life is guaranteed. To remain successful, a city must keep reinventing itself against great odds. A city like Cleveland may appear tough and gritty, but it is a fragile organism—a complex web of interdependencies among fellow citizens and the natural ecosystem. Countless individual acts of faith and despair accumulate over the years and, in the balance, build a proud city or squander its potential.

Many of these acts involve seizing opportunities presented by geography and history. In Cleveland's case, its favorable location on the Great Lakes at the northern terminus of the Ohio and Erie Canals propelled its early growth as a mercantile center in the 1830s. After oil was discovered nearby in western Pennsylvania in 1859, Cleveland became the oil refining center of the country under John D. Rockefeller. Similarly, the city capitalized on its strategic location between iron ore and coal deposits to become a leader in iron and steel manufacturing. It capitalized on history, too, as its industries profited and grew on demand created by the Civil War and the two world wars. Historical forces also supplied the waves of immigrants—hundreds of thousands of hopeful people without whose labor the city and its industries could not have been built.

Within a hundred years of its founding in 1796 at the swampy, disease-ridden mouth of the Cuyahoga River, Cleveland had become one of the great commercial and industrial centers of the nation. By 1930 more than nine hundred thousand people called the city home. The growth was astonishingly rapid. But it was also reckless—largely unplanned, heedless of environmental consequences, a creator of extremes of wealth and poverty.

As a result, acts of despair began to weigh against acts of hope. Around the turn of the century the city's wealthier residents began to abandon the city. They established new, independent suburbs with restrictive zoning and real estate covenants that would insulate them from the problems of the city. By 1932 the city was surrounded by suburbs and could no longer grow by annexing land.

Moving to the suburbs became the natural thing for all "sensible" middle-class people to do. And the more natural it became, the more it was supported by public policy and investment. New highways made it easier to commute longer distances. A host of tax policies and aid programs promoted new development rather than the maintenance of older neighborhoods. Government-sponsored "urban renewal" projects actually wiped out whole neighborhoods. By 1965 there were more people in the suburbs of Cuyahoga County than in the city of Cleveland. The exodus, which peaked in the 1970s and 1980s during the massive contraction of heavy industry in the Rust Belt, left behind a city trapped in an insidious spiral of decline as the tax base shrunk and demands for social services grew to meet the needs of an increasingly impoverished population. Although the decline seems to have leveled off in the 1990s and Cleveland has cultivated an image as the "Comeback City," the desperate challenges of poverty, loss of blue-collar jobs, failing public schools, and blighted neighborhoods remain.

Thus, during its second century Cleveland transformed again. From a central, dominant city in which citizens of all incomes and ethnic backgrounds shared a common destiny, the city became a sprawling, multi-county, metropolitan area increasingly divided by race and class.

As Cleveland enters its third century, its fate now depends on a web of interdependencies on the regional scale. People and communities throughout the region are being forced to adjust to new civic roles. The city of Cleveland must understand how it fits into Greater Cleveland. And suburbs must understand their dependence on the historic central city and be drawn into the Cleveland community.

Overcoming the political fragmentation of Greater Cleveland and forging a regional identity will be extremely difficult, but there are recent signs of progress. In fits and starts, people are beginning to ask a new set of questions: Will the new highway entice more people to move from the city to the country? How can polluted industrial land in the city be cleaned up and redeveloped? How can we protect farmland? How can a multicounty region coordinate development so that infrastructure and services can be provided economically in the long run?

Such questions really are not new, but it is new that they are being asked seriously by growing numbers of people in Northeast Ohio. This book captures some of the new thinking bubbling up about Cleveland and its region. The first three chapters—from Cleveland Bishop Anthony Pilla and land use authorities Henry Richmond and David Rusk—are adapted from addresses made at a Cleveland Bicentennial Symposium, "Into the Future: Greater Cleveland 2046," on October 22, 1996, at Cleveland State University. The remaining chapters are contributions from faculty members and staff of CSU's Levin College of Urban Affairs and Urban Center, with an additional contribution from staff of the Citizens League of Greater Cleveland.

A theme running through many of the chapters is the continuing geographic spread of the region. Even though we are not growing much in population or employment in Northeast Ohio, we are consuming more and more land, moving farther and farther out from established urban areas, and all the while providing public subsidies and investments to perpetuate the process. This prompts Bishop Pilla to ask:

> Does this well-established trend represent good stewardship of our valuable agricultural lands? Does it lead to a cleaner environment? Does it strengthen the social fabric of our communities? Does it make cohesive, vibrant family life easier? Does it foster greater civic participation? Does it wisely utilize our fiscal resources? Does it increase our economic competitiveness? Does it further a healthy appreciation of multicultural diversity? Does it better ground our young people in a rooted, meaningful sense of identity marked by

solid values? Does it help break down the isolation of people by race, income, and culture? Does it help bridge the widening gaps that separate rich, poor, and middle class? Does it advance social justice and the common good? I don't think so.

In response, this book offers a new vocabulary for what is possible and necessary. We hear such terms as urban growth boundaries, reducing economic disparities between cities and suburbs, fair and affordable housing requirements, and regional tax-base sharing.

These are the controversial issues with which Northeast Ohio—and metropolitan regions across America—will have to grapple in the coming decades. It won't be easy to summon the political will, for example, to change zoning or to require a growing suburb to share its new tax base with older communities (as they do in the Twin Cities area of Minnesota). But, as David Rusk says, "There are no soft paths to regionalism, only hard choices."

In the end, we will have to make these hard choices if we want to succeed as a region—and if we want to regenerate the heart of the region, the city of Cleveland.

Thanks to all the contributors for allowing their work to be included in this book and for enduring the editorial process with good spirits. David C. Sweet, dean of the Maxine Goodman Levin College of Urban Affairs at Cleveland State University, conceived of the book and assisted its publication. Kathryn Wertheim Hexter, Urban University Program director in the college, was an indefatigable co-editor. The editors wish to acknowledge Susan Petrone, editor, and Barbara Lesiak, administrative assistant, for their exceptional editorial work and administrative skills.

And thanks to all the civic leaders of Northeast Ohio who are grappling with the complex issues of regionalism.

Part of the above passage about Moses Cleaveland trees can be found in *Images from the Heart: A Bicentennial Celebration of Cleveland and Its People,* copyright 1995 by the Cleveland Bicentennial Commission.

Introduction

David C. Sweet and Kathryn Wertheim Hexter

In 1996 the city of Cleveland celebrated its bicentennial. As part of Cleveland State University's contribution to this historic event, the Maxine Goodman Levin College of Urban Affairs convened local and national experts for a symposium on the future of the city and the region. The symposium was part of "Bicentennial Cleveland: 1796–1996 & Into the Future," a public policy series presented by the Levin College, the Citizens League, and the City Club and with the generous support of Herbert Strawbridge, president of the John P. Murphy Foundation. It provided a forum for experts to interact with key decision makers and the general public to create a vision for the future. Equally important, the symposium began to identify the public policies that will be necessary to move us toward that vision.

This book captures the wisdom and insights presented at the symposium and throughout the multipart public policy series. It also draws on the expertise of faculty and researchers in the Levin College and throughout the community, as well as the visions of Greater Clevelanders, to explore how Cleveland can be a leader among its sister cities in beginning to counter the negative effects of urban sprawl. It is hoped that this book will inform the ongoing public debate and dialogue and will stand as a useful guide for civic and political leadership for the twenty-first century.

The City of Cleveland, 1896 and 1996

Prepared by:
Northern Ohio Data & Information Service,
  a member of the Ohio GIS Network
The Urban Center, Levin College of Urban Affairs
Cleveland State University
September 1998 JCW

Figure 0.1. *The city of Cleveland, 1896 and 1996*

In 1896, the Women's Department of Cleveland's First Centennial Commission wrote a letter to the women of 1996 that was placed in a time capsule and was opened as part of the yearlong celebration of Cleveland's bicentennial. Their challenge: "We make you heirs to all we have and enjoin you to improve your heritage."

They described the Cleveland of 1896 (Figure 0.1) as prosperous and beautiful, yet far from ideal. Many of the conditions they described as true for 1896 still hold true one hundred years later: "Many of the people are poor and some are vainly seeking work at living wages . . . sometimes the reigns of government slip from the hands of the people and public honors ill fit some who wear them." They asked: "How are these things with you? What have you done?" Their words, reaching across a century, gave us cause to reflect on the condition of our city. We, too, are prosperous and beautiful, yet far from ideal.

The Cleveland of 1996 is experiencing a pattern of development common among older cities in the United States. Following a period of rapid growth after World War II, the central city since the 1960s has been losing population to its suburbs and outlying counties. At the same time, the population of the Northeast Ohio region has been stable, with little real growth. This pattern of out-migration has come to be called "urban sprawl." It is a complex phenomenon fueled by many factors, such as jobs and the economy, public education systems, race relations, land use, environment, and transportation, and it requires regional solutions that comprehensively address all these factors.

In the spirit of the challenge and the questions posed by the women of 1896, this book looks at the Cleveland of 1996, assesses the condition of the city and region today, and identifies actions to improve our heritage for future generations.

Many of the problems of 1896 are still with us in 1996, but on a much larger geographic scale. Instead of a city, we are concerned with the Northeast Ohio region. The idea of thinking regionally is not new, but it is enjoying renewed attention. Bishop Anthony Pilla has been a key figure in raising public awareness of the importance of this issue through his "Church in the City" initiative. The Bishop and his staff have been working closely with the Levin College and the Ohio Housing Research Network of the Urban University Program, the Citizens League through its "Rating the Region" benchmarking studies, the Regional Environmental Priorities Project at Case Western Reserve University, and others. These programs are working to better understand and document how current patterns of growth and development impact Cleveland, its inner and outer suburbs, and surrounding rural and agricultural land, patterns that will impact the entire region long into the future. As the far-reaching impacts of these regional dynamics become more widely understood, the way in which cities and their regions grow and change is rising in importance on the national, state, and local policy agendas.

Since its founding in 1979, the Levin College has been a neutral convener for public discussion of issues confronting the city and the region. This role is consistent with the college's commitment to nationally recognized excellence in the education and development of leaders, in the search for solutions to urban problems, and in the enhanced understanding of public policy issues. The Levin College provides academic and professional education, expertise, and research capabilities to enhance the quality of life in urban communities.

As part of an urban university, the college takes very seriously its mission to link the university to the community. This linkage is made possible, in large part, by the Ohio Urban University Program (UUP), a statewide program founded by the college in 1979. Since that time, more than $50 million has been invested by the state to establish and build the capacity for urban research and outreach at eight urban universities in Ohio. With Cleveland State's Levin College as the flagship institution, the UUP links the resources of Ohio's eight urban universities with their communities through centers of excellence on each campus and collaborative research networks.

In carrying out this mission, the college sponsored in 1980 its first conference to explore the issues of Cleveland and its future. What emerged was an early call for public-private partnerships. Then, in 1982 the college convened the "Cities Congress on Roads to Recovery" in conjunction with George V. Voinovich, then Cleveland's mayor, and Tom Vail, then publisher and editor of the *Cleveland Plain Dealer*. The event was chaired by Paul Porter, former assistant administrator of the Marshall Plan and author of the book *The Recovery of American Cities* (1976). At that time, Porter was Albert A. Levin Professor of Urban Studies and Public Service. The nationally known developer and urban visionary James W. Rouse was keynote speaker.

The event was the first nationwide congress of cities to focus on the success stories, not the problems, of cities—assets, not deficits. Case studies were presented on fifteen of the fifty-three U.S. cities that had populations of at least 150,000 people in 1970 but that lost population between 1970 and 1980. (These case studies can be found in the book *Rebuilding America's Cities: Roads to Recovery,* edited by Paul R. Porter and David C. Sweet [New Jersey: Rutgers, 1984].) Many of the cities invited to present case studies had initiated self-help programs that did not rely solely on federal aid.

Porter had a clear definition of recovery: "Concretely, recovery means three things: a city's regained ability to compete with suburbs as a place to live; a regained favorable climate for investment and a consequent growth of jobs; and as a consequence of these two, a regained independence from external subsidies" (xii). He continued: "Recovery does not mean a return to any past condition of cities except one. That one is good health, defined to mean a quality of living as good as will be found anywhere else" (xiii). These are useful measures as this book examines the Cleveland of 1996.

Table 0.1. **Cities* that lost population from 1980–96**

City	State	Population (thousands)					
		Change 1970–80		Change 1980–90		Change 1990–96	
		#	%	#	%	#	%
St. Louis	MO	−169	−27.2	−56	−12.4	−45	−11.3
Cleveland	OH	−177	−23.6	−68	−11.8	−8	−1.6
Buffalo	NY	−105	−22.7	−30	−8.4	−17	−5.2
Detroit	MI	−311	−20.5	−175	−14.5	−28	−2.7
Pittsburgh	PA	−96	−18.5	−54	−12.7	−20	−5.4
Rochester	NY	−53	−18.0	−12	−5.0	−8	−3.5
Louisville	KY	−64	−17.7	−28	−9.4	−9	−3.3
Flint	MI	−33	−17.1	−19	−11.9	−6	−4.3
Dayton	OH	−40	−16.5	−21	−10.3	−9	−4.9
Washington	DC	−119	−15.7	−31	−4.9	−64	−10.5
Cincinnati	OH	−69	−15.2	−21	−5.5	−18	−4.9
Minneapolis	MN	−63	−14.5	−3	−0.8	−9	−2.4
Newark	NJ	−53	−13.9	−54	−16.4	−6	−2.2
Akron	OH	−38	−13.8	−14	−5.9	−6	−2.7
Syracuse	NY	−27	−13.7	−6	−3.5	−8	−4.9
Philadelphia	PA	−261	−13.4	−102	−6.0	−108	−6.8
Norfolk	VA	−41	−13.3	−6	−2.2	−28	−10.7
Gary	IN	−23	−13.1	−35	−23.0	−6	−5.1
Baltimore	MD	−118	−13.0	−51	−6.5	−61	−8.3
Richmond	VA	−30	−12.0	−16	−7.3	−5	−2.5
Milwaukee	WI	−81	−11.3	−8	−1.3	−37	−5.9
Chicago	IL	−364	−10.8	−221	−7.4	−62	−2.2
Warren	MI	−18	−10.1	−16	−9.9	−7	−4.8
Bridgeport	CT	−14	−8.9	−1	−0.7	−4	−2.8
Toledo	OH	−28	−7.3	−22	−6.2	−15	−4.5
New Orleans	LA	−35	−5.9	−61	−10.9	−20	−4.0
Birmingham	AL	−17	−5.6	−19	−6.7	−9	−3.4
Kansas City	KS	−7	−4.2	−9	−5.6	−9	−5.9

*Cities with populations greater than 150,000 in 1970, but which lost population by 1980.

The 1980s and 1990s were decades of rebuilding in Cleveland through public-private partnerships. Through these partnerships, it can be argued, we started to slow down or turn around the massive population losses. This is clearly illustrated in Table 0.1, which presents the rate of population loss for the 28 of 53 cities in Porter's study that continued to lose population from 1980 to 1996. Among these cities, Cleveland's rate of population loss slowed dramatically from 23.6% (1970 and 1980) to 1.6% (1990–96). While we have not solved all of our problems, substantial progress has been made, and the next set of challenges is clearly in focus.

In Cleveland in 1982 Rouse challenged the cities in attendance at the conference to develop a long-range vision of what a city might become. He inspired those in attendance to look beyond the day-to-day problems of the city and to develop a vision for the future—"A Civic Vision."

Between 1982 and 1996 the city of Cleveland did in fact create a civic vision that served as a plan for development of the downtown and neighborhoods. Drawing on a nationally renowned public-private partnership, the city, county, and state governments, foundations and business leaders, using significant federal funding and tax incentives, set about implementing that vision.

By 1988 Cleveland was being hailed as the comeback city. The economic base was more diverse, industries were more competitive, and the region as a whole was more attractive to industry and business. In the 1990s close to two thousand new housing units and several retail centers were built in Cleveland neighborhoods. These additions, along with the Gateway sports complex, the North Coast Harbor, and other major downtown developments, were physical evidence of the success of that partnership.

However, the question remains—are Cleveland and the region competitive as a place to live and invest? A great deal was accomplished in the 1980s and 1990s, but much of it was in the downtown and outside the city limits. Looking beyond the physical development, we find that the region is characterized by political fragmentation, racial division, large income and education differentials, and interjurisdictional competition. For the region, the bottom line is the lack of a shared sense of community and common destiny. With the recognition that the future of Cleveland in many ways depends on the strength of the region, the biggest challenge for the future is to create a vision for the region that will enable us to achieve regional viability.

In 1996 the Bicentennial Symposium challenged participants to focus on creating their vision for the future fifty years hence—a comprehensive vision that went beyond bricks and mortar. It brought together professionals working on these issues in the public and private sectors, civic leaders, local and state political leaders, students, and the general public. Participants represented the central city, inner suburbs, outer suburbs, and rural and surrounding counties.

In his keynote address Bishop Anthony Pilla articulated his vision for a new pattern of development in the region, one that is healthier, sounder, fairer, and wiser. This moral imperative set the tone and provided the framework for the other presenters and the following discussions. David Rusk and Henry Richmond, both nationally recognized urban strategists, guided the participants in identifying the steps needed to move toward that vision. The Citizens League made its first public presentation of its updated report "Rating the Region," which set the stage for panel discussions of the issues.

This book draws on the information presented at the symposium and supplements it with the findings and policy implications of researchers and practitioners who are looking seriously at the broad spectrum of issues that will impact the future of the region.

Part 1 of the book sets the stage and details the challenge. Bishop Pilla argues that we are all in it together; people living in the suburbs cannot isolate themselves from the people living in the city and vice versa—their futures are inextricably linked. Rusk and Richmond offer such strategies as regional land use planning, urban growth boundaries, tax-base sharing to narrow the disparities, and regionwide requirements for fair and affordable housing. Bier, Krumholz, and Hexter provide a perspective and a context in which to better understand the dynamics of the region.

Part 2 sheds some new light on the complex issues that will need to be squarely addressed in the civic dialogue about our regional future. Hill takes a hard look at the region's economic trends, challenging us to create a balanced economic recovery that does not leave behind a large part of the region's population. Chandler looks at race relations; Star and Rittenhouse look at leadership development, citizenship, and civic participation. Weisblat, Slone, and Petrone offer strategies for engaging our youth in civic affairs. Bryant looks at the collaborative economic development efforts by Northeast Ohio's corporate and business leaders.

Part 3 describes two efforts to engage citizens in a dialogue about the future of the region. Purdy and Eugene, both formerly of the Citizens League, present benchmarking as a tool for comparing the performance of the region with other regions across the country. The final chapter, by Kaufman and Kellogg, summarizes Levin College's community-wide visioning exercise that encouraged people living in the region to develop and share, in writing, their vision for its future in the year 2046. More than fifty people submitted their visions of the future, including who must act and how. In the conclusion, Sweet calls for the creation of a civic vision for the region.

In 2046, at the midpoint of Cleveland's third century, the city and region will have changed in ways we cannot even imagine today. However, as we learned from the women of 1896, the fundamental, quality-of-life issues are likely to remain. This book has tried to capture some of the best thinking about these issues as we seek to position the region for the next century. The contributors challenge us to look beyond the political, social, and economic barriers that separate us and to work together to forge a shared vision for our future.

Part 1

Toward a New City

*We are at a very crucial fork in the road. . . . We now have
an opportunity to continue our united thrust to address the still
unsolved issues of our public schools, improving race relations,
strengthening job training, upgrading urban housing, and promoting true regionalism.*

*It is totally in our hands which fork in the road we take—a
return to the past with missed opportunities or that New American City shining brightly on the hill, on the North Coast Harbor,
in the heart of America.*

—Robert Gillespie, co-chair, Cleveland
Bicentennial Commission and CEO and
Chairman of the Board, KeyCorp, Cleveland

Chapter 1

Toward a New City of
Justice and Peace

Bishop Anthony M. Pilla

*In 1993 Cleveland Roman Catholic Bishop Anthony M. Pilla caused a
local and national stir by releasing "The Church in the City," a paper
that challenged the nearly one million members of the Cleveland diocese to consider the moral dimensions of urban sprawl in Northeast
Ohio. Pilla argued that public policies that promote development at
the edge of the metropolitan area also promote the decline of the
urban core, and he urged all members of the Greater Cleveland community to come together, recognize their interdependence, and work
for more balanced development. As Pilla says, "Our fates are intertwined economically, socially, and spiritually." For everyone's benefit,
therefore, we need a change of policies—and a change of heart.*

This chapter is adapted from Pilla's address at "Greater Cleveland 2046: A
Bicentennial Symposium" at Cleveland State University on October 22, 1996.

I would like to start with a quote from the famous Athenian statesman
Pericles: "All things good on this earth flow into the city because of the
city's greatness." What a contrast such a view provides with what we so
often hear, see, and perceive about American cities today. It is a sign of

our times that such a venerable perspective can sound incongruous or even jarring to many across our country. Our region, Northeast Ohio, home to nearly two and a half million people, is no exception to the national mindset so wrapped up in the pattern of development described as out-migration or sprawl. Indeed, local and national studies point to our area as a prime example of the dramatic demographic and social shifts that have occurred in the United States over the past decades.

In November of 1993 I issued a statement that tried to analyze and address the challenge of sprawl in Northeast Ohio from my vantage point as bishop of the Cleveland Catholic diocese. What has come to be called "The Church in the City" vision challenged the almost one million Catholics who live in the eight counties of our diocese to recognize the fundamental interdependence in our lives as a church and as a metropolitan community.

In 1996 we celebrated our 150th year as a diocese. Over that time span I believe we have made remarkable contributions to the three central cities of our diocese and region. Catholic parishes, schools, social services, and social action have enriched the Akron, Cleveland, and Lorain/Elyria urban centers through the ministries of dedicated women and men. Those contributions must continue, but they are seriously affected by years of out-migration.

Many factors have fueled the complex phenomenon of out-migration. No doubt deep societal issues of color, class, and culture have been and continue to be powerful influences. Surveys note the importance of fear of crime and concern about educational quality. For much of our national history, moving up the socioeconomic ladder has meant moving out. Nevertheless, careful study indicates that, over the past few decades, unbalanced public and private investment decisions have accelerated out-migration. Not too long ago some 900,000 people lived in Cleveland, while approximately 450,000 lived in the suburban parts of the diocese. Now the numbers are virtually reversed. As population has changed, so, too, have the tax bases of our cities. At a time when there are growing concentrations of poverty in our urban cores, fiscal resources are strained, if not scarce. Recent research points to the spread of this pattern in our inner ring of suburbs.

Support for the maintenance and redevelopment of central cities, and now inner-ring suburbs, has simply not been comparable to the underwriting of sprawl. Unbalanced investment promoted housing and economic growth in outlying areas to the detriment of older urban neighborhoods. That kind of unbalanced investment did not provide people with fair choices if they wanted to remain in more established neighborhoods. That pattern of unbalanced investment has brought us to an anomalous situation in Northeast Ohio—we basically have flat regional population growth yet we spread out over more and more land. We have sprawl without growth.

Does this well-established trend represent good stewardship of our valuable agricultural lands? Does it lead to a cleaner environment? Does it strengthen the social fabric of our communities? Does it make cohesive, vibrant family life easier? Does it foster greater civic participation? Does it wisely utilize our fiscal resources? Does it increase our economic competitiveness? Does it further a healthy appreciation of multicultural diversity? Does it better ground our young people in a rooted, meaningful sense of identity marked by solid values? Does it help break down the isolation of people by race, income, and culture? Does it help bridge the widening gaps that separate rich, poor, and middle class? Does it advance social justice and the common good? I don't think so.

Within our Catholic diocese, we have 237 parishes. But whether people belong to an urban, suburban, exurban, or rural parish, we are all called to be one body with one mission. In the context of our faith, this call to unity is not an option. It is who we are as a Catholic Church. We are called to be a single-faith community, respecting our diversity but united in solidarity with the whole human family. No matter where we live or who we are, we have gifts and talents to build upon and share with others. We also all have needs and challenges to face. We need each other to grow and develop into the fullness of who we can be as individuals, as families, as communities, and as a people. That is all rather easy to say but much harder to translate into reality, as you can well imagine.

I issued "The Church in the City" statement to motivate an attitudinal change that could help people take different steps in the personal, public, and social arenas of their lives. As a pastor and teacher, I hoped it could be a lens through which to see our church, our community, our region, and ourselves in a fresh way. We are far more interdependent than our many civic or organizational boundaries would lead us to believe. Increasingly, we share one economy and one environment. Whether we live in city, suburb, or country, we are one metropolitan society. Our fates are intertwined economically, socially, and spiritually. Our geographic boundaries can be illusions that distract us from the real needs and the real capabilities of the region in which we live.

For example, a growing body of scholarly literature shows that regions where the income of suburban residents has been growing the least are areas where the income of city residents has grown the least. Suburbs and cities are linked in a single economy. Employers will invest where negatives are fewer. The negatives that have resulted in our region from more than forty years of building new suburbs while abandoning older cities have accumulated to where they are serious obstacles to economic growth. All of us are paying the price for sprawl.

Our social and economic separation is problematic not only because of its personal and social destructiveness, but because it is costly. Communities in the urban centers—inner-ring suburbs as well as the central city— struggle with out-migration. They face aging infrastructures, declining revenue bases, and growing concentrations of people with reduced income. At the same time, previously rural communities struggle with rapid population growth, increasing demand for expensive services and infrastructures, and an often disruptive pace of social change, as well as the serious issue of prime farmland being lost for agricultural use.

The challenge to stem sprawl and redevelop our urban centers is not simply a task for the people of Cleveland or Akron or Lorain. It is a challenge and task for the whole metropolitan region. It is foolish to think that we can have a thriving region and a continually declining urban core. We miss a crucial opportunity in carrying forth our responsibility to build a good and just society when we do not recognize this common responsibility. The wisdom, talents, and resources of all the people of our cities, suburbs, and rural areas are to be appreciated and shared in service to the whole of our regional community. Too often we isolate rather than share these resources. I believe that the isolation of the poor and vulnerable members of our community particularly wounds the whole community. We are all impoverished when society fails to incorporate into its political and economic policies measures to empower those left out of the mainstream. At the same time, no public policy can totally rebuild what is broken in our families and communities. We must rebuild the moral fiber of neighborhoods as we rebuild the economic and social fiber. That will take new partnerships as well as new policies.

Creating those kinds of empowering partnerships and advocating for more rational, just public policies are key components of the ongoing implementation of "The Church in the City" vision. The people of our diocese were asked to submit recommendations for an implementation plan through the first half of 1994. A task force was then formed to develop that plan. A broad consultative process took place through 1995 across the eight counties of the diocese. Parishes, schools, colleges, religious congregations, interfaith gatherings, and civic and business groups came together in various formats to discuss "The Church in the City" vision and plan. A few months ago we announced the completed plan.

At the heart of the implementation plan is a call to a change of heart that recognizes the reality of interdependence in all areas of our lives as residents of Northeast Ohio. As might be expected, some are not comfortable with that challenge. For some the image of our cities is based on flight and fear rather than solidarity and compassion. Some feel overwhelmed with the stresses and strains of their own lives. But we have also heard a multitude of voices from all around the diocese that give me great hope. Overall, the responses indicate basic acceptance and support for our implementation plan as a guiding framework for what we can do as a church over the next five to ten years. I believe that more people than ever are asking the right questions and are more willing than ever to reflect on our responsibilities as believers and as citizens. What does it mean to be a church in our time? What does it mean to be an active citizen in Northeast Ohio? What does it mean to work for the common good?

Many people evinced an openness to exploring new kinds of partnerships. One of the major action priorities relates to developing parish-to-parish partnerships. I am especially pleased with some of the emerging models of urban-suburban parish partnerships. These involve relationships that reflect a true sense of mutuality, of respecting each other's gifts, of listening and learning from each other, no matter where people live or what their background is. We have established a new Church in the City grants program to assist parish and school partnerships of that type. People from very different realities have begun to gather regularly. I am very encouraged by these steps, because if we know each other, and especially if we are friends, a great deal is possible. If we are strangers, little is possible.

Another priority area involves ongoing education, prayer, and leadership training that emphasizes "we are all in this together." We will give special attention to experiences that bring people together, bridge the gaps that separate us, and transcend the racial and economic tensions that too often divide us. We will also continue educational forums about "The

Church in the City" vision with special attention to the complex, multi-faceted nature of regional sprawl. We hope to further understanding about how we already are interdependent in Northeast Ohio, as well as help create more common ground for unified, cooperative responses. Regions that are divided against themselves will languish and decline.

Redevelopment of our central cities is a third major priority area. For us as a church, redevelopment means joining with a wide range of part-ners—neighborhood groups, business, labor, government—to create greater housing and job opportunities. It means acting as conveners, catalysts, and anchors for community-based economic development initiatives. We can-not do such work alone. Nor do we want to. We are committed to collab-oration. Our mission and work in the revitalization of our urban com-munities are paralleled in significant ways by the commitments of other faith traditions. Our common mission as people of faith and our mutual concern for those most at risk challenge us to cooperate rather than com-pete with each other. I welcome opportunities for interfaith dialogues and partnerships. Similarly, I hope that we can do much more to create a respectful and cooperative spirit between Catholic and public schools so that we can provide the best possible educational opportunities for all chil-dren, especially those in the poorest and most disadvantaged situations.

The fourth and final priority area I want to touch on is advocacy. We are building on our already extensive advocacy efforts for social justice based on the substantial body of Catholic social teaching by forming a new diocesan regional land use committee. It will promote and advocate public policies that are economically, environmentally, socially, and mor-ally responsible. This is not only a new advocacy arena for the Cleveland diocese but the first such step nationally.

I am very pleased with what is happening with "The Church in the City" process. I know that we have a long, long way to go. But in the early days of this journey, it is clear that this initiative continues to be challenging and inspiring. In the public sphere, both locally and nation-ally, it has received remarkable attention. That says to me that we have touched a real chord in people's lives, one that seems to resonate with their hopes for a future pattern of development that is healthier, sounder, fairer, and wiser.

Nurturing that kind of hope is extremely important. Some studies have shown that today we live in one of the most cynical of times. Negativity, criticism, and disrespect seem to have no boundaries. Cynicism runs so deep that it appears to choke the hope and life from many of our youth, especially in our cities. I believe the loss of hope is a major societal problem today. It paralyzes rather than catalyzes effective action.

I believe that each one of us can make a difference. Our choices and actions can help lead to a different future. We can create new cities, the kind our society longs for—cities where people of different incomes, races, and cultures can live together and be enriched by each others' presence. We can begin to build a new city of justice and peace if we really commit ourselves to that noble task. If we undertake that challenge, we will also reclaim Pericles' vision of the polis as a community of citizens with a full, rich, dynamic understanding of the responsibilities of citizenship. The polis referred to more than a place; it referred to a way of behaving and living in community.

Too many in our society today feel outside the polis, feel alienated and cut off from even thinking about full participation and mutual responsibility. Let me be clear: this is not only an inner-city issue. Disaffection with the civic arena and the political process, as well as social irresponsibility, is rife all across our society, across all kinds of locations and backgrounds. I believe we have to rediscover that older meaning of citizenship as an everyday activity and common responsibility. It means much more than voting, and we know it is not even that for more and more Americans. I fear we are losing the sense that our society is built by and rooted in ordinary citizens who day in and day out lead their private lives and make public contributions in the polis with integrity, commitment, and pride. Citizenship should once again be a badge of honor, a cherished title, an emblem of hard work and dedication to social justice. Our ancestors did it. Why can't we?

Can we really say that our times today are more difficult than those faced by our forebears? Are they more difficult than those faced by African Americans who survived slavery and segregation? Are they more difficult than those faced by Hispanics who survived colonization and discrimination? Are they more difficult than those faced by European immigrants who survived poverty and prejudice? My own father came to this country with a nickel in his pocket. Literally one nickel. Growing up in the city, I know well the struggles he and so many others like him and my mother—good, hardworking people of all races, religions, and backgrounds—faced.

They built our cities brick by brick. Today we, their sons and daughters, are called to build and rebuild—not so much buildings and streets as lives and relationships, one by one.

I believe that together we can meet that challenge; we can plant more seeds and lay more of the right foundations for a better future, one marked by more peace, harmony, and justice for all the people of our metropolitan community. Then we will truly be able to reclaim the view of cities set forth by Pericles for our time and place. In doing so we will not only strengthen our region and revive our city, but we will also enliven democracy and advance justice. Finally, we will then be coming closer to the biblical vision of "the Holy City, the place where God is encountered, the promise of the city which comes from on high." That is our challenge, that is our responsibility, and that is our opportunity.

Chapter 2

Model Strategies
for Greater Cleveland

Henry R. Richmond

Suburban sprawl and urban disinvestment are undermining national goals of prosperity, equal opportunity, and environmental quality. Fortunately, Greater Cleveland and other metropolitan areas can rein in sprawl with such strategies as urban growth boundaries (UGB), programs for fair and affordable housing, farmland protection, and regional tax-base sharing. Contrary to popular belief, these strategies are compatible with a free real estate market, protect the rights of the majority of property owners, and are prodevelopment in the long run.

Henry Richmond was a founder and longtime executive director of 1000 Friends of Oregon and is a nationally recognized expert on land use issues. He also has chaired the National Growth Management Leadership Project, a network of state and regional organizations promoting development that conserves land, is fiscally responsible, and is environmentally sustainable. This chapter is adapted from his address at "Greater Cleveland 2046: A Bicentennial Symposium" at Cleveland State University on October 22, 1996.

Think Patiently, Act Locally

In talking about model growth management strategies for the Greater Cleveland metropolitan area, the year 2046 time frame you have set for our discussions is on target. The patterns of development that concern you are the result of forces that have been at work for many decades. There is no law or policy of any kind that can fix these problems quickly or easily. Even if we assume everyone wanted change, even if we assume everyone wanted the same change, there is no switch that can be flipped to change what we have. This situation we face is physical in nature. Changing that situation is thus essentially a question of how development will occur in the future. As I will discuss later, we have to build, not regulate, our way out of the problems we face.

The long-range time frame is a challenge. Decades don't fit into election cycles very well. The political benefits of politically difficult action on regionwide issues don't usually occur before the next election. Thus, the long-range time frame requires both persistence and patience.

A state and local focus is also important. It's true, federal money for highways, public housing, mortgage interest deductions, and many other federal programs contribute to local sprawl and disinvestment. However, if state legislatures reformed the local zoning and property tax systems that states created long ago, the geographic consequences of federal policies and dollars would be largely benign. So the focus is really state and local. From a national perspective, that makes the land use reform effort rather untidy. From the perspective of local communities, it means that both problems and solutions are within reach.

In other countries, land use—how societies develop as a physical matter, how development happens in Gloucestershire, Oslo, or Hamburg—is a subject of national policy. We don't have that in this country. We can't have that in this country—because of our federal system. Indeed, we probably shouldn't have it in this country. Local land use patterns are too varied and too voluminous in their administrative detail. So, a state and local focus is definitely appropriate.

What Are Our Purposes?

We are all deeply indebted to Cleveland Bishop Anthony Pilla for reminding us that any strategy we may want to talk about must be judged in terms of higher social purposes. Whether we are talking about tax-base sharing or urban growth boundaries—which I will discuss in some detail—land use strategies are not ends in and of themselves. We should refer to these purposes when we are evaluating our existing patterns of development, whether in Cleveland; Portland, Oregon; Tallahassee; or wherever. We also should use those purposes when evaluating or advocating alternative development patterns.

Importantly, the purposes of land use policy should not be derived from technicians or planners or advocacy groups. Our purposes, our criteria, so to speak, should be basic social goals most Americans agree on — consensus goals, duly chosen long ago, through established majority rule procedures. These include goals of prosperity and economic strength, the goal of equal opportunity found in the U.S. Constitution and many state constitutions, and the goal of environmental quality.

There are other goals, but these three probably should be the key criteria for judging the performance of our land use patterns, as well as for judging the strategies to bring about alternative patterns. With these purposes in mind, we can ask, "How well do existing patterns serve households and businesses? How might alternative patterns better serve communities?"

Bishop Pilla is providing great national leadership. He is helping us all see how and why development patterns have powerful social impacts. He is teaching us how to judge land use patterns. The criteria he advances are not essentially different from those I just mentioned. Equal opportunity is rooted in the idea of the inherent dignity of each human being. That principle is at the core of Catholic social doctrine, as is the idea of the common good that Bishop Pilla emphasizes so eloquently. The idea of protecting the environment, of conserving natural resources, has a similar religious root — the ancient concept of man being a good steward of a holy gift, the earth, the creation.

So there isn't much of a gap between our society's fundamental policy goals and the religious or moral principles Bishop Pilla speaks of. These two sources of guidance should be joined for purposes of framing a regional conversation. What are people and communities getting from development patterns? How does the physical reality we all see and live in stack up against what most of us want as a society?

Local Land Use Patterns
Are Undermining National Goals

My purpose is to discuss strategies — eight of them — that will advance basic social goals. These are strategies that can ameliorate the social harms caused by the kinds of land use patterns typically seen throughout America today. While my assignment here is to point out strategies and not the gloomy enormity of land use problems, my suggestions need context.

First of all, it's important to bear in mind that local land use patterns are undermining basic national goals. Suburban sprawl and urban disinvestment undermine prosperity, equal opportunity, and environmental quality. Second, it's important to understand how public policy at all levels of government directly and indirectly causes these local land patterns. Direct government subsidies for sprawl include highways and sewers. Indirect government subsidies for sprawl include support for single family residential (but not multifamily) mortgages; utility rate systems that require cheap-to-serve urban ratepayers to subsidize costly-to-serve suburban customers; and tax treatment of house sales (now less of a problem since the 1997 changes in capital gains tax law).

Sprawl and urban abandonment are also due to the inability of the market to ensure that the prices of sprawl development incorporate all the costs of sprawl development. Or as the economists would say, the ability of suburban development to "externalize" costs—to push them off on other people. Government's failure to respond to this "market failure" is another type of subsidy. It has the same effect as highway-building and mortgage benefits because fobbed-off costs don't have to be reflected in price. The lower prices that result confer a competitive advantage.

The combination of government policies favoring sprawl and government's failure to respond to market failure results in a regionwide dynamic: development patterns characterized by the constantly outward-moving location of private investment—a dynamic that creates jobs and boosts tax bases in one part of the metropolitan region and eliminates them in other parts.

In the Chicago region, for example, from 1970 to 1990, 81 percent of the region's new jobs were created in a few northwestern suburbs where only 18 percent of the region's people live. Jobs are going farther and farther out, in many cases beyond where existing public transportation operates. The low rate of car ownership of people in inner cities means this phenomenon is a problem for both workers and employers.

Equal Opportunity

How is this government-induced movement of investment undermining national goals? Equal opportunity is an example. There were about four million slaves in 1860. There are now 5.9 million African Americas living in "the ghettos" in American cities. A "ghetto" is defined by sociologists and urban geographers as a place where the poverty rate is at least 40 percent. Think of that. Think of where you live. Think how it would be if at least 40 percent of the households in your neighborhood were poverty households, neighborhoods with high crime, failing schools, and the joblessness that William Julius Wilson describes so powerfully in his new book, *When Work Disappears*. The neighborhoods Wilson analyzed were not just poverty neighborhoods. These neighborhoods have been poor for a long time. However, they are now poor and jobless—a combination that introduces an entirely different dimension of economic and social isolation and a lack of important mechanisms of community support, like PTAs, youth centers, and informal social and economic networks that middle-class people take for granted.

Ghetto conditions raise fundamental questions of justice for individuals. But ghetto conditions also have a negative impact on the whole region, an impact far out of proportion to the geographic and population size of the ghetto—which is about 5 percent of the nation's population. Unfortunately, the geographic size of ghettos has expanded dramatically in recent years—54 percent nationwide in the 1980s alone, based on census tract measurements. The most important out-of-proportion impact these expanding ghetto areas generate is that the worse the conditions become, the more they repel the very thing they need most: job-creating private investment.

If that's the recent track record of land use patterns and equal opportunity, what's the outlook for American race relations? In many respects, solid progress has been made. There is a growing black middle class. We have seven thousand black elected officials and many black college graduates, but we all know another part of black America is sinking. Apart from that, the race issue is much more complicated than it used to be because the Hispanic and Asian populations are growing so fast.

Today our nation is in the midst of its third great challenge of racial justice. The first one was slavery. It took one hundred years to change that. Next was prohibiting legal segregation. That took another hundred years. We're forty-five years or so into the third challenge. Unlike the first two, this third challenge is not going to be fought out on battlefields, or in the Supreme Court, or in Congress. It is going to be resolved in state legislatures and in regions like Cleveland. Our third great challenge of racial justice is the access of people of color—people who soon will be the majority in this country—to jobs, housing, and education in America's highly fragmented metropolitan areas.

This change is happening fast. An overwhelmingly white society for two centuries, only 11 percent of the population was nonwhite when *Brown vs. Board of Education* came out forty years ago. But America will be half white, half nonwhite in fifty-two years. As Bishop Pilla says, if you don't know people you can't make progress on issues all people care about. But the kind of urban disinvestment and suburban sprawl projected in Michigan and elsewhere portends greater, not less, isolation of urban minorities from new jobs, good schools, affordable housing, and safe streets.

Environment

The same regionwide development patterns that undermine equal opportunity also hurt the environment. The same outward movement of job-creating, tax-base-boosting private investment that causes disinvestment in the inner city also needlessly destroys open space, farmland, and wildlife habitat at the edge of suburbia and beyond. Coupled with excessive regulation of suburban development, that same outward investment is also a major cause of air and water pollution. Whether in Cleveland or elsewhere, pollution and traffic congestion are largely consequences of development patterns that separate every suburban destination by a distance that can be navigated only by a car.

Again, policy plays a major role in these auto-only patterns of development. This is because zoning laws require that suburban land uses be separated and that suburban densities be low. This fabric of suburban development is the main reason vehicle miles traveled have increased four times as fast as population in the last four decades nationally. We can't build highways fast enough to keep up with the auto travel generated by suburbs. Wholly apart from the money employers spend for employee parking, and wholly apart from environmental impacts or energy consumption, we don't have enough money to build and maintain enough highways to handle all the auto trips that will come from suburbs generating twelve to fourteen trips per house per day.

Economic Strength

Let's look at the economic side. How do development patterns affect society's goal of prosperity? Macroeconomic numbers like the high stock market, low unemployment rate, and low inflation are not the best indicators of strength. Productivity growth is the critical measure of economic health. Productivity growth increased 2.7 percent from 1946 to 1973. Politicians dismiss this period as an anomaly, a time when America boomed because Europe and Japan were flat on their backs. Okay, let's take 1909 to 1969, when productivity growth averaged 1.9 percent. Compare that to 1973 to 1995, when productivity growth averaged only 1.1 percent. Productivity growth is the social muscle on which our true economic strength depends. As our nation's productivity growth has slowed, incomes have been flat for half the nation's population. At the same time, income disparities have increased. The slowdown in productivity is partly why we hear so much about Social Security and Medicare. Our economy is not only not generating the employment income households need to support families, our economy is also not generating the public revenue at low tax rates that the government needs to finance basic public programs.

Some of this decline in productivity has to do with our development patterns. The ability of private investment to be productive is dependent on infrastructure. Something like $1.9 trillion of the nation's $4 trillion in nonresidential capital is public capital. The most important category of public capital is core infrastructure—highways, transit systems, airports, railroad stations, water lines, and sewers. It is on this base of public capital that the profitability of private capital partly depends—for its efficient operation and for its high rate of return.

In terms of an annual increase in the value of core infrastructure, America's investments in core infrastructure have gone from 4.2 percent for the period 1960-69, to 2.6 percent for 1969-73, to 1.6 percent for 1973-79, and to 1.3 percent for 1979-87. That is a downward slope.

Sprawl patterns have contributed to this slowdown in core infrastructure investment, on which productivity, economic growth, household income, and public revenue all crucially depend. Core infrastructure investments are sensitive to factors of density and distance for their initial feasibility, as well as for their efficient operation thereafter. However, regions like Cleveland, New York, Philadelphia, and San Francisco are expanding in area so fast, and at densities so low, that efficient infrastructure investments are costly and difficult to justify.

You know the numbers here in Cleveland: 11 percent population loss as a region from 1970 to 1990, but a 33 percent expansion of the region's urbanized area during that same period. Pittsburgh's history is similar.

Other big regions have at least grown a little population wise, but their urban areas have expanded even more. Chicago's numbers are 4 percent population increase, 46 percent residential area expansion, and 67 percent commercial and industrial expansion. Whether we're looking at Atlanta or Los Angeles, at small towns up and down the Front Range in Colorado, or the cities of Michigan, the numbers and the trends are similar.

The Michigan Society of Planning Officials (MSPO) projects that all of Michigan's urban areas will expand somewhere between 63 percent and 87 percent from 1990 to the year 2020. The MSPO also reports Michigan has a $67 billion backlog in infrastructure finance for the last generation of sprawl—either needing repairs or playing catch-up for deferred maintenance. Michigan's infrastructure "balloon payment" must now be paid—or vast suburban areas will deteriorate. Instead, Michigan is on the verge of allowing another thirty years of sprawl and making an already huge problem even worse.

We think about Detroit. The mental image is of a hollowed-out Detroit. The flip side of hollowed-out Detroit is a very low density, rapidly expanding urbanizing, suburbanizing area. Development is sort of like jam. If you spread it too thin, you lose the benefit of it. A lot has been written about sprawl in the West, but it's at least as bad in the Midwest. Detroit and Michigan are extreme cases, but they mirror what we're doing all over this country.

I mentioned the decline in core infrastructure investment. Schools are not part of core infrastructure, but education relates to productivity, and sprawl and disinvestment have a similar effect on the efficiency of this critical social investment too. At the same time that disinvestment and sprawl intensified, we saw a twenty-five-year decline in SAT scores. Once-great central city public schools are now engulfed in poverty. For example, 73 percent of the kids in Chicago's school system are from low-income households. The citywide dropout rate is 56 percent, and of those who graduate, 25 percent read at only a sixth grade level. At the same time, in regions across the United States, new schools are being built at the edge of the region while physically functional schools are being closed in the center and the population of school-age children regionwide declines. That kind of waste makes no sense economically and drives up education costs systemwide. It leads voters to say "no" to bond measures and is one reason kids are going to school in trailers. These land use patterns not only undercut national goals, such as the environment, equal opportunity, and economic strength, but also the ability of local government to carry out basic functions, like education and transportation.

Public Safety

Let's look at public safety. Private investments depend on the efficient operation of local government functions like public safety, but police departments can't function efficiently given the kinds of land use patterns America has encouraged since World War II. We used to have a cop on the beat. Then we went to the squad car. Now we're in the 911 mode at a time when the average burglary takes three minutes and the average police response time is fourteen minutes. During this period, expenditures on public safety increased 50 percent faster than the rate of inflation and crime rates soared. As America has sprawled and the inability of public safety agencies to deter and respond to crime has become apparent, companies have had to hire their own police forces. Business essentially has had to shoulder a responsibility government should be handling, but can't. The result is that today there are two and a half times more people working in private security companies than in all the nation's municipal police forces put together.

Strategies That Advance Many Goals

Each of the eight strategies that follow advances all the social goals we have discussed. In different ways, all these strategies advance economic goals because they support private investment. They also make feasible investments in critical public functions, like education and transportation. They also support environmental quality and equal opportunity, all in different ways.

Urban Growth Boundaries

The first strategy is foundational, and it strikes some as radical, but it deals with the national phenomenon of rapidly outward-expanding development that underlies all the socially harmful consequences of local development patterns: jobless inner cities, unstable blue-collar inner suburbs, unfeasibility of investments in core infrastructure, and damage to the environment.

In Oregon, the legislature requires every city to have an urban growth boundary (UGB). The Portland region has twenty-four cities and parts of three counties falling within its UGB. The purpose of UGBs is not to stop growth, or even to slow it down. Portland's economy is booming, and we like it that way, thank you. Slowing growth is not the point. On the contrary, UGBs are prodevelopment and promarket.

A UGB addresses two questions: "Where are we going to do a good job of being an urban community?" and "How big of an area can we afford to make the investments we need to make in order to be a functioning, healthy, fair, sound community?" Those are the criteria, the purposes Bishop Pilla urges. The UGB makes this critical "where-we-will-be-urban" cut. It's the kind of community decision most other free industrial societies insist local governments make. We don't do it in this country. If you travel to England or France or Scandinavia, you see the stark distinction between the urban and the rural. That is not happenstance. Nor is it because greed lurks any less prominently in the human heart in those societies. Rather, it's because they all have drawn lines on maps. Those societies call those lines different things. But all those lines say, "This is where we are going to be urban. Outside that line we're not going to be urban, at least for the time being. We will move the line out only as needs be."

That's what an urban growth boundary is. Portland's was put in place in 1979. All of Oregon's 241 cities have them. They were controversial then. Nearly everybody loves them today. As stated earlier, Michigan's urban area is projected to expand 63 to 87 percent by 2020. Portland's boundaries have been in place for almost twenty years. There is a process now underway to consider how much to expand the boundary around the Portland metropolitan area, where nearly half of the state's population lives. How much should we expand it to accommodate new development and population growth—about 33 percent—until the year 2040? The range of the debate is from 0 percent on the low end to about 3 or 4 percent on the high end. And the decision is probably going to end up closer to 0. As needed, the state will specify areas outside the UGB where that 3 to 4 percent expansion may occur in the future. As for the rest, over the next half century we won't see any kind of urban scale development. That's what the urban growth boundary does. It contains the outward movement that prevents the infrastructure investment that private investment needs; undercuts police and education functions; needlessly consumes natural resources at the urban fringe; and separates jobless people in the city from the job-rich suburbs at the region's edge.

UGBs are absolutely pro-development. The UGB says, "Inside this line we want development." Development inside the line has the blessing and the affirmation of public policy and is formally declared to be in the public interest. Because of that affirmation, and because of specific pro-residential and proindustrial land policies that apply inside the UGB, Oregon's residential and commercial developers have come to accept UGBs. They didn't previously, but they accept them now, because of the benefits they receive.

Affordable Market Housing

The benefits to developers lead to the second model strategy: easing zoning restrictions on affordable housing. In the 1970s, the Portland area was experiencing a trend similar to many other metro regions: residential zoning was out of whack with economic and demographic reality. As was the case nationally, household size in Portland was getting smaller and smaller due to later marriages, fewer children, more seniors, and more people living alone for various reasons. At the same time, incomes were flat or falling for 50 to 60 percent of the population.

Despite these changes, suburbs used zoning that required houses to be larger and larger, mainly by requiring bigger and bigger single-family lots. In addition to large lots for single-family homes, we had a zoned shortage of sites for multifamily homes. Even though half the demand for housing was for multifamily, only 7 percent of the vacant, residentially zoned land in the region was zoned multifamily—93 percent was zoned single family. The state land use program forced the issue, asking: "Is this what people need and want?" "Is this where the market is?" and "How does our zoning stack up in terms of what people can afford for housing, what builders want to build, and what banks want to finance?"

The state's land use program helped the Portland region get zoning for housing back to normal. It was not something new and radical, just normal. In 1978, the average size of a built single-family lot in Portland was 5,700 square feet, but the average size of a vacant lot in the region had increased by 13,000 square feet. The state's affordable housing land use policy required all the cities in the Portland metropolitan area to revise their zoning to better reflect economic and demographic reality. Eventually, the average single-family lot size in the region shrank back down to about 8,500 square feet. In addition, the amount of land zoned for multifamily quadrupled. The end result was that in 1983, 305,000 housing units could be built on the same residential land base that in 1978 could hold only 129,000.

Thus, the second reason the urban growth boundary is a pro-development concept is that it made possible a nationally unprecedented, metropolitanwide deregulation of the housing market. The higher density zoning that resulted from Oregon's state-mandated relaxation of zoning restrictions on residential development benefited many interests. The new market-sensitive zoning increased affordability for consumers and profitability for developers. It also reduced development pressure on the urban fringe. Because we have the urban growth boundary, and because vast amounts of land outside of it are zoned for forest and farm use, Oregon builders and home buyers have the political and operational possibility of an inside-the-UGB policy that says, "We're going to reduce the interference in residential markets that local zoning is causing."

For those reasons, UGBs are pro-development, but they are also "pro-market." I referred earlier to the process that, in part, fuels sprawl: residential developments, office parks, and shopping malls being able to push costs off onto other people. Several studies have documented the kinds and amounts of costs thus able to be "externalized," as the economists say. Such development projects don't have to bear these "externalized" costs. Somebody else has to pay them—a taxpayer, another business, a nearby property owner, someone commuting in a traffic jam. By being able to push off those costs, these products are able to be sold at a price that is below full-cost pricing.

The advantage of below-full-cost pricing attracts investment capital these projects wouldn't otherwise attract. That's a misallocation of resources—the biggest "no-no" in any economics 101 textbook. Economists from Milton Friedman to Lester Thurow would say, "Well, we've got to make projects internalize these costs." Well and good. The problem is, it's difficult to internalize costs because of the anarchy of our land use patterns. So, the economist says, "Well, if you have pervasive externalities, if you have hundreds of people externalizing costs, and you don't know where those costs are landing, or when they are going to land, then you need some kind of systemic intervention to allow the market to perform its most vital function, which is to efficiently allocate society's scarce economic resources."

Thus, the economic view of sprawl is that it is a misallocation of resources. Suburban projects are able to push their costs off onto other people and be sold at below-full-cost pricing. Suburban projects have a distinct advantage because urban projects don't have the luxury of externalizing costs. To make matters more difficult, urban projects must internalize costs that were actually externalized a long time ago, such as brownfields and deferred maintenance of crumbling infrastructure. The result is very unlevel playing fields for private investment across metropolitan areas. The urban growth boundary can at least contain the geographic area where the phenomenon of cost externalization occurs. That containment helps restore the market to its position of being an efficient allocator of resources.

Modernizing Industrial Land Inventories

The third strategy is modernizing industrial land bases. By establishing the urban growth boundary, communities are in a position to designate the kinds of sites industry will need to be efficient twenty-first-century operators and to support those sites with infrastructure—to actually get the infrastructure in the ground. The UGB requires localities to compare notes in terms of their industrial inventories and their infrastructure plans. The state's industrial land policy requires local governments to set economic development goals and to compare those goals to how they have zoned land. With these tools, a region can accelerate the process of modernizing its industrial land base.

In the 1970s, Oregon's industrial land base was heavily dominated not just by brownfields but by old-style heavy industry next to railroad tracks. That's not the kind of high technology companies need—the kinds of companies our legislature was targeting to diversify our economy. With the planning system we were able to increase our industrial land base 79 percent within the UGBs of Oregon's ten largest cities. That increased supply provided the kind of campus-type sites electronics companies said they needed. More important, we were able to expedite the process of getting infrastructure to those sites. Today, Oregon has $13 billion worth of electronic and high technology plants planned or under construction.

That would have been a pipe dream twenty years ago. Oregon is a timber state. We produce more lumber and plywood than any other state. If somebody had said in 1975 that technology companies were going to be Oregon's leading manufacturing employers by the turn of the century, people would have laughed. But, as of mid-1996, that statement is true. Top leaders in the electronics industry credit Oregon's land use system for the industry's ability to make facilities investment decisions quickly and predictably. That, and the low-cost housing we've locked in with our housing affordability strategy. By giving people more choices for smaller lots, and making it easier to build the multifamily housing many people want to buy and many builders want to build, we created a huge economic development "draw." Housing in Portland costs half what it does in California's Silicon Valley. We also have lower housing costs than Denver, which has no urban growth boundary. The average house price in Denver is $163,000. It's $135,000 in Portland. Our housing costs are lower because our cities have become efficient producers of lots inside the boundary, and because we approve projects quickly, which also cuts costs. Yes, our housing prices are rising, but they are rising more slowly than Denver's, even though both regions are experiencing similar booms.

Subsidized Housing

The fourth strategy is subsidized housing. HUD says people have an affordability problem when they spend over 30 percent of their income for housing. There are now five million American households spending more than half their income for housing, an all-time high. These are people who are not getting public housing assistance. These people have a housing affordability crisis. The hurt is greatest in the chunk of the population where incomes have been falling. To understand what's happening to income in America, you have to look at it in quintiles. Incomes at the bottom 20 percent have been going down sharply, the next 20 percent have also been going down, if less sharply. The next 20 percent have almost held their own. Then there's another 20 percent going up a bit, and the top 20 percent going up fast. So, even though home ownership is now at a fifteen-year high, people in the bottom 35 percent are having real problems paying for housing.

One of the most successful subsidized housing programs in the country is in Montgomery County, Maryland, a wealthy county of about 750,000 people in a state where 28 percent of the population is black—compared to 16 percent in Illinois and a little less than that in Ohio. Since 1970, any housing project in Montgomery County with more than 50 units is required to provide 15 percent of its units as low and moderate affordable units. As of 1994, 8,840 units have been created. Of those, two-thirds were sold, one-third were rented. The average sale price from 1980 to 1991 for one of these affordable units was $69,900 compared to the county average of about $208,000. Over 60 percent of the buyers of affordable units were minority members whose household incomes were $26,400, compared to the county average of $62,000.

Montgomery County is still one of the richest counties in the United States. Its minority population has increased considerably over what it was twenty years ago. The dropout rate in the county's schools runs about 2 percent a year—one-tenth the national average. It is a tremendous success story. The implications of this success are significant. Assume the United States adds 1.5 million housing units a year in the private market. Add to that 1.5 million the 50,000 units all of the nonprofits, the community development corporations, and the public housing authorities and so forth are creating, and assume further, that we did as a nation what Montgomery County has done for the past twenty years. If we had done that, we would have provided about five million housing units in eighteen or twenty years—something like that. In other words, an amount equal to the five million households now paying over 50 percent of their income for housing.

Some of our seemingly daunting, big-ticket social problems are manageable. The beauty of the Montgomery County policy—a strategy I commend to you—is that the county didn't say, "Well, this city has to do this, and this city has to do that." Instead of assigning quotas, the county set up a builder-driven process. The builder says, "Let's see. The county is going to give me a density bonus that will allow me to add about 22 percent more units to my project, because I've included 15 percent affordable and low income units in my project. Where can I do that?" The developer pencils it out. Except for the support from the county, it is all happening essentially in the market.

Faster, More Predictable Decisions

The fifth strategy addresses an important process point: the "time cost" of money, as developers put it. If you have the UGB, and if you've made the industrial and residential designations inside the UGB, why should it take two years to get a permit? The legislature asked itself, "Why should it take so long?" and concluded, with the UGB and with the new designations, that the process could be much faster. So, the 1983 legislature imposed a 120-day time limit on getting an answer to a completed development application. And it's typically taking a lot less time than that. By placing the policy debate about where development should into the planning process—not at the point in the process when the developer steps up to the counter in the zoning office—Oregon has created the nation's fastest, most predictable development process. The result is lower real estate product costs, whether residential, commercial, or industrial.

Preserving Farmland and Forestland

My sixth strategy addresses the conservation side of the issue. I know that in Ohio Governor Voinovich initiated a farmland preservation discussion. One of Ohio's most important industries is agriculture. Agriculture is big in Oregon, too. So our legislature decided to protect the foundation of that industry—the state's productive agricultural soils. Our laws say that certain types of soil outside an urban growth boundary have to be protected for farming. Some good farmland has been chewed up inside the boundaries, but outside the UGB, where there are good soils for growing crops based on U.S. Soil Conservation Service (SCS) criteria, those soils must be protected. The SCS has mapped soils, county by county, in most of Oregon. This soil data provides a good criteria for conservation—one that farmers, extension agents, and local officials are all familiar with. The objectivity of the SCS soil maps is also valuable. It helps wring the politics out of the rural zoning process. Probably most of Ohio's farmland has been mapped by the SCS too. You can use those soil maps to identify Ohio's best soils.

In Oregon, where good soils exist in "large blocks" outside of UGBs, the legislature required counties to zone those soils exclusively for farm use. Oregon is a state of some 60 million acres, about half of which is owned by the federal government—national forests and the Bureau of Land Management. There are about 30 million acres of private land. Pursuant to the state's land use laws, 26.5 million acres of farmland and forestland were rezoned to exclusive farm use or exclusive forest use. That's just slightly larger than all of Ohio. This zoning was done county by county, and area by area within each county. It took about ten years. To change the farm designations created by this process requires a review by the state. The results have been dramatic. There hasn't been a subdivision, or a shopping center, or a commercial development outside of an urban growth boundary in Oregon for fifteen years.

The Farm Bureau was a little unsure about this in the beginning, but now they're solidly in favor of it. Indeed, in recent years they have pushed in the legislature to tighten state restrictions on development.

Again, the urban growth boundary doesn't get you home. It's the critical start, but it's just a start. Affordable housing policies must exist inside the boundary to accomplish something for housing. The same for the industrial land and for transportation. Similarly, UGBs can't save farmland by themselves. UGBs just say where the farmland policies apply: outside the UGB. To save farmland, Ohio will need policies that limit partitioning and that limit the placement of dwellings, either for farm or nonfarm. The state will need a system like the UGB to say where those policies apply.

The reason Oregon's UGBs and farmland policies are relevant to Ohio is because Ohio's agricultural economy, like Oregon's, is diverse, large, and prospering. Agriculture is Ohio's number one industry. Its 74,000 farms on 15 million acres contribute $56.2 billion to the state's economy each year and employ one in six Ohioans. Oregon farmers support the program for the usual reasons. They don't want new urban neighbors next to them complaining about smoke, dust, smells, or slow-moving farm equipment on narrow, farm-to-market roads. But basic money reasons are more important. First, land is the biggest capital input in farming. Farmers who want to expand their profitable operations can't afford to buy agricultural land if "anything goes" zoning allows development value prices to radiate out over the countryside.

Second, and less obviously, stable land uses are critical to farming operations in terms of maintaining efficient economic units. About one-third of the farmland in commercial production in the United States is held in lease—not owned in fee. A farmer will own a couple of hundred acres and lease another ten or fifteen parcels of varying sizes in efficient proximity to the home place. The combination of fee and leased land makes up that farmer's economic unit.

Unfortunately, the owner of a leased parcel can say, "Well, I'm not going to have another handshake deal with you next year, Claude, or with any other farmer. The dentist in town wants to come out and live in the country because you've done such a nice job keeping it pretty out here. I'm going to sell him my ten acres. Sorry, but it won't be part of your farm next planting season." That's the sort of dicey situation farmers live with: They worry leased parcels are going to get sold out from under them for homesites.

Thus, two reasons relating to stable land uses are why production farmers in Oregon support the state's land use program. Farmers need to be able to invest in silos, tractors, tiling systems, fencing, and other things with some confidence about future revenue flows generated by fixed or expanding amounts of land in production. Stable land use patterns give farmers the confidence they need to make the investments that drive farm sector income growth. Over the past two decades, farm sector income has grown steadily in Oregon while other sectors of the state's economy have gone up and down. That steady growth is a huge plus for the state economy, as well as for individual farmers. Keeping it that way is why farmers and legislators support the program—the whole program. They know that if development isn't efficiently accommodated inside the UGB, conservation and stability outside the UGB will be unrealistic economically and unachieveable politically.

The forest products industry long has been the dominant political interest in Oregon. That industry also strongly supports the program, for many of the same reasons, though land costs are less important to the foresters than to farmers. Some freshman legislators are surprised when farmers and timber managers show up in the legislature and testify that they like the restrictions on the land they own. And, of course, these are the major landowners in the countryside.

Protecting rural land benefits heavy-duty economic players. It also protects Oregon's heritage of beautiful open space. Less obviously, saving rural land also deflects investment and demand for new development back inside the urban growth boundary, where it is most needed. As I said, we have to build our way out of the problem of sprawl. The urban growth boundary and the farmland zoning outside the boundary, together, help us do that. They do it by focusing and channeling development back inside. Like all the other strategies we are talking about today, in a comprehensive system, farmland preservation generates many benefits, inside the UGB as well as outside.

Tax-Base Sharing

The seventh strategy is tax-base sharing. The best example is in Minneapolis/St. Paul. Again, like UGBs, at first blush this idea may sound radical. But, if you think about it, not pooling revenues is perhaps more radical. American society depends on property tax revenue to finance basic public services like schools and police. How does that system compare to our income tax system? Income tax revenues are pooled and used throughout the state or national community. The property tax system is different. Take a region like New York. And I say *region* because the region is the true community, socially and economically. Our regions are chopped up for property tax purposes. New York has 765 taxing jurisdictions. Chicago has 269. Philadelphia has 245. That's just municipalities; it doesn't count the hundreds of school and special districts in each of those regions that also have the power to tax property. Among the nation's tens of thousands of taxing districts are enormous disparities in taxable property wealth. This raises obvious questions about inequity. Education is the most prominent example. In thirty-nine states today there are lawsuits saying states are violating provisions in state constitutions that require state government to provide adequate public education. One is here, in the Ohio Supreme Court. As in other states, the issue has been ping-ponging back and forth between the courts and the legislature, unresolved, for twenty years.

There is more involved here than just inequities. The disparities in our property tax system also fuel sprawl across metropolitan regions. We have a situation where, as in the Chicago region, the property tax bill on a 100,000 square foot office building is $500,000 to $900,000 each year in the central city, but the same building pays only $100,000 to $200,000 each year in the suburbs. Suburbs have low rates because they have a lot of tax base and relatively low social costs. The city and older suburbs have high rates because they have weak tax bases and high costs. The relative tax burden of these places sends clear and powerful signals to people deciding where to invest in commercial or residential property. Not surprisingly, people respond quite rationally to those signals with investment decisions that create sprawl.

I suggest you consider the strategy that has worked in the Twin Cities. Under a 1971 state law, 40 percent of the increase in commercial and industrial tax base is pooled annually. They could have pooled 100 percent or 60 percent. They could have pooled residential instead of commercial and industrial. They could have done some combination. Since 1971 this policy has gradually reduced disparities between taxing districts—there are 185 cities in the Twin Cities region—from about fifty to one to about twelve to one. Something like $395 million now goes into the pool each year and is distributed. Apart from questions of school funding equity, the whole region is a place where, from the perspective of property taxes, private investments are a little more feasible throughout.

Somewhat surprisingly, tax base disparities have become so great in places like Chicago, Philadelphia, Pittsburgh, and Baltimore that, region-wide, majorities of residents would be on the receiving end of tax-base sharing programs, as they are in the Twin Cities.

Why are suburban tax bases so high in the first place? Did they get that way the old-fashioned way—by being earned? Or has the "invisible hand" of the government provided a helpful, if unremarked upon, boost? One clue might be $67 billion of real estate taxes and mortgage interest deducted nationally from taxable income every year. The vast majority of these deductions are in the suburbs. These deductions amount to a $67 billion reduction in residential operating expense. State-set utility rates that subsidize costly-to-serve suburbanites also reduce suburban residential operating costs. These two policies that reduce suburban operating costs make suburban houses more valuable. That increased value shows up in tax bases and allows suburbs to reduce property tax rates.

Infrastructure investment, which boosts property values, also allows suburbs to lower rates. Like the income tax deductions, the lion's share of new infrastructure also occurs in a narrow range of "favored quarter" suburbs, as Myron Orfield and Christopher Leinberger have shown. In the 1980s, 90 percent of new highway construction in the Twin Cities region, for example, and a slightly lower proportion in the Chicago region, went to suburban parts of those regions where only 25 to 35 percent of the population lives.

There are other examples of government policy that reduce suburban operating costs, such as mortgage insurance and subsidies to auto use—each enjoyed more in the suburbs than in the central city. The point is, there are issues of fairness, beyond obvious issues of need, that justify considering the idea of regional tax-base sharing. Strong suburban tax bases are not simply the result of sweaty suburban brows. Urban sweat—in the form of intraregional transfers established by Congress and by state legislatures—is also part of the mix.

Connecting Land Use and Transportation

The eighth and the final strategy can best be termed as "transit-shed planning." Again, this is dependent on first having said, with an urban growth boundary, "This is where we're going to be urban." In the mid-1980s we had a situation in Portland where only 16 percent of the future development inside the urban growth boundary was going to be within walking distance of existing or planned bus or rail service. This disparity meant that even with the 1979 UGB and the increased residential densities put in place from 1979 to 1983, we weren't going to get any kind of an access or mobility benefit. Instead, we were going to get more congestion. The increases in density made from 1979 to 1983 to achieve housing affordability goals were theoretically high enough to justify transportation investments. The problem was, future development inside the UGB—higher density or not—wasn't going to happen in the right location.

In response, 1000 Friends of Oregon sponsored a "transit-shed" analysis. The question was, "Where would additional transportation investments make sense if future development happened differently?" To make a long story short, without increasing densities, an alternative land use pattern was configured so 65 percent of the new residential development and 78 percent of the new jobs would be near where transit is going to be, or where, if you make those land use shifts, transportation investments become feasible. The alternative land use pattern allowed the same money to be spent on a different form of transportation capacity that can produce more mobility, less congestion, less energy consumption, and less air pollution than would spending the money on a freeway. As a result, the freeway that had been proposed outside the urban growth boundary has been scrapped, and the money used to improve arterials in close-in suburbs and invest in improved bus service, express bus service, and light rail. A $1 billion, seventeen-mile light rail system west of Portland is now half built. It's like the fifteen-mile rail system built east of town in the early 1980s—also built with money originally budgeted for a freeway.

As time passed, the "transit-shed" concept shifted from being an analysis conducted by 1000 Friends of Oregon to stop a freeway to being a land use strategy to maximize the return on desired transportation investments. The alternative made transit-oriented development around rail stations feasible. Cities are now changing their zoning to allow this form of development. The alternative won support because it was based not on some planner's idea of what he or she wanted, but on market analysis keyed to household incomes, consumer preferences, absorption rates, etc. Similar market analysis has prompted the electronics industry in Silicon Valley to ask municipal governments to change zoning to permit development that will achieve the industry's transit feasibility and housing affordability goals.

The Silver Lining of Sprawl

So those are the eight strategies. In different ways, each one advances basic social goals, including economic strength, equal opportunity, and environmental quality. I want to close with two thoughts. The first is that gloom is not the right mood for talks about land use reform. True, the "parade of horribles" described earlier can seem overwhelming. But, as Bishop Pilla says, we need to hear from exponents of hope. Fortunately, there is a political flip side, a silver lining, to all the difficulties our development patterns are causing us. The flip side is there are a whole lot of people out there being hurt in different ways by suburban sprawl and urban disinvestment, and those people compose a majority coalition just waiting to be formed, in region after region, all across the United States. The key point is not how bad things are. The key point is that the people affected form a potential majority in most U.S. metro regions, and that each of the eight strategies discussed can benefit all the people being hurt. That's what we should focus on because that's what shows us what needs to be done.

Granted, it would take a lot of work to build and sustain those majorities. People have to understand why disinvestment in the city and auto-only sprawl in the suburbs are two sides of the same coin. They also need to see that individual interests are too weak to deal with the situation acting in isolation. Environmentalists can't get it done by themselves. Urban advocates can't get it done by themselves. Neither can business. Business in northern California tried and came close in the California legislature, but they didn't have enough allies to get over the hump.

Those of us seeking change must take advantage of this silver lining. We must constantly define the land use problem so all stakeholders see their connection to it. Also, we must frame solutions that create many winners.

Freeing the Debate of Myths

Finally, by talking about the issues in the way that I've just described, we can slay four conceptual dragons that have throttled and stymied the land use debate for thirty years. First, we must dispel the widely assumed, and mistaken, notion that land use policy reform is at odds with free economic markets. We don't have to have a fight with the market to implement these strategies, as they are compatible with the market. But our position is stronger than that. Most of our strategies amount to peeling back interference in real estate markets caused by federal or state policies that distort the free operation of markets. These policies send people signals that induce them to make personal or business investments that, taken together, lead to sprawl. So, our approach is more to free, rather than to fight, the market, and to level investment playing fields.

Second, land use reform doesn't mean having a fight with local governments. Unfortunately, we made this mistake in Oregon. The way the land use issue first surfaced was that the state was going to come in and tell local governments what to do. Happily, we've gotten beyond that, but it was nearly fatal. More and more local governments, particularly small suburban jurisdictions, recognize they are not masters of their own fate. They see themselves being increasingly bumped and buffeted by forces beyond their control. State policies providing regional frameworks—for tax-base sharing, or fair share affordable housing, or rural land conservation—help insulate and stabilize local governments. Suburban jurisdictions in the Portland region are now the strongest supporters of the urban growth boundary. They were hostile to it in 1975, when it was first proposed. Done right, land use reforms can strengthen local fiscal independence and stability and bolster local legislative discretion. Those should be explicit goals of reform.

Third, we are not hostile to property rights. We have to broaden the now very narrow notion of property rights, at least the way the idea has played for so long in the land use debate. Some of you winced when I discussed the urban growth boundary—when I said subdivisions aren't allowed outside UGBs. What about those poor guys who own all that land out there? Well, you know, there are not that many of them. But the more important point is there is a much larger group of people whose property values also are at stake in the debate over regional land use patterns. These are people who own real property inside the boundary, in the center of the region and in the established suburbs. What about their balance sheets? What about their house values? What about the sale value of their businesses as a concern when the owner is ready to retire? The pattern of sprawl not only creates an opportunity for speculation for a tiny handful of landowners at the urban fringe. It also depresses or stagnates the residential and commercial values of a much larger group of property owners in the interior of the region. This is particularly true for regions—like Chicago or Cleveland—where population growth is slow or declining in absolute terms, but the urbanized area is nonetheless rapidly expanding.

The land use reform movement is concerned about property rights. That's not a problem for us. We're for property rights. We've got to focus attention on all the property owners of a region, and not just on the noisy few who will benefit from a continuation of sprawl.

Finally, land use reform is not against development. We want to revitalize the inner city. We want to cure the auto-only suburban development fabric that pollutes air and water. Achieving both these objectives depends much more on development than on regulation. Regulation can help say where we are going to develop. But the solution to the problem of the city and the suburb fundamentally is one of investment and development. That's not a problem. It's a plus.

So let's take those four demons off of our backs. Let's make allies out of those concepts and the people behind them. Let's also remember the broad social goals, the consensus goals we're trying to serve when we evaluate land use patterns and when we work for alternative land use patterns that will better serve Greater Cleveland and other American communities.

Chapter 3

Sprawl and Race

Today's Winners Become Tomorrow's Losers

David Rusk

Ohio's urbanized areas are consuming land almost five times faster than the state's population is growing, a disparity that contributes to the abandonment of central cities and inner suburbs. The problems of urban disinvestment, concentrated poverty, and racial isolation can't be solved by the cities alone: regional solutions are required. The time is ripe for the broad coalition of interests who have been hurt by Ohio's sprawling development patterns to create the political will for change.

David Rusk is the former mayor of Albuquerque, New Mexico, and author of *Cities without Suburbs*. As a consultant to the Ohio Urban University Program, he has analyzed the economic and racial disparities between central cities and suburbs of Ohio's metropolitan areas. This chapter is adapted from his address at "Greater Cleveland 2046: A Bicentennial Symposium" at Cleveland State University on October 22, 1996.

In the past two years, I have come to appreciate much more the adverse impact of urban sprawl on my concerns about social inequity. When I originally wrote *Cities without Suburbs,* my general view was that sprawl has been universal, but that about half the cities in the country have effectively defended their market share in a region growing ever outward by growing outward themselves. What I came to call "elastic" cities expanded their boundaries by annexation or, in a few cases, through city-county consolidation. Most elastic cities are still pretty healthy cities.

In analyzing metro areas with elastic cities, I also found significantly lesser levels of racial and economic segregation. I associated that phenomenon, in part, with the elasticity of cities. I didn't like sprawl as a matter of style in urban form but felt that if elasticity and sprawl are associated with greater social equity, I could accept sprawl. My own Albuquerque, New Mexico, was a prime example of the association of sprawl, elasticity, and higher social equity.

I've now concluded that sprawl is *not* associated with greater social equity. Sprawl is a pattern of development that constantly segregates society more and more by income class with an adverse impact on racial segregation as well.

Consuming Land

In 1995, I studied the growth of populations and land for all urbanized areas in the country from 1960 to 1990. In 213 major urbanized areas, population increased 47 percent but land increased 107 percent. In other words, nationwide we consumed land at over twice the rate of net population growth.

Ohio's urbanized areas experienced a 13 percent increase in urbanized population but a 64 percent increase in urbanized land. In other words, in Ohio sprawl has been consuming land at almost five times the rate of net population growth. Ohio's ratio is exceeded on a statewide basis only by Michigan, where land is being gobbled up at six times the rate of urbanized population growth.

In this context I coined what I modestly call "Rusk's Rule of Urban Sprawl," which states that the greater the rate of sprawl compared to net household formation, the greater the rate of abandonment of core neighborhoods in central cities and inner suburbs. Conversely, the more sprawl is controlled, the more the viability and marketability of older housing in central cities and inner suburbs is maintained.

Since the advent of Oregon's statewide land use planning law in 1973 (which took full effect in 1979), Portland has been able to contain sprawl.

For that same 1960–90 period, when Ohio's urbanized areas were gobbling up land at five times the rate of population growth, the Portland area experienced an 80 percent population growth, but only a 103 percent growth of urbanized land—in other words, almost a one-to-one ratio. In the decade of the 1980s, when an urban growth boundary around metro Portland was fully in effect, urbanized population increased 14 percent while urbanized land increased only 11 percent. By popular demand, the Portland area is becoming more densely developed, not less densely developed like almost everywhere else.

Inside Game, Outside Game

The notion that through strong sprawl controls the value of older communities is maintained was a statement I felt comfortable making but didn't have evidence to support until recently. In mid-1996, the *Oregonian* came out with a front-page story about the Albina area of the city of Portland. An old blue-collar lumber mill community absorbed by the city back in the 1890s, Albina has historically been Portland's poorest neighborhood. After World War II, Albina also became the neighborhood where much of Portland's small but growing African American population lived. Of Albina's twenty census tracts, six are majority black. In those six census tracts, the poverty rate increased from about 30 percent in 1970 to 39 percent in 1990.

I toured Portland in February 1996, one of about fifty such neighborhood tours I've taken around the country. Albina didn't look like a neighborhood with a 39 percent poverty rate. There was just too much evidence of reinvestment, renovation, and new commercial and residential development. Albina felt more prosperous than the six-year-old census reports indicated.

The *Oregonian*'s front-page story closed the circle for me. From 1985 to 1995, the government spent about $145 million in the Albina area (60 percent on housing renovation programs, 20 percent on commercial development, and 20 percent on job-training employment programs). However, private investment in Albina in just the past five years had almost doubled the assessed evaluation of all property from $1.4 billion to $2.6 billion.

Think of Albina as a little bit better-off Hough, the Cleveland neighborhood hit by riots in the sixties. Albina has doubled its property values fundamentally because, to a substantial degree, Portland's regional growth management policies have turned development and growth pressures toward existing communities and existing neighborhoods.

The Portland area is far from perfect, but no neighborhoods or political jurisdictions are being systematically abandoned. In addition, there are not major gaps in income levels by jurisdiction, although there certainly are richer and poorer communities.

In the Albina area the average home price went from $61,000 to $120,000 in a five-year period. That increase is causing some real strains for low-income white and black renters, and Portland area officials are trying to develop more vigorous affordable housing policies. However, the majority of Albina's African American residents are homeowners, and they are experiencing something almost no African American community in the country has ever experienced: a sustained increase in the value of their biggest asset, their home. Through this maintenance of largely segregated housing markets, American society has robbed African Americans of the opportunity to create family wealth the way most white families have created wealth—that is, through appreciation in home values.

Almost $145 million of government money has been invested in Albina—that's the traditional "inside game." But Albina is winning today because Portland is playing the "outside game"—regional growth management—better than anybody else.

Community Development Corporations

I've been studying how the nation's best examples of the "inside game" have worked. I compiled census records for target neighborhoods served by thirty-four of the nation's best community development corporations (CDCs), as recommended by knowledgeable national organizations. Of these thirty-four target communities, from 1970 to 1990, in only three did average household income improve at all as a percentage of regional household income. These successful neighborhoods were San Francisco's Mission District, Cincinnati's Walnut Hills, and Boston's Jamaica Plain—all of which experienced substantial gentrification.

Of the thirty-four CDC target areas, twenty-eight had higher poverty rates by 1990 than they did before the programs began. For the newer CDCs the average poverty rate rose from 25 percent to 29 percent over a ten-year period. For older CDCs the average poverty rate increased from 23 percent to 28 percent over a twenty-year period.

Of the seventeen areas that had majority African American populations in 1970, all but two lost between 10 and 45 percent of their households. The two exceptions were the Jamaica area of Queens, New York,
where Hispanic and Asian in-migration offset African American out-
migration, and the Miles neighborhood here in Cleveland. The Miles
area has been a solid African American, middle-class neighborhood for
decades. I think the Miles Ahead CDC has probably done a fine job of
helping maintain the strength and stability of what was already a middle-
class neighborhood.

The overall picture is that incomes are lower and poverty rates higher
almost universally in target neighborhoods served by the very best of the
nation's community development corporations.

It's not that the CDCs have been ineffective. CDCs have undertaken
many successful housing projects and revitalized neighborhood shopping
centers, but the task CDCs face is akin to trying to help a crowd of poor
people run up a down escalator. No matter how hard they run, that escalator comes down faster and faster and faster. There will be some individuals, often helped by effective programs, who succeed in running up to
the top of that down escalator. Then they will jump off. Successful people
will move from poor neighborhoods because they have new options and
choices in life they didn't have before. Why should they put up with the
rising crime and delinquency rates, poor local schools, and all the other
problems endemic to high-poverty neighborhoods? Thus the more successful residents move away, and the less successful are carried back down
to the bottom of that escalator—often to a deeper hole than before, from
which the climb out gets steeper and steeper.

The challenge is not just helping more people run up that down escalator. The challenge is to rewire the direction of the escalator, to change the
way that sprawling development patterns and racial attitudes combine to create high-poverty neighborhoods that trap so many low-income minorities.

Comeback City?

In the past two years, in particular, Cleveland has received glowing acco-
lades as the "Comeback City." When I was here in December 1994,
Jacobs Field was just completed—its first season truncated by a strike.
(The Indians have been to the World Series since.) The Gund Arena was
just opening. The Rock and Roll Hall of Fame still lay in the future.

On a neighborhood tour I saw something I hadn't seen in other cities—large, new homes being built for black professionals right in the middle of Hough. These professionals were former Hough residents who had forsaken being scattered in suburbia for reunification back in the old neighborhood. Right up the street was Lexington Village—a very successful, moderate-income rental project. Now there are more new developments, and recent studies suggest a quickening of the market for home buyers in the city.

In my previous appearances I've talked about Cleveland as a city past the point of no return. I'm sure that statement raised some hackles—not only those of the mayor but also of the business community, who both have so much to be proud of regarding downtown Cleveland's redevelopment. Someone once described Cleveland as "Detroit with glitz." But let me assure you: the glitz is important. You're much better off having the glitz than not having the glitz.

I had described Cleveland as a city past the point of no return because of my statistical analysis of all American cities. I found that when major population loss, a disproportionate minority population, and a large income gap between central city and its suburbs all come together, the city has nowhere to go but down.

For example, I calculated that in the city of Cleveland the number of poverty census tracts (that is, those with greater than 20 percent poverty levels) grew from 64 census tracts in 1970 to 147 by 1990. Looking at such indices of misery, I couldn't get enthusiastic about Cleveland's title of "Comeback City."

The rejoinder by Cleveland boosters is that I'm looking at old data, and that the city has turned around. Maybe. Nobody would like to be proved wrong on this point more than I, because Cleveland's success would argue for some alternative strategies. However, I have looked at current reported property valuation and updated population estimates. Cleveland now has 28 percent of the region's population but only 13–14 percent of the region's total value of commercial, industrial, and residential property. The city's share, though low, may have stabilized over the past three to four years.

The percentage of children in the Cleveland Public Schools who qualify for free or reduced-price lunch is still very high (81 percent) but also seems to have at least stabilized somewhat in recent years. Again, it is difficult to get excited about Comeback City when the state (and, more recently, the mayor) have taken control of the city school system.

However, whereas the city of Cleveland was in absolute economic and social free fall in the 1970s and 1980s, that rate of decline seems to have slowed. Cleveland may indeed have stabilized, although there isn't anything in the numbers I see to suggest that things have turned around. Stabilizing Cleveland's free fall is still a significant achievement.

Playing against a Stacked Deck

In June 1996 I participated in a daylong workshop sponsored by the Northwest Indiana Federation of Interfaith Organizations, a group of black and white churches banded together across Gary, Hammond, and East Chicago, Indiana, to defend their communities (which, by the way, are the most racially segregated metropolitan areas in the nation).

While there I met with former Gary mayor Richard Hatcher (who, along with Cleveland's Carl Stokes, was one of the first two African Americans elected mayor of a northern industrialized city). He and I were mayors together back in the late 1970s. I recall that in 1978 we were on *Meet the Press* together. I remember very vividly the confidence, the optimism, and the pride that Mayor Hatcher expressed about his community. He was convinced that a new day had dawned when the African American community took political control of city hall, and he expressed confidence that "we are indeed turning Gary around."

Seeing former Mayor Hatcher almost twenty years later, I reflected that Gary had not been turned around. It continues to decline at a dramatic rate, but Mayor Hatcher and Mayor Scott King in Gary, Mayors Coleman Young and Dennis Archer in Detroit, and Mayors George Voinovich and Michael White in Cleveland are always forced to play poker against a stacked deck of cards. Mayors of cities like Gary or Detroit or Cleveland are always being dealt a hand in which, to win, they must always draw to fill an inside straight. By contrast, suburban leaders in south Lake County, Indiana, or Oakland County, Michigan, outside Detroit, or Geauga, Medina, Portage, or northern Summit Counties in Northeast Ohio are always being dealt a couple of wild cards off the bottom of a marked deck.

When you're playing poker and one side has to fill an inside straight every time to win and the other side always starts with a couple of wild cards, you know how most of the hands are going to turn out. You've got to get rid of the marked cards and be dealt a fair hand before there can be real competition. You must somehow change the rules of the game.

Cities past the point of no return, like Gary, Detroit, and Cleveland, are not hopeless cases, but they can't turn around alone. Such cities are suffering from intense economic and racial isolation they cannot end simply through a series of unilateral actions.

The key policies to rewire that down escalator, or to take the marked cards out of that deck and get a fair deal, are all regional policies—building an outside game to complement the strong inside game needed through strong, neighborhood-based redevelopment organizations. The major elements of the regional outside game (which Henry Richmond laid out in the previous chapter) include the following:

- Fighting urban sprawl through regional land use planning, like Oregon's statewide land use law

- Fighting fiscal disparities through regional tax-base or revenue sharing, like the Twin Cities Fiscal Disparities Plan

- Fighting the concentration of poverty through mandatory, mixed-income housing in all new construction, as best exemplified by Montgomery County, Maryland's Moderately Priced Dwelling Unit ordinance

Today's Winners Become Tomorrow's Losers

To win—to rewrite the rules of the regional development game—central cities need allies. Minnesota State Representative Myron Orfield, who forged the nation's first inner-suburb/central city political coalition in the Minnesota legislature, once told me that inner-city problems have no "political legs" as long as they are viewed as strictly city problems. When inner-city problems can be shown to be suburban problems (at least for some suburbs), then you've got the potential for putting together a winning political coalition.

A great deal of my work in the past couple of years, particularly during my tour of Ohio's metropolitan areas, has focused on the message I have appropriated from Myron Orfield. I have emphasized the point that inner-city problems—concentrated poverty, crime, etc.—are reaching out to affect many inner-ring suburbs. The corollaries to Rusk's Rule of Urban Sprawl are that "the new beats out the old" and that "today's winners become tomorrow's losers" unless the region as a whole has better balanced development.

Let me give you some examples from the Cleveland area of today's winners becoming tomorrow's losers. I'll express the average household income of a community as a percentage of the regional average, first in 1970, then in 1990.

Back in 1970, the average household income of residents of the city of Cleveland was 72 percent of the regional average; by 1990, city residents' average income had dropped to 60 percent of the regional average. Likewise, for East Cleveland, average household incomes dropped from 77 percent in 1970 to 57 percent in 1990.

Let's talk about some others:

Community	Percentage of Regional Income	
	1970	1990
Cleveland	72	60
East Cleveland	77	57
Lakewood	99	93
Bedford	101	87
Euclid	103	82
Garfield Heights	100	82
Maple Heights	103	85
Parma Heights	114	89

All of the above are inner-ring communities in decline. We can see the same phenomenon in older, established communities in counties farther out.

Eastlake	103	93
Wickliffe	109	95
Willoughby	104	98
Willowick	119	93

Why this decline? First, as established communities their households are aging. Second, because of urban sprawl they are no longer top-of-the-line communities of choice. There are newer communities farther out with new homes, new schools, and a closely controlled range of family incomes appealing to upper-income families. Third, since the newer communities are not accommodating any low- and moderate-income households, inner suburbs are now providing a growing share of the hand-me-down housing for lower-income groups. At first, lower-income whites move out of the city and into inner-ring suburbs; in time, lower-income blacks move into inner suburbs as well.

I have not run the numbers on all jurisdictions in the Cleveland metropolitan area, but I would expect that one-quarter of your communities are on the rise and three-quarters are on the decline. That kind of math holds for the Cincinnati area, the Columbus area, the Dayton area, the Akron area, the Youngstown area, and the Toledo area as well.

From my analyses and visits, I can assure you that there is a statewide political coalition waiting to be formed between Ohio's central cities and many, many inner-ring suburbs who may have been winners once but have been converted now into losers by Ohio's constant sprawling development patterns.

To this coalition of central cities and their inner suburbs could be added environmental groups, which so often recognize that preserving the natural geography also requires greater stability in the human geography. Business organizations have a natural regional perspective. Farm bureaus can become allies. Religious leaders and church coalitions are also important allies. At the heart of this struggle are not only economic issues but moral issues.

Sprawl and Race

Sprawl and race are the two defining factors that have shaped development patterns in urban America. Race is the underlying basis of the emergence of major disparities. In urban America there are as many people who are poor and white (10.8 million) as who are poor and black (6.9 million) and poor and Hispanic (4.8 million) combined.

One of the ironies of current political discourse, which is so disparaging about the Great Society, is that we actually won major battles in the War on Poverty. In 1960, for example, over 40 percent of the elderly in

America were poor. Now the poverty rate among the elderly is 11 percent. The elderly population today is economically better off than the population as a whole. In 1960 the poverty rate among urban whites was 13–14 percent; now their poverty rate is less than 8 percent. In effect, we won the War on Poverty for the elderly and urban whites.

We didn't win where race was a factor. Now we have an urban America where less than 8 percent of whites are poor but 24 percent of Hispanics and 28 percent of blacks are poor. Moreover, although there are almost 11 million poor whites, almost no poor whites live in neighborhoods where concentrated poverty creates a critical mass that promotes social meltdown. Nationwide, fewer than one out of four poor whites lives in a poor neighborhood. In other words, three out of four poor whites live in middle-class neighborhoods scattered all over metro areas. When poor white children go to neighborhood schools, they typically aren't in classrooms dominated by other poor children but in classrooms filled with middle-class children.

By contrast, nationwide, two out of three poor Hispanics and three out of four poor blacks live in poor neighborhoods. When their children go to school, they find themselves in classrooms with 60 percent, 70 percent, 80 percent, 90 percent poor children. This convergence of poverty and race creates the toughest political issue in America. Don Hutchinson, the former Baltimore County executive and now head of the Greater Baltimore Committee, told a Baltimore audience recently that "if regionalism isn't dealing with land use, fiscal disparities, housing, and education, regionalism is not dealing with the issues that count."

Voluntary versus Mandatory

There is no warm and fuzzy path to achieving regionalism on these hardest of issues. Take the possibility of voluntary tax sharing. The most extensive voluntary tax sharing arrangement is located in the Dayton, Ohio, area. Through vigorous effort and long negotiations, using $5 million in annual economic development grants as an inducement, Montgomery County government managed to get twenty-nine of their thirty local cities, villages, and townships to sign a nine-year contract on joint economic development and tax sharing. But this tax sharing component is only symbolic, amounting to barely one dollar per resident of Montgomery County per year in pooled revenues. By contrast, for the Twin Cities area, where the state legislature mandated tax sharing twenty-five years ago, about one hundred dollars of revenues per resident per year is pooled.

Take the case of regional land use planning. The only effective, voluntary program of joint land use planning where local governments have established voluntary urban growth boundaries is in Lancaster County, Pennsylvania. Lancaster County is a very special place. With 4,700 family-owned farms (including many Amish and Mennonite households) Lancaster County farmers outproduce thirteen entire states, including New Jersey, the self-styled "Garden State."

You couldn't find another American community with a stronger commitment to farmland preservation. For many Lancastrians, the farming way of life is literally a religious commitment. Lancaster County is the only place in the country where, on a voluntary basis, they've succeeded in forging growth management alliances. Otherwise, wherever there is strong land use planning, such as in Oregon, state law has made it mandatory.

Regarding fair share low- and moderate-income housing, all the non-profit housing groups, all the community development corporations, all the church organizations, and all the local public housing authorities build about 50,000 low-income housing units a year, out of a total annual production of 1.5 million housing units. That's about 3 percent of all housing built. Only where state or local law mandates that the housing industry produce a proportionate share of low- and moderate-income housing is there significant construction of affordable housing.

There are no soft paths to regionalism, only hard choices. Take transportation policy, for example. The easy choice is to keep building highways everywhere. This serves the interests of both highway contractors and construction workers unions. Building more highways is perceived as spurring economic development and has been a constant pattern in Ohio and around the country.

The hard choice is what, a generation ago, Oregon Gov. Tom McCall did, what all Oregon governors since have done, and what Neil Goldschmidt did as mayor of Portland. They viewed transportation investments as merely one tool of rational land use planning and shifted highway funds to light rail and bus systems.

Mayor Richard Hatcher and a succession of African American mayors newly arrived to power asserted the easy political cliché: "we can make a difference." The hard path was taken by Mayor Willie Herenton, first black mayor of Memphis. Confronted with the fact that Memphis's average income had fallen from 97 percent to 76 percent of its suburbs in just one decade, Mayor Herenton said, in effect, "This dog don't hunt. I propose that we dissolve the city of Memphis and make Shelby County our unified government."

Or take the example of Mayor Larry Chavis, African American mayor of Richmond, Virginia. After twenty years of black control of Richmond, he saw that 80 percent of black households of above-average income lived outside the city itself. In other words, the very people such a majority black government would look to as the primary source of civic involvement—middle-class, African American families—have been leaving. Mayor Chavis advocates consolidating Richmond with surrounding Chesterfield and Henrico Counties.

In the Cleveland area there won't be any resumption of annexation or city-county consolidations, like Memphis or Richmond. However, it is certainly possible to move toward a stronger system of shared responsibilities in the region. One key would be a clear statement from Cleveland's own political leadership that says, "Yes, we need to actively search out regional solutions and not rely solely on programs and policies directed at Cleveland itself."

It is the easy political choice for suburban officials everywhere to pretend that their communities can really isolate themselves from the central city's problems. The hard political choice was taken by the Association of Northern Municipalities outside Minneapolis and St. Paul. They vigorously supported both regional tax sharing and fair share low- and moderate-income housing.

The easy choice is for major business leaders and major foundation executives to champion modest investment not only in the central business district but also in older, inner-city neighborhoods, complying with the Community Reinvestment Act. The hard choice is for that same leadership to recognize that part of the solution for the problems of the inner city must involve the very suburban communities where they live and the suburban school systems where their children go to school.

The easy path for religious leaders is to acquiesce to the fact that the most racially segregated hour in American life is 11 A.M. on Sunday mornings. The hard path has been embraced by Cleveland's Bishop Pilla, who states that dividing the metropolitan community by race and class is not only economically wrong, it is morally wrong. "We are all one community," the bishop said, "within the context of our faith, a call to unity is not a choice, it is an obligation."

In other parts of the country, where major reforms such as those discussed above have occurred, state legislatures have made them happen. The key barriers are not legal, but political. In Ohio the question is: How can a sufficiently broad-based coalition of interests be organized to secure from the Ohio legislature regional reform laws addressing urban sprawl, fiscal disparities, and concentrations of poverty in inner cities and older blue-collar suburbs?

This coalition should join central city and inner-ring suburban residents with taxpayer groups, environmentalists, farm interests, chambers of commerce, religious leaders, public transportation advocates, affordable housing advocates, and many others. The coalition should explain how all the people losing under the present system can be turned into winners.

By reducing wasteful sprawl and reducing economic disparities and racial segregation, the entire state will benefit. But it will take the state legislature to change the rules of the game. The challenge before you is to develop the will to change. No one can do that for Ohio but Ohioans. No one. You must take steps on that path of hard choices.

Chapter 4

Cleveland and the Region

A Planning Perspective

Norman Krumholz and Kathryn Wertheim Hexter

The suburbanization of Greater Cleveland is based on race and class as much as on geography. Reducing inequalities will require new programs for fair and affordable housing, improved public education, and regional governance. If we don't address these issues of fundamental injustice, the resulting social and economic problems may drag down the entire region.

Norman Krumholz is professor of urban studies at Cleveland State University's Levin College of Urban Affairs and former director of planning for the city of Cleveland. Kathryn Wertheim Hexter is the Urban University Program director at the college.

Growth and Suburbanization

Cleveland began as a commercial city. For its first few decades the city lived on trade with its surrounding hinterland. At a very early stage (1840–50), however, Cleveland became an industrial city, making its living by manufacturing and exporting. It was also a self-contained, integral political unit, incorporating virtually all the population and development in Cuyahoga County. In 1900, for example, over 381,000 of the 439,000 people in Cuyahoga County lived in the city of Cleveland. While there were rich and poor residents in the city, employers and employees, and identifiable neighborhoods of different ethnic groups and classes, they all worked and lived in the same small space and under the same political administration.

The major spur for the growth and development of Cleveland—as with many other American cities—was jobs and economic activity. The city was not deliberately planned or built as much as it was the result of the agglomeration of jobs. Figure 4.1 suggests the strong relationship between Cleveland's economic development and population.

Until the 1950s Cleveland enjoyed great success as an industrial city. Industry was booming, the city was growing, and most of its people were employed and earning above-average wages. But the very success of the industrial city and the resulting densities produced high prices for land and made it difficult for manufacturing firms to expand. As early as the 1920s employers began considering moving to outlying sites where they could expand their businesses without worrying about high-priced land or resistance from surrounding neighbors. In addition, the relatively wealthy members of the population became conscious of the deterioration of the industrial city as a place to live. They noted the deteriorating environments, the obsolete infrastructure, and the possibility of social unrest in the city and began to consider other options. Their mobility options, however, were constrained, as they had to depend on inadequate transportation technology. But transportation, and resulting mobility, improved rapidly. First the trolley, then the commuter train, then the automobile exploded the older "walking" city and opened up previously undeveloped suburban areas for industry and housing alike.

To an extent, suburban proliferation was encouraged by the political power of the automobile, oil, housing, and road-building industries. As powerful private entities, these industries were free to ignore the social or public costs associated with the impact of their policies on the city. The public costs included environmental damage and harm to the social and fiscal integrity of the city that suburbanization would bring in its wake. Public policy, especially in transportation, urban renewal, and the provision of mortgage capital, also facilitated the suburbanization of the white middle class.

The movement to Cleveland's suburbs involved far more than just deconcentration of the population. Lowering of densities in the city might

City and area population, 1810-1990
Cleveland, Cuyahoga, and Five-County Area*

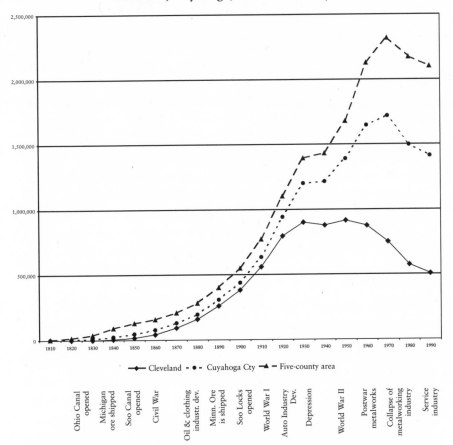

*Five-County Area includes: Cuyahoga, Geauga, Lake, Lorain and Medina counties

Source: U.S. Dept. of Commerce, Bureau of the Census

Figure 4.1 *City and area population, 1810-1990*

have been considered desirable because, one could argue, it provided the remaining city residents with more parkland and open space. The early industrial city had been overbuilt, the argument could continue, and some suburbanization provided it with "breathing space." But suburbanization also has a powerful class dimension and produces social and territorial polarization, since suburban communities enjoy political autonomy and total control over zoning and land use. Through large-lot zoning, deed restrictions, and other exclusionary means, they are free to screen out the poor and determine that the lower-income population of the region will live in older, deteriorated housing in Cleveland and, more recently, in the near-in suburbs.

The poor, especially the minority poor who are not only burdened by poverty but also by racial discrimination, are left with deteriorating housing, polluted vacant land, and an obsolete infrastructure that is now deficit ridden. The city of Cleveland can levy taxes on employee earnings in the city but cannot tax suburban real estate. Outlying communities, however, with tax bases enriched by new industrial and commercial properties and the relatively expensive dwellings of the affluent, can afford first-rate public schools for their children, fine parks, roads, and other services.

So it is clear that suburbanization is as much a class process as a spatial process; it makes a geographic, political, and economic fact out of the hierarchy inherent in the economy. This creates not only a high-income class in the Cleveland region but also high-income suburbs like Pepper Pike, Hunting Valley, Gates Mills, Rocky River, and others, which are separate and privileged. It also creates working-class suburbs like Lakewood, Garfield Heights, Parma, Euclid, and others, as well as poor suburbs like East Cleveland.

Although significant numbers of jobs in manufacturing, retailing, and wholesaling have left the older city of Cleveland, downtown Cleveland and University Circle have retained their primacy because of access and agglomeration. Cleveland still has facilities that cannot be replicated (at least so far) in the suburbs—museums, theaters, sports and entertainment venues, and universities. These appeal mainly to suburbanites but are now partially supported by city residents through "sin" taxes and various forms of tax subsidies.

The greatest employment attraction of downtown Cleveland to suburban dwellers is the concentration of office employment. It is well-paid work in such fields as law, real-estate, finance, insurance, and government, and it requires higher level training rather than manual skills. Office work is pulled to the center of the region because of great agglomeration economies and thrives there despite the distances its workers may travel. The population living closest to these downtown jobs in city neighborhoods like Central, Hough, and Tremont are generally excluded from these good jobs because of inadequate education and job skills or class or racial prejudice (John D. Kasarda, "Urban Change and Minority Opportunities" in *The New Urban Reality,* ed. Paul E. Peterson [Washington: Brookings Institution, 1985]).

So the Cleveland region's poor and their needs are concentrated in the city of Cleveland, which has diminished resources and power to help the poor or help them find work. Suburbia benefits from what the city provides but avoids most of the costs the city bears. A process whose roots are in market determination of housing supply, industrial and commercial location, and interurban transportation modes is reinforced by a class-specific system of government.

As one direct result of this process, the public institutions in education, housing, and transportation that serve the people of Cleveland also lack the resources, power, and, indeed, the interest in serving the basic needs of their clients. For example, the Cleveland Public School system, which has been in disarray for decades, was put into state receivership in 1994 and is now under the leadership of the mayor. Students in the system, on average, perform poorly on state proficiency tests. Of all the students who enrolled in the eighth grade in 1990, the school system graduated only 32 percent four years later; fully 68 percent dropped out, moved, or otherwise disappeared. The Cuyahoga Metropolitan Housing Authority (CMHA), which in 1980 housed more than twenty-five thousand people in twelve thousand traditional public housing units, was in 1995 housing many fewer families while demolishing or "thinning down" their inventory and in 1998 had about two thousand fewer units. CMHA had also left unused part of its Section 8 allocation. The Greater Cleveland Regional Transit Authority has built rail lines like the two-mile, $72 million Waterfront Line to service downtown development projects and has placed high priority on developing a regional commuter rail network while neglecting the basic mobility needs of Cleveland's population, about 35 percent of whom depend on public transit for their total mobility around the Cleveland metro area.

As noted above, the city was not deliberately planned or built; an agglomeration of jobs and private decisions combined to shape the city of 1996. Like so many other American cities, Cleveland's development was the result of a process that was inherently unfair and exploitative of the poor, especially the minority poor. In the 1960s, rapidly declining population, the increasing isolation of the poor in the central city, and increasing levels of unemployment and crime were accompanied by a decline in the assessed value of the tax base and a decline in the local general fund operating revenue. In fact, the fiscal and economic disparities between central city and region were wider in Cleveland in 1980 than in almost any other place in the United States. Unemployment, poverty, crime, inadequate education, rotting housing, and the other elements of the urban crisis were concentrated in the city, particularly in the city's low-income neighborhoods.

There was very little that the local political structure could do to address these problems. The roots of the problems—concentrated poverty and racial segregation—were national in their scope. Furthermore, Cleveland's resident population had very little political influence in the region. However, several initiatives related to mass transit, land banking, and lakefront development were undertaken by the city's planning department the 1970s and 1980s, and these made a small but significant impact in addressing some of these inequities and reshaping the future development of the city.

In 1975 the Cleveland Transit System was transferred to the Greater Cleveland Regional Transit Authority. A high priority in negotiating this transfer of a city asset to a regional authority was to improve the mobility of Cleveland's transit-dependent population, those families who lacked automobiles and who depended entirely on public transit. At that time, about one-third of all Cleveland families had no car; among families over age sixty-five or earning less than six thousand dollars a year, about one-half had no car. Part of the agreement was the improvement of service frequencies and route coverage within the city and the initiation of Community Responsive Transit, a door-to-door, dial-a-ride service.

Also in the 1970s Cleveland planners drafted, introduced, and saw passed a new state law that shortened and simplified the foreclosure procedure for tax delinquent and abandoned property. The new law also allowed the city to land bank these foreclosed parcels as trustee for the other two taxing bodies, Cuyahoga County and the Cleveland Board of

Education. By the early 1990s the land bank owned up to 15 percent of all the land in certain east side neighborhoods, thus greatly enhancing the city's ability to redevelop property.

In 1977 a similar effort was undertaken to address the problem of the neglect and decay of the city's once elegant lakefront parks. The mayor's task force on lakefront development, headed by the city planning director, established a new state park in Cleveland using as the core of the park three lakefront parks—Edgewater, Gordon, and Wildwood—that the city could no longer afford to maintain. In agreeing to set up this park, the Ohio Department of Natural Resources reversed its historic policy of only building state parks in rural areas. The impact of this action went beyond the cleanup of the city's three lakefront parks. Since 1977 the state has maintained and expanded the park and added the North Coast Harbor, catalyzing the future development of the Rock and Roll Hall of Fame, the Great Lakes Science Center, and other attractions.

Flaws in the Growth Strategy

For better or worse, Cleveland is where it is today mainly by observing five growth-related precepts that have dominated development in this region for the past forty years:

- The widespread ownership of private property, more specifically single-family, detached housing on a plot of land, extending indefinitely outward from the central city.

- The almost universal ownership and use of private automobiles for mobility. (There are now in the United States more registered vehicles than drivers; soon there will be more registered vehicles than people.)

- Building places for working and shopping that are widely scattered and low density and have plenty of adjacent free parking.

- Providing housing for low-income households largely through the trickle-down process. This concentrates the poor—especially the minority poor, who suffer from racial discrimination as well as institutional custom—into backwater neighborhoods near the urban core.

- Supporting all of the above with a highly fragmented governmental structure that consists of many small and virtually autonomous local governments, each with its own mayor, council, school board, and absolute control over local land use and zoning in its locality.

The result of this pattern of metro development has been traffic congestion in certain growth locations, difficulties in paying for new roads and sewage systems, shortages of affordable housing in growth areas, loss of green space in the region, air and water pollution, and difficulty in locating new sanitary landfills and other essential but locally undesirable land uses (LULUs). None of these problems, however, approach in severity the systematic isolation of the minority poor and the continued growth of two societies—separate and unequal—that the Kerner Commission warned us about twenty-five years ago. This problem is inherently unjust; it is wasteful and inefficient; and it may soon threaten the social peace of our society.

The typical metro growth pattern takes place through an uncoordinated, seemingly chance set of local public policies and individual private actions carried out by separate governments and private parties. This almost random process is cherished by many Americans who reject the ideas of coordination and regional planning as near-socialism. However, none of the growth-related problems Cleveland is encountering can be solved by fragmented local governments, each acting to maximize the interests of its own citizens without regard for the rest of the region. Our failure to develop mechanisms for regionwide decision making is a major fundamental flaw in the metropolitan development of our region.

Another major developmental flaw is that Cleveland's growth strategy focuses far too much on physical and economic activities and far too little on critical social issues. In particular, Cleveland's civic and political leaders focus much too much on big-bang projects, such as the Gateway stadium and arena complex and the Rock and Roll Hall of Fame, which divert scarce public capital to projects that make only marginal improvements while much more serious problems are allowed to fester. Although they claim to produce jobs for city residents and net taxes to the public treasury so that the city can continue to provide public services, there is little evidence that these large-scale projects result in such public benefits. Instead, there is evidence that they contribute to widening inequalities. Civic leaders must confront and attack the immense disparities between the incomes and educational levels of its black citizens on one hand and its white citizens on the other. Without this leadership, the rising tide of the Cleveland region's overall prosperity has failed—and will continue to fail—to carry with it a substantial part of the region's African American residents.

Widening Disparities

The disparities are substantial. For example, the average 1989 income for the region's white families was $40,862; for the region's black families it was $24,069. For black families in the city, the average 1989 income was $17,822. Poverty rates in the city and in the county have been growing rapidly: between 1980 and 1990, the county's poverty rate went from 13.6 percent to 18.5 percent and then increased to 19.3 percent in 1995. The city's poverty rate rose to 42.2 percent in 1990. Both figures are all-time highs (Council for Economic Opportunities, "Ohio Poverty Indicators," vol. 10, 1995). Although blacks make up about 25 percent of the region's population, 80 percent of all children in our region living in poverty are black. In 1992, almost a third of Cleveland's African American population lived in neighborhoods beset with extreme poverty. In fifteen of these neighborhoods, over 50 percent of all families lived under the poverty line in 1994. Poor blacks are left behind in neighborhoods of concentrated poverty. In 1990, 91 percent of poor blacks in Cleveland lived in poverty tracts, isolated from jobs, decent schools, middle-class role models, and the larger community.

The city's crime index was among the highest of the nation's seventy-five largest cities in 1990, and the region's public schools remain ineffective and highly segregated by race. Even though African American households have been moving out of the city and into the eastern suburbs, the exodus has not improved their access to new jobs, which are shifting to the far eastern and far western periphery. Indeed, the inner-ring suburb of East Cleveland is now in worse shape than the center city itself. The reality of overwhelming poverty results in innumerable social problems and also sharply weakens the ability of the city to redevelop its neighborhoods.

Cleveland's failure to face these problems squarely has been obscured by several positive aspects of its race relations. One is the exercise of important powers by African Americans within the city, where they control both the municipal government and the school system. Another factor is the emergence of a sizable black middle class, much of which has moved to the suburbs. But Cleveland's reputation for good race relations is only partly deserved. Much of the region's black community, especially within the city, has been and is being left out.

The tendency to evade dealing directly with racial inequality has been strengthened by three other circumstances. First, many members of the region's white majority benefit from maintaining the inequities. This may not be deliberate, but they do not want to change certain institutions that benefit them at blacks' expense, especially racial segregation in housing and schools.

Second, some of the institutions that enable the white majority to maintain its advantages—particularly zoning and local legal arrangements that help maintain residential segregation by race—were not ostensibly adopted for that purpose, so they are somewhat hidden from view. Because these institutions are not in plain sight, it is easy for most people to ignore their existence and disregard their disastrously unfair effects.

Third, even if most Clevelanders wanted to change things, it would not be easy. Some important problems such as high rates of out-of-wedlock births among black teenagers, high rates of crime, and widespread drug abuse seem to resist solution by public policy.

To those who are willing to consider long-term development, a regionwide approach to social issues seems essential. However, the more common practice in most relatively affluent suburbs has been simply to ignore the social problems of Cleveland and poor suburbs like East Cleveland. Yet all suburbs are economically dependent on the city for the jobs of many of their residents, for low-wage workers, and for many vital services. And most suburbs have adopted exclusionary zoning regulations that make them partly responsible for the inner-city concentration of poverty that generates many of Cleveland's worst problems. So all suburbs have a responsibility to—and indeed stand to gain economically—by helping to solve the problems of the entire metropolitan area community that sustains them all economically.

If Cleveland is to grapple effectively with its crucial social problems, its citizens also must explicitly recognize the importance of race in generating social and economic inequalities. They must also genuinely want to reduce major racial and economic inequalities. There is no shortage of planning reports with data confirming the economically inferior position of the region's African American population. But they remain largely silent about whether that condition is good or bad, and what, if anything, should be done to change it. True, the incomes and status of many African Americans in the Cleveland region have improved in the past decade, yet they still have much lower incomes, education, and status than the region's whites and a much larger proportion of them are poor. Not specifically recognizing the need to improve this situation amounts to accepting present racial inequalities in the region as essentially inevitable.

Reducing Residential Segregation

Reducing residential segregation by race is essential to resolving nearly all of the Cleveland region's social problems. It is crucial because where a family lives affects four key aspects of life—schools, access to jobs, personal safety, and the speed at which home investments appreciate and create household wealth. All four are less favorable in most mainly black neighborhoods than in most mixed or mainly white neighborhoods, in part because black incomes are so low compared with white incomes and in part because of continued racial discrimination in the dual housing market.

Effectively attacking racial segregation in Cleveland would mean adopting explicitly race-based policies encouraging more blacks to move into western suburbs and other largely white areas. How might that be accomplished? One way to reduce racial segregation is to seek out and penalize widespread racially discriminatory behavior by realtors and homeowners, especially racial steering. Discriminatory behavior, which is already illegal, could be easily discovered, severely punished with expensive fines and jail sentences for violators, and highly publicized. Perhaps then it would cease. The necessary laws are already on the books; what is needed is the political will to enforce the law with vigor.

A second tactic would be to provide numerous inner-city black households with federal housing vouchers to be used in mainly white city neighborhoods and suburbs. Since 1976 the Gautreaux project in Chicago has moved more than four thousand inner-city, black, low-income households to mainly white suburbs with very positive results for the people involved. The Cuyahoga Metropolitan Housing Authority could assign some of its housing vouchers to that approach. Or the vouchers could be managed by another agency interested in desegregation, as is done in Chicago.

Roughly seven thousand new homes are built each year in the Cleveland metropolitan area, most of which are in the outer suburbs. If just 2 percent had been occupied by low-income, inner-city households using housing vouchers, the city of Cleveland could move more than 140 poor households of all races per year from its concentrated poverty areas into new suburban dwellings. It is not too late to begin now.

But why would suburban housing developers make even 2 percent of their new units available to low-income families? They probably wouldn't without some strong incentives. One such incentive would be inclusionary zoning that would require all developers of housing subdivisions of a specified size to include a certain percentage of those units to be rented or sold to low-income households. To make up for any resulting economic loss, developers could increase their overall density above normal levels. These tactics would have to be enforced throughout the metropolitan region, not in just one or a few localities. One agency would thus have to implement them on a regional basis. Montgomery County in Maryland has had just such a program for many years, but it requires commitment by the region and strong support by the state.

Indeed, any long-term strategy would require the state government to play a crucial role. Only the state can design and pass a regional governance structure that can cope with both growth-related and basic social problems at the metro-area level. But private sector leadership is also essential. Elected officials in our democracy mainly follow existing public opinion rather than creating it. New ideas that upset the status quo must spring mainly from and be promoted by the private sector—business, labor, citizens groups, the media, and academics. If Cleveland is going to change, its own community is going to have to assume responsibility for stimulating that change. This means that the leadership of Cleveland must turn away from the easy and often glitzy so-called economic development projects that don't produce either jobs or taxes and emphasize other, more difficult goals. Top priorities would be to (1) reduce racial segregation in housing; (2) reform and improve the public educational system; and (3) establish a regional structure of governance to address regional issues and control growth.

Finally, a truly long-term perspective will be essential. Even a quarter of a century will not be enough to end most of these problems. Americans hardly ever think in such long terms, but such an approach is absolutely essential to correct a fundamental injustice and to keep social problems from gravely weakening our entire society.

Chapter 5

Rebuilding Cleveland

A Regional Undertaking

Thomas Bier

*In its first two hundred years, Cleveland went through phases of great
building and great abandonment. Cleveland's third century could be
a time of rebuilding—if the metropolitan region can work together
for balanced development.*

As director of the [Housing Policy Research Center at Cleveland State
University's Levin College of Urban Affairs,] Thomas Bier studies the migration of households and tax base in the region.

The history of world cities, cities much older than Cleveland, tells us that
they typically go through various phases of growth, decline, and population change, and that such phases can last hundreds of years. In comparison, Cleveland, at just two hundred years old, is a newborn infant.
Nonetheless, Cleveland can be viewed as having gone through two
phases, each about one hundred years in length, and as entering a third.
This chapter will consider briefly the first two phases and focus on the
third, which concerns the path that the city and its surrounding region
could take over the next one hundred years.

Building and Abandonment

The first phase of Cleveland's history fits neatly into the nineteenth century. It began in 1796 with Moses Cleaveland and his surveyors, who configured a village in the wilderness. It continued through the massive economic development, construction, and growth that resulted from the industrial revolution. And it ended when the first suburbs began to form around 1900. Given the extent of development and expansion, this first phase of Cleveland's history can be termed "building."

Abandonment followed building. Although it would not begin to show seriously until the 1950s, the roots of abandonment touch the turn of the century. Before 1900 there were no such places as "suburbs" — there was just Cleveland and beyond it scattered villages. Around the turn of the century, Cleveland's wealthy industrialists began to move from their elegant Euclid Avenue homes to communities that were independent units of government, such as East Cleveland, Bratenahl, Lakewood, Cleveland Heights, and Shaker Heights. With those moves began the abandonment and disinvestment of Cleveland and the creation of the present-day region that is highly fractured by scores of independent suburbs.

It is important to note that the city's wealthy, who created the first suburbs, did not move willingly. They felt forced out of Cleveland because of city hall's inability to protect their residential streets from traffic and encroaching commercial and retail development. Those were the days before zoning, when property owners could essentially do whatever they wanted, including establishing nonresidential activities in the middle of a residential area.

When the wealthy left Cleveland they vowed never again to allow their place of residence to be so violated. They protected themselves by moving to "new" governmental jurisdictions—suburbs—where laws and property deed restrictions would prevent what had happened to them in Cleveland from happening again. And, because the city's economically powerful left Cleveland feeling forced out and violated, it is not surprising that support for living in Cleveland, as a matter of principle, waned across the following decades. "Sensible" middle-class people were expected to live in suburbs. Their actions set the tone and initiated the momentum for the second phase of Cleveland's history: abandonment and disinvestment in favor of suburbs.

Cleveland's second century, particularly after World War II, was dominated by abandonment and disinvestment as more and more people found that they, too, could afford to live in a suburb and receive protection (and other "benefits," such as distance from racial minorities) that they could not get in the city. The result was a city whose economic strength was largely drained away. If in recent years Cleveland had not been able to tax the earnings of suburbanites who work in the city, it would be truly decimated.

As Cleveland enters its third century, it is faced with the legacy of abandonment and disinvestment: thousands of acres of vacant land (some of it chemically contaminated by previous use) where buildings once stood; thousands of empty and obsolete buildings, most of which, in time, may have to be demolished; tens of thousands of abandoned people; and the city's estrangement from the numerous suburbs and the adjacent counties of the metropolitan area.

It is a staggering legacy with which to cope but not an inherently impossible one. Numerous activities have been under way to strengthen the city, and progress is evident. Overshadowing all activities is the fundamental requirement that abandonment be reversed in order to reestablish the city's economic and social strength. Cleveland's future depends on its being occupied to a major extent with residents (and employers) who can afford to locate in a suburb. To accomplish that, much of the city must be rebuilt and, to the extent feasible, existing buildings must be modified to suit contemporary needs.

Rebuilding

Because of the scale of the needed rebuilding, ultimately involving one-half or more of the city's land area (one-half would be thirty to forty square miles), rebuilding could span much of the next one hundred years. Indeed, rebuilding needs to be thought of as a never-ending, continuous process. Rebuilding already has begun, as evidenced by recent housing developments downtown and in neighborhoods, by Gateway, Society Center, Tower City, and new hotels. Rebuilding has begun, but outside of downtown the surface has barely been scratched.

A key feature of most of these projects is that they require public funds to bring them to life. Urban rebuilding or redevelopment is fundamentally different than new suburban development, which typically is located on what had been farmland. Rebuilding usually involves demolition of old properties, digging out foundations, assembling numerous small parcels of land to form a sufficiently large site, cleaning up contamination—all costs that new suburban developments do not have to face.

In 1996 the demand for land for redevelopment in Cleveland was estimated to be 150 acres per year (150 acres annually for 100 years totals 23 square miles). Nowhere near that amount is being produced. It can cost on the order of $20 million to prepare 150 acres of used land for redevelopment, or about $133,000 per acre, compared with a purchase price of $50,000 per acre for undeveloped land 25 miles out in Geauga or Medina Counties. Unless the gap of $83,000 per acre ($12 million for 150 acres) is filled by public funds, most urban redevelopment projects will not happen.

The pace at which Cleveland will be able to rebuild will be dictated by the funds available for the preparation of sites for redevelopment. The city does not have $12 million annually to apply to that need. Funds must come from other sources: the federal government, state government, or the suburbs of the region.

One might ask: "Why should government or suburban residents pay those extra costs and subsidize projects? If redevelopment in Cleveland is not economically feasible, then it should not happen. Let development occur where developers can make it happen." The answer is that government already subsidizes suburban development through the provision of roads, highways, bridges, water, and sewer systems. People (and businesses) that move to new suburban developments don't pay the full costs of the infrastructure that enables them to make their move. The public at large bears the cost. Most development occurs not where developers can make it happen, but where government enables it to happen.

Will suburbanites in the Greater Cleveland region be willing to pay to help meet the special costs associated with redeveloping Cleveland? Probably not, if the only purpose is Cleveland's redevelopment. If the issue is not just the future of Cleveland but the future of all suburbs as well, then a majority may be willing to support it.

The Situation of the Suburbs in Cuyahoga County

Although the intention of the original suburbanites in 1900 was to secure a place of residence that would never be disrupted as their homes in

Cleveland had been, and although all suburbs that came to life and grew to maturity since then have held that outlook, the reality is that no suburb is inherently protected. Suburbs age and can decline just like big central cities. Suburban real estate is no different than urban real estate; it too deteriorates (if not adequately maintained) and it too can lose favor in the marketplace as tastes and preferences shift. And suburban streets, curbs, sidewalks, water, and sewer systems age and deteriorate just as in the big city.

The older original suburbs that abut Cleveland—suburbs such as Lakewood, Parma, Garfield Heights, Cleveland Heights, Euclid—are now fifty to seventy years old and have aged to where they are changing. They are battling decline and are in competition with the new, growing suburbs. And they won't be the last; they will be followed by more suburbs— such as North Olmsted, Middleburg Heights, Lyndhurst, Highland Heights—as they, in turn, age to fifty, sixty, seventy years.

It so happens that at the same time that Cleveland's future depends on major redevelopment, the future of a growing number of suburbs depends on increased maintenance and, to some extent, on redevelopment as well. Suburbs are faced with doing, on a smaller scale, exactly what Cleveland is faced with: maintenance, modernization, and redevelopment. But do suburbs have the fiscal resources for that? Somewhat, but not fully. Most could not tax their residents and businesses enough to accomplish what needs to be done. Higher taxes would precipitate moves out to lower-tax communities, which in turn would precipitate more decline. A positive future for declining suburbs depends on financial assistance from state and federal governments and from the developing suburbs in the region.

Some suburbs are, for now, ideally situated—such as Solon, Beachwood, Strongsville, Avon. They are largely new; they have been developing and growing with new residents and businesses; and they have been able to hold down the tax burden on residents through industrial and commercial developments. However, although their decline may be fifty or more years off, they can be hurt in the near term by the situation in which Cleveland and the older suburbs now find themselves.

If Cleveland and the older suburbs are not able to strengthen their property tax bases through redevelopment and maintenance, taxes needed to support Cuyahoga County government will have to come more from the Solons and the Beachwoods. If that were to happen, residents and employers in those communities could be pushed to adjacent counties where taxes are lower. Therefore, all communities within Cuyahoga County have much to gain through the redevelopment and maintenance of Cleveland and the older suburbs and much to lose in the long run if that does not happen.

The Situation in Adjacent Counties

In the counties adjacent to Cuyahoga—Lake, Geauga, Portage, Summit, Medina, and Lorain—there are conditions that are similar to those in Cuyahoga County, and there are conditions that are completely different. Similar are the central cities of Akron, Lorain, and Elyria, and older communities such as Barberton and Painesville. Although smaller in scale, needs for redevelopment and maintenance exist across the counties and parallel the situation within Cuyahoga. The rural areas, small towns, and villages are, however, completely different.

All six counties are being dramatically affected by Cuyahoga County. In the portions of the six counties that are closest to Cuyahoga, 40–50 percent of the people who purchase homes are movers from Cuyahoga. The homebuilding market is being fueled by movers out of Cuyahoga, the number of which increases each year. Many of the businesses locating in the six counties are movers from Cuyahoga. Much of the growth and development occurring there is the result of proximity to Cuyahoga County. Because of the scarcity of undeveloped land in Cuyahoga suburbs, and the plentiful supply of land in the adjacent counties, development will continue to increase in those counties.

In the adjacent counties, development is a blessing to some and a curse to others. Rural areas and small towns are being transformed into extensions of urban life. Some bemoan the change, others hail it as economic growth. One thing is certain: unless there is more redevelopment in Cleveland and older suburbs, unless there are more people and business that choose to locate in the urban core, the development pressures in adjacent counties cannot lessen, nor can the possibility of Cuyahoga County's economic decline.

The prospect facing Cuyahoga County is that its suburbs will be abandoned and disinvested just as Cleveland was. That, indeed, is what has begun to happen. The prospect facing the adjacent counties is that over the next forty to fifty years all farms and large open spaces will be lost to development. Under existing trends that future is a certainty.

Development in the seven-county region is not balanced. Communities with undeveloped land are growing while communities that do not have undeveloped land but rather have aging real estate are either declining or are facing the prospect of decline. The challenge is to change the imbalance; to achieve redevelopment and maintenance of cities and older suburbs across the region while having development in rural areas that is less disruptive to communities and rural interests.

Regional Commitment

The next phase in the evolving life of Cleveland, the city's third century, should be characterized by a regional undertaking that addresses the future of all communities in the multicounty region. A regional commitment is needed to serve three objectives simultaneously: (1) rebuild and maintain the central cities of Cleveland, Akron, Lorain, and Elyria; (2) maintain and redevelop older suburbs; and (3) preserve as much farmland and open space as possible.

To accomplish these objectives, public policies and programs will have to be reoriented and tax dollars will have to be expended accordingly. This may appear, at first thought, to be a monumental political challenge, but it could be exactly what most of the residents of the region would prefer, particularly if they see it leading to (1) community stability and security and (2) improved race relations and relations in general among the public.

One of the consequences of the past fifty years of development and movement has been community instability. It is difficult for many people to feel secure about the place where they live. Lack of a sense of community stability and security has become a hallmark of the American way of life—a feeling spawned by spreading decline, racial change, "growth," and, of course, crime. How many can say with unshakable certainty that in fifty years their home community will not be "run down" or "a slum" or completely changed racially, or, for those in rural areas, ten times larger or totally devoid of farmland?

Underlying the concern for quality of life is a strong need for a feeling of community stability. Stability began to erode when Cleveland began to be abandoned: when new communities began to be favored over old communities, when moving began to be favored over staying, and when public policy was oriented to promote all of that. Community stability can be reestablished by rebalancing the development of the region. As Cleveland is rebuilt and becomes much more attractive as a place to remain in and move to; as older suburbs are maintained, redeveloped, and become more attractive; and as rural towns grow and develop at a pace and in a style that most residents endorse, then a sense of stability can flourish across the region. Not to rebalance is to invite more instability.

This chapter touches the two most sensitive and potent nerves in American society: real estate development and race. To some extent they are linked. As whites have retreated from living with minorities, they have fueled the development of new communities. The retreat continues, adding to the vulnerability of some of the older racially changing suburbs, such as Euclid, Cleveland Heights, Lakewood, and Maple Heights, where minority residents are growing in number.

But not all whites are impassioned racists; far from it. A mayor of a racially changing inner eastern suburb that is still very much white said recently, "The racists are gone. The people living here now aren't bothered by the color of their neighbor's skin. They just want no crime, good schools, and good services." The same mayor knows that the financial burden facing his community because of aging streets, curbs, water lines, sewer lines, and some obsolete real estate has made the odds against long-term stable racial integration very high. Many whites are willing to stay, and want to stay, but if racial integration is going to survive, that suburb must have financial assistance to cope with needed maintenance and redevelopment.

Cleveland has the same need, and it also has a sizable population that has been abandoned as a result of the region's imbalance of development. Abandonment by the larger society is bound to foster destructive and criminal behaviors. Many of the abandoned live in or near neighborhoods with large amounts of vacant land and obsolete real estate. They live at the doorstep of needed redevelopment. A way to begin drawing them, particularly the youth, back into mainstream society is to reverse their abandonment through rebuilding with occupants who could live in a suburb if they wished.

One can only truly feel better about one's self through one's own actions, but a strong influence in that direction can be affected by others who say through their actions: "We're not abandoning you." The new homes being built in Cleveland's Hough neighborhood by people who could easily afford to live in a suburb, some of whom are white, make the statement (intended or not) to the poor living nearby: "We are willing to live near you; you are not as abandoned as you thought."

Race relations can be improved through suburbanites helping to rebuild Cleveland (and Akron and Lorain) and helping to maintain and stabilize older suburbs. It may turn out in the long run that the breakthrough on race relations will come through people, white and black, who can afford to live in a suburb choosing instead to live in the city in new developments. The key word in that sentence is *choosing*. All suburban racial change, even in the most open of suburbs, occurs within a defensive atmosphere because it is change that happens to a suburb and its existing residents—change that they did not choose. Even if many residents are willing to live with the change, it is still something happening to them.

In contrast, when whites and blacks choose to move into a development knowing that it will involve living with people of the other race, a proactive, positive atmosphere is created, which is much more likely to result in a permanent, stable racial mix. Perhaps the greatest potential that rebuilding Cleveland offers is the strengthening of racial and community social cohesion.

The great cathedrals of Europe took many years to construct—one hundred years in the case of Notre Dame in Paris. The long, continuing process involving succeeding generations of designers, laborers, and craftsmen fostered community cohesion. The character of Paris and the way Parisians feel about each other had to be shaped by the building of Notre Dame.

The best of construction projects will cause people living in the community to feel better about each other, will tend to bridge social estrangements, and will enable people who feel uneasy in each others' presence to feel more comfortable. Can that type of community cohesion happen under modern-day conditions in the rebuilding of Cleveland? It should be the goal. The challenge and opportunity in rebuilding Cleveland is to do it in ways that serve to heal the economic, racial, and social fractures of the region. The road to that healing begins by making the undertaking a regional commitment.

Mechanisms for Regional Commitment

A regional commitment involving at least the seven counties that make up the core of the region is needed to address the three objectives discussed previously: (1) rebuild and maintain the central cities of Cleveland, Akron, Lorain, and Elyria; (2) maintain and redevelop older suburbs; and (3) preserve as much farmland and open space as possible.

To accomplish these objectives, new plans are needed and government policies and programs must be reoriented. State government, for example, promotes development at the rural edges of the region (primarily through roads and highways) but gives relatively little support to the redevelopment of housing in the city of Cleveland and to the maintenance and redevelopment of older suburbs.

A rebalancing in the use of government funds is needed, but the state cannot be expected to change what it does unless local officials call for that change. Their willingness to do so depends on their willingness to commit to the above objectives. As the reality of the situation facing older suburbs becomes more apparent, and if resistance to hopscotch development of farmland at the outer edges of the region grows, then an increasing number of officials can be expected to support the above objectives. Turning that commitment into effective action requires the creation of a regional development plan and, quite possibly, the establishment of regional tax-base sharing.

Regional Development Plan

It is not possible to achieve the above objectives without cooperative action among the seven counties of the region and their local units of government. Each county, on its own, must work out what it wants in the way of its long-term future. Does Geauga County, which is now zoned almost entirely for residential development, want to preserve any of its farms? Do the suburbs of Cuyahoga County really want to support the redevelopment of Cleveland if it means losing suburban residents to the city? Does Lorain County want a new State Route 83 if it will mean the development of all of the land in the eastern half of the county?

Each county has questions like these that need to be answered. In addition, each county needs to consider regional issues. For example: Where is the best place to locate a new airport? Are there sites in the region where industrial development would best be located? Where, in the long run, will the seven thousand units of housing that are built each year in the region be located?

The last question is directly linked with the future of each county. If more of the seven thousand units are not located in Cleveland and older communities, the pressure on regional farms for development cannot be reduced. What portion of the seven thousand would each county like to have annually for the next fifty years?

After each county arrives at its preferred future, the seven counties then need to come together, lay their future before the others, and see how the seven futures fit together. Do they form a coherent and consistent whole? They probably won't at first. If they don't, the seven then will need to negotiate adjustments to where they can come to agreement on separate and joint futures.

Describing that process is easy; for officials, residents, and leaders in each county to actually implement it would be revolutionary. The process would not be impossible, but such dealings are far beyond established ways. In the first place, under Ohio law, each city, village, and township has no obligation whatsoever to any other unit of government, and each is protected from intrusion from the others. The home community rules the home community.

Further, the entire two-hundred-year history of local governments in Ohio is dominated by competition. Local governments have always competed with each other for residents, businesses, and tax base. That is how the state constitution has structured the rules of the game for local governments: go forth and compete with each other, and to the victors go the spoils. County A gets a new coliseum and a professional basketball team moves from County B; County B steams. County B gets a new arena and a professional basketball team moves from County A; County A steams. Suburb A offers more tax abatement to a business than Suburb B can offer; A gets the move from B. It happens daily.

Competition for tax base among the local governments of the Greater Cleveland region is so strong that it may be impossible for them to cooperate for the purpose of creating and implementing a regional development plan or to cooperate on anything of consequence. The pressure to compete must be reduced. One way to do that is through a system to share the tax benefits of development.

Tax-Base Sharing

To the victors go the spoils—as if the spoils were produced exclusively by the victors. When it comes to development of real estate, often nothing is further from the truth. For example, a suburb with undeveloped land attracts a shopping mall developer who likes the location because of its proximity to a highway interchange. The landowner sells the site to the developer for $100,000 an acre after having purchased it twenty years earlier for $500 an acre. The developer constructs a $100 million mall, and the suburb collects the new taxes.

Did that happen entirely because of the efforts and resources of the victors? Not at all. If the highway interchange had not been built at that point, the mall would not have been built and the property owner would not have been able to sell for $100,000 an acre. Without the interchange he might have gotten $10,000 an acre. The public investment in the interchange enabled the property owner and suburb to profit as they did.

Further, suppose the interchange had been built at that point but few people lived within twenty miles of it. Would the mall have been built? Quite likely not. The proximity of many people living in other communities created the demand for the mall—and created the increased value of the land and the value of the development itself.

If the public in general and the residents in other communities in particular created the possibility for the mall to be located in that suburb and created the value of the real estate, why should the suburb keep all of the tax revenues? It should not. It should keep some because the mall must receive public services, but not all. Since so much of the value of the land and the mall was created not by the developer or the property owner or the suburb itself but by the region, why not share half of the tax benefits with the communities that need to redevelop and modernize their real estate so as to prevent their tax base from declining?

If there were regional sharing of the tax benefits produced by development, the pressure on communities to compete would be greatly reduced. Communities and their counties would be better oriented to participate cooperatively in a regional undertaking to rebuild central cities, maintain older suburbs, and preserve farmland and open space.

Conclusion

Cleveland's third century will involve a great deal of rebuilding. In the best of futures the undertaking will have broad regional support—through which social and racial wounds that were aggravated as a result of abandonment can be healed. This reconciliation should be the point of it all: don't just rebuild, but do it in ways that cause people across the region to feel better about each other.

Part 2

Issues for the Region

My ideal Cleveland of the future runs to the intangible qualities that, in my view, make a community great. Chief among these is, in fact, a real sense of community: a sufficiently shared spirit of appreciation and aspiration that enables forward progress. This is especially difficult in a city as diverse as Cleveland.

Such a sense of community demands celebration of our diversity without permitting it to be divisive. It requires a broadly based effort to break down racial and economic isolation. It calls for continuous effort to maintain open communication between all sectors of the community, for dialogue is the foundation for any form of partnership or common action.

—David Abbott, executive director,
Cleveland Bicentennial Commission
(1993-97)

Chapter 6

Comeback Cleveland by the Numbers

The Economic Performance of the Cleveland-Akron Metropolitan Area

Edward W. Hill

If Greater Cleveland is to extend its comeback beyond glitzy down-town revitalization, it must overcome a number of underlying economic challenges—especially the lack of employment growth in its major industries and the relatively low educational attainment of its workforce. The overall challenge will be to create a balanced economic recovery that won't leave behind a large part of the region's population.

Edward W. Hill is professor of urban studies and public administration at Cleveland State University's Levin College of Urban Affairs and senior research scholar in the college's Urban Center.

What does "Comeback" mean? It's largely physical development focused on the downtown; that's what the feds gave us the money for.

—Janis Purdy, executive director of
The Citizens League of Greater Cleveland

Cleveland's economic "comeback" is complex, and the perception of the successes that the city and region have experienced in developing a new economy has been hurt by the very term that has been used in the promotional effort—*comeback*. The word has generated unreasonable standards for success, even though it has proven to be both a winning marketing tag line and a successful piece of alliteration. Comeback, after all, implies returning to what was. But Cleveland hasn't returned to its past, nor should it aspire to do so. America's role in the global economy has changed, and with it so has Cleveland's role in the national econ-omy. Like Humpty Dumpty, the old economy cannot be put back to-gether again.

What would be required to produce a "comeback Cleveland?" The region would have to return to being a prosperous center of heavy indus-trial production—where poorly educated, semi-skilled labor could share in the oligopoly profits of corporations that are insulated from serious domestic or international competition. This, of course, will not reoccur in the foreseeable future because the tremendous market power of those cor-porations has been reduced; oligopoly profits have decayed in concert with their loss of market power; and, as oligopoly profits have declined, so have the wages available to labor.

If not comeback Cleveland, then what? Cleveland's economy is revi-talizing. Downtown Cleveland has witnessed a wave of building since 1983. The unemployment rate shows that the regional economy has suc-cessfully changed. However, an index of employment growth and data on poverty indicate that work remains to be done. Each of these indicators of economic restructuring is examined below.

Downtown Construction

From 1980 to 1996, building construction contracts in downtown Cleve-land totaled about $3.7 billion in 1994 real (inflation-adjusted) dollars. Nearly 60 percent of this amount was invested in buildings that were ded-icated to office and retail activities, and 21 percent was invested in enter-tainment or visitor attractions. (See table 6.1.) Another indicator of the rebound of Cleveland's downtown is the real dollar increase in property values. The real value of downtown private property holdings more than doubled between 1979 and 1990.

Table 6.1

Annual spending on major building projects in downtown Cleveland, 1980–96

	Reported contract amount	
Year	Current dollar (millions)	1994 Real Dollar (millions)
1980	64.5	106.9
1981	22.5	35.4
1982	12.4	18.8
1983	137.8	204.8
1984	124.0	178.9
1985	236.0	331.8
1986	69.9	96.9
1987	98.5	132.6
1988	128.2	166.5
1989	60.3	74.9
1990	672.2	789.8
1991	689.4	772.1
1992	16.6	17.9
1993	0	0
1994	401.4	401.4
1995	268.9	268.9
1996	244.9	244.9
TOTAL	3,160.5	3,700.3

Source: Greater Cleveland Growth Association

There is little question that this investment remade the public face of the downtown area and that the public sector participated substantially in financing these projects in the form of various subsidies, write-downs, and tax breaks. The largest investors were county and state governments, followed by the city and federal governments. No single accounting is available of the investments made by each governmental unit, and I was unable to find an accounting of the various building projects that identified the participation of each unit of government, the not-for-profit sector, and private investors, but some examples are available.

North Coast Harbor: North Coast Development Corporation is the not-for-profit organization that controls the North Coast Harbor site, home to the Rock and Roll Hall of Fame and the Great Lakes Science Center. The initial $10 million investment in North Coast Harbor came from the state's capital budget and accounted for 55 percent of the project investments as of 1991. The state funds were linked to an early grant from the Economic Development Administration to make the harbor a reality. Thirteen percent came from federal sources and 6 percent from county and city government. Corporate donations accounted for 10 percent, and local foundations contributed 10 percent. Once the inner harbor was completed, the Rock Hall's architect selected the harbor as its location. The reported contract amount for the hall was $45 million, and Cleveland's alternative newspaper, *The Free Times*, reported that the exhibits cost $22 million. These funds came from an $8 million state capital grant and $64 million in bonds issued by the county Port Authority, the county, and the city. These bonds are to be repaid in part by tax increment financing from Tower City's property taxes, the county hotel bed tax, and admissions fees.

Tower City: Along with North Coast Harbor, Tower City Center is one of the cornerstone projects in Cleveland's downtown redevelopment. It was a high-risk venture and was the project that, in the words of one city economic development official, "taught us how to put together packages." Tower City was first announced in 1985, construction began in 1987, and the project opened in 1990. The project received five Urban Development Action Grants (UDAGs), valued at $31.5 million, and at least $54 million in transportation grants from federal and state sources. The project is reported to have let construction contracts valued at $400 million. Tower City was of such size and complexity that it took deep pockets to make the project possible, and the bulk of the patient public money came from the federal government. Most other projects in Cleveland's downtown, however, received their funding from state and county governments. Playhouse Square and Gateway are good examples.

Playhouse Square: The federal government did not directly participate in the development of the Playhouse Square theater complex. The county and city provided nearly half of the funds, and the state contributed another quarter, using the bonding authority of the higher education budget as the shell to transfer the funds. The final piece came from corporate contributions (13 percent) and local foundations (7 percent).

Gateway: Gateway is a half-billion-dollar sports complex whose final sources of funding are not yet clear. The bulk of the funds come from a countywide sin tax on cigarettes and alcoholic beverages that is used to retire bonds issued by the county government. Infrastructure finance came from gasoline taxes and from a statewide infrastructure bond issue called Issue 2. The city of Cleveland also abated property taxes as a development incentive. The federal government contributed indirectly by allowing the issuance of tax-free bonds for the project. Funds from loges, club seats, and naming rights completed the financing. Unfortunately, the not-for-profit development entity that holds title to the complex was insolvent in 1995 due to $22 million in cost overruns, and neither the final tally nor the final financial structure of this project is known. However, the sin taxes were extended, some property was sold, and Gateway toughened its bargaining with its two major tenants—the Indians baseball team and the Cavaliers basketball team. So as of late 1997, it has managed to avoid bankruptcy.

There are two points to be made from all of this detail. First, doing capital-intensive civic projects—which is what many of the visitor-destination projects are—is expensive and requires spreading the risk and cost among many participants. In all of these cases, participation started with a risk-absorbing unit of government. In the case of the rock hall, the governments were the state of Ohio, with its $10 million grant for the harbor and initial capital grant of $8 million for the hall itself, and the federal government in the form of the grant from the Economic Development Administration. These grants were due to the personal involvement of then-Governor Richard Celeste. Playhouse Square was made possible due to risk taking on the part of the county commissioners, as was the case with Gateway. Tower City was a political risk taken by the federal government. In each case there was a project advocate who lobbied for the grants. The Playhouse project was initiated by three civic activists, who were later supported by the Cleveland Foundation and the corporate leaders of Cleveland Tomorrow. The Hall of Fame was advocated by George Voinovich, mayor of Cleveland at that time. Gateway was initiated by Cleveland Tomorrow and the mayoral administrations of Voinovich and Michael

White, but the county commissioners and the state of Ohio made the project happen under the threat of the Indians leaving the region.

Public participation continued in private sector projects as well. Key Tower, headquarters to KeyCorp, received historic restoration tax credits, a UDAG, and tax abatement. Most other commercial buildings completed after the mid-1980s have received property tax abatement. Despite the subsidies, the city benefits because it receives wage tax revenue from the workers. (A former city finance director told me that getting the Cavaliers downtown was a victory for the city because the major cost of the new basketball arena was borne by county taxpayers while the city received the wage taxes.)

Could these projects have succeeded without the public's participation? The complicated early projects, such as Tower City and Key Tower, most likely would not have been undertaken. It is highly unlikely that Gateway could have been built solely with private participation due to the fierce inter-city competition for sports franchises. And the waterfront projects—the Rock Hall and Great Lakes Science Center—could only work with public money.

It is also very likely that these projects secured the financial health of the city government because approximately 40 percent of the city's general operating budget comes from suburban wage tax payers. If these projects were not built, downtown's competitive position vis-à-vis suburban office sites would have worsened. And if the employment base were lost in downtown Cleveland, the city's finances would markedly deteriorate. Granted, much of the development has been financed through property tax abatements that primarily affect the financing of the city's schools. The system of public finance encourages the city to abate to garner wage taxes, even though the abatements might harm the financial structure of the public school system. But the real issue at hand is whether or not the development downtown would have taken place without the public subsidies, and there is no way to know the answer to this question. In all likelihood the early projects—such as Tower City and the sports arenas—would not have been built, and that would have changed risk perceptions for the downtown investments that followed.

The unanswered question is about the development road not taken: Would the city have been better off with a different mix of projects? Should the city invest in its neighborhoods versus its downtown? The choice is presented in casual conversation as a choice between the downtown "gorilla" projects—large complicated projects that barge onto the development scene and demand political attention—versus investing in smaller neighborhood businesses outside of the downtown. In Cleveland's case, during the late 1980s and 1990s, framing development options in this way presents a false dichotomy.

Start by examining the opportunity costs—political costs, development costs, and forgone taxes—involved in catering to the large downtown projects. What was lost in the neighborhoods by devoting time and attention to the large downtown projects? The largest cost is the expenditure of administrative time and attention on the part of the mayor and city officials. The gorilla projects make it difficult to devote time and attention to other, smaller projects and they are not conducive to forming development strategies and policies. They drive the city into a transactional, economic development, "deal-making" mindset. The result is that the most likely losers are not small projects in the neighborhoods, but smaller, in-fill projects downtown and the management of other large development resources, such as the airport.

The largest danger the gorilla projects present is that downtown will become an opportunistic collection of architectural icons that are not connected by a fabric of buildings, shops, and street-level activities that promote a vibrant streetscape—the very elements that make downtowns competitive with suburban shopping malls and office parks. The gorilla projects have the opposite effect from that posed by the usual neighborhood versus downtown rhetoric. The gorilla projects gave the administration of Mayor Michael White leverage over the members of Cleveland Tomorrow to invest in neighborhood development activities in which they would not normally have an interest.

The second part of the downtown versus neighborhood dichotomy that is typically posed involves taxes and public expenditures. The argument is made that the gorilla projects consume deep pools of subsidy, which they do, and that these moneys would be better spent on other economic development resources, such as education, that would make the region more competitive with other locations. The argument is largely correct, but the choice presented is false. It is easier to argue this point with an example. The Cuyahoga County commissioners put an increase in sin taxes on the ballot to subsidize the construction of the sports stadiums. The tax increase was approved countywide but lost in the city of Cleveland. Would the tax increase have passed if suburban voters in the county were instead offered the choice of spending the money on the city of Cleveland's public school system? This outcome is extremely doubtful; suburban voters will tax themselves for projects in the central city only if they see tangible benefits from the projects flowing back to themselves. The benefits that they would receive from a better-educated workforce coming out of Cleveland's public school system are too abstract, distant, and tainted by issues of race and class to support a tax increase. On the other hand, there were two sets of benefits from voting increased taxes for the sports stadiums. The first is fan interest and the second is that they are voting to retain the facilities downtown, which remains a place suburbanites still support. The tax increase was approved by a narrow majority of voters.

What has been the impact of these projects on the core of the city? Many of the office projects opened their doors just as a number of prominent downtown employers were cutting back on employment to improve their efficiency and in reaction to the 1990 recession. Ameritrust merged with Society Bank, which later merged with Albany's KeyCorp Ameritech, formerly Ohio Bell, experienced a long and deep set of layoffs to improve its competitive position, as did East Ohio Gas Company. And a longtime downtown bellwether company, BP, went through a painful downsizing that had profound effects on its Cleveland operations. All of these layoffs reflected national and international market conditions and were independent of local actions. However, these cutbacks, combined with the boost in the supply of office space, increased the local vacancy rate for downtown office space from approximately 8 percent to a range from 17 percent to above 20 percent through much of the early 1990s.

Since that time, rates have drifted downward. In 1996 the vacancy rate for Class A office space, according to commercial real estate brokers Grubb & Ellis, was 11.3 percent. In 1997, that rate dropped by a full percentage point and the overall vacancy rate for downtown office buildings dropped from 18.4 percent to 16.6 percent.

Most of the new office space that was filled, with two prominent exceptions, came from local firms that moved from existing downtown office space. The exceptions were the United Church of Christ, which moved its headquarters from New York City to Cleveland, and KeyCorp. KeyCorp has increasingly centralized its operations in Cleveland, moving activities out of a number of locations, including Albany, New York, where KeyCorp was headquartered before its merger with Society Bank. The firm has become the largest employer in the downtown area.

Employment

The unemployment rate makes an unabashed case for the dramatic recovery
of the regional economy (defined as the Cleveland-Akron-Lorain-Elyria Con-
solidated Metropolitan Statistical Area [CMSA], which includes Ashtabula,
Cuyahoga, Lake, Lorain, Medina, Portage, and Summit Counties). The differences between the state and national unemployment rates displayed in
figure 6.1 were constructed by subtracting the national unemployment rate from
the rate for the state of Ohio and the CMSA respectively. If the percentage-
point difference is positive, the local unemployment rates are greater than the
national rate and, if negative, they are lower than the national rate.

Annual unemployment rates: 1972–96
(Ohio less U.S. and CMSA less U.S.)

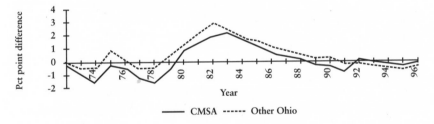

Year	CMSA	Other Ohio	Year	CMSA	Other Ohio
72	−0.2	0.0	85	1.4	1.7
73	−0.9	−0.5	86	0.9	1.2
74	−1.3	−0.6	87	0.5	0.9
75	−0.2	0.9	88	0.3	0.6
76	−0.4	0.3	89	−0.2	0.4
77	−1.1	−0.5	90	−0.2	0.4
78	−1.2	−0.5	91	−0.5	−0.2
79	−0.5	0.3	92	0.0	−0.1
80	−0.9	1.4	93	−0.1	−0.3
81	1.5	2.3	94	−0.4	−0.6
82	2.2	3.1	95	−0.7	−0.9
83	2.5	2.6	96	−0.3	−0.5
84	1.9	2.0			

Figure 6.1. *Annual unemplopment rates: 1972-96*

From 1972 to 1979, the unemployment rate for the CMSA was lower than that of the state, which was, in turn, below the rate for the nation (1979 was also the year of peak employment in the region). The unemployment rate for the nation was significantly below that of both the CMSA and state for a decade, from 1979 to 1989. Generally, the unemployment rate for the CMSA was below that of the state until 1993, and fell below the national rate in 1989. This latter event marked the recovery of the regional economy. The state's unemployment rate fell below the national rate in 1991.

Movements in the unemployment rate mark three of the four periods of recent economic history, the fourth period is only evident when employment figures are examined. The regional economy moved cyclically, in concert with the national economy, from 1972 to 1979, but signs of structural problems were evident. The economy crashed in 1979, bottoming out in 1983, and did not stabilize until 1986, when the restructured economy was firmly in place.

The flip side of the region's economic recovery is marked by employment growth. To best display fluctuations in the number of people employed, I constructed an employment index using the annual average number of people employed in 1979 as the base of the index (1979 was chosen because it was the employment peak of the old Cleveland economy). The index can be interpreted as the percentage point difference in a given period's level of employment from the 1979 level. If the index is below 100, employment is less than it was in 1979; if above 100, the number of jobs is greater than in 1979. The employment growth rate can be observed by looking at the slope of the index, or changes in the position of the index, between any two points in time. Data are not displayed for the state of Ohio; instead they are displayed for Ohio less the Cleveland-Akron-Elyria-Lorain CMSA. This is labeled as "Other Ohio" in figure 6.2.

Four distinct periods are evident in the second figure: before 1979, 1979 to 1983, 1983 to 1989, and 1989 to 1996. The first time period is marked by generally positive employment growth rates that move with the national business cycle. Here, the growth rates for the CMSA and the other Ohio move together. The decline of Ohio's regional economies from 1979 to 1983 is evident, but the parts of the state that are located outside of Northeast Ohio pull out of the decline a year before the region, and the other Ohio's decline is not as deep as that of Northeast Ohio. The nation

Annual employment index: 1972–96

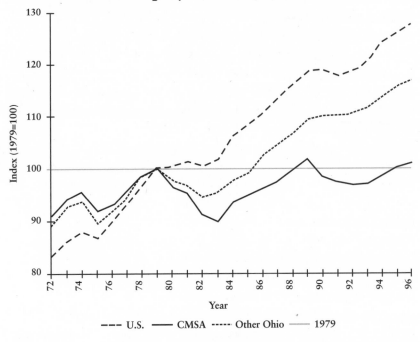

			Other					Other	
Year	U.S.	CMSA	Ohio	1979	Year	U.S.	CMSA	Ohio	1979
72	83	91	89	100	85	108	95	100	100
73	86	94	93	100	86	111	97	103	100
74	88	96	94	100	87	114	98	105	100
75	87	92	89	100	88	116	100	107	100
76	90	93	92	100	89	119	102	110	100
77	93	96	95	100	90	119	99	110	100
78	97	99	98	100	91	118	98	111	100
79	100	100	100	100	92	119	97	111	100
80	100	97	98	100	93	121	98	112	100
81	102	96	97	100	94	125	99	114	100
82	101	92	95	100	95	126	101	116	100
83	102	90	96	100	96	128	102	117	100
84	106	94	98	100					

Figure 6.2. *Annual employment index: 1972-96*

as a whole suffered a slowdown in employment growth, but never an absolute annual decline, over this time period. From 1983 to 1989, the regional economy slowly recovered the number of jobs it had had in 1979 and resumed a growth track that roughly paralleled the state and nation until 1989, when the regional economy appears to have stalled.

Figure 6.3 depicts the employment index quarterly from the first quarter of 1990 to the second quarter of 1997. This figure contains three comparison groups: the nation, other Ohio, and an aggregation of thirty-four other metropolitan areas from around the nation. The figure is designed to more closely examine regional job growth.

Nationally, the recession of 1990 was relatively shallow (unemployment did not increase as dramatically as it did in past recessions), and the recovery became notorious as the "jobless" recovery. Northeast Ohio entered the recession late because the national recession was triggered by regional events that were located largely outside of the Midwest, such as the savings and loan industry collapse and cutbacks in defense spending.

The message contained in figure 6.3 is clear: during the most recent business cycle employment growth in the region, the rest of Ohio, and the comparison group of metropolitan areas roughly mirrored that of the nation; the region merely started from a lower employment base and lagged in its recovery—both the region's recession and recovery started about one year later than the nation's. The nation began to pull out of the recession in the early 1993; the recovery in the other Ohio began in late 1994 and continued until late in 1996. The recovery in the CMSA began later than it did for the other Ohio, and employment growth has been faster outside of the CMSA. Movements in the employment index for the CMSA over the entire period covered in figure 6.3 largely represent seasonal fluctuations in hiring (employment peaks in the summer months) until the recovery set in the second quarter of 1994. Of concern is the increasing gap in the employment index between the other Ohio and the CMSA.

There is an apparent inconsistency when the unemployment rate for the region and employment growth data are compared. The unemployment rates make an unabashed case for comeback Cleveland, while the employment growth data indicate that the regional economy has stagnated. The only way in which these two sets of data can be reconciled is by stating that a growing share of the population exists outside of the labor force. One indicator of this would be the incidence of

Quarterly employment index: 1990(1) to 1997(2)

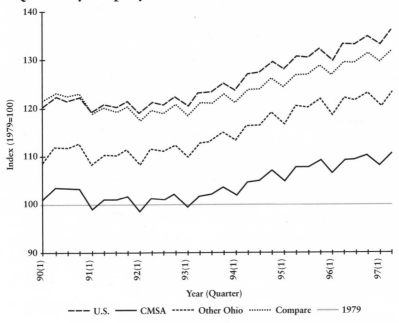

Year (Quarter)

--- U.S. —— CMSA ----- Other Ohio ········ Compare —— 1979

Quarterly Index of Total Employment				
Year: Qu	U.S.	CMSA	Other Ohio	Compare	1979
90(1)	120.2	100.9	108.8	121.4	100
	122.6	103.7	112.0	123.2	100
	122.0	103.6	112.0	122.8	100
	122.4	103.4	112.5	123.2	100
91(1)	119.5	99.3	108.5	119.3	100
	120.8	101.0	110.3	120.3	100
	120.4	101.2	110.5	119.6	100
	121.3	101.8	111.5	120.6	100
92(1)	119.0	98.7	108.7	117.7	100
	121.2	101.2	111.8	119.6	100
	121.0	101.1	111.3	119.3	100
	122.4	102.2	112.6	120.8	100
93(1)	120.7	99.7	110.1	118.8	100
	123.3	101.8	112.8	121.1	100
	123.6	102.2	113.4	121.3	100
	125.4	103.8	115.3	123.2	100

Quarterly Index of Total Employment *(Continued)*				
Year: Qu	U.S.	CMSA	Other Ohio	Compare	1979
94(1)	123.9	102.3	113.5	121.3	100
	127.1	104.9	116.7	123.9	100
	127.7	105.3	116.9	124.3	100
	129.7	107.2	119.4	126.3	100
95(1)	128.2	105.2	117.2	124.7	100
	130.7	107.9	120.5	126.9	100
	130.7	108.1	120.4	127.0	100
	132.3	109.4	122.1	129.1	100
96(1)	130.4	106.9	119.1	127.1	100
	133.3	109.5	122.3	129.7	100
	133.5	109.6	122.1	129.9	100
	135.1	110.6	123.7	131.8	100
97(1)	133.2	108.6	120.8	130.1	100
	136.2	110.9	123.5	132.2	100

Figure 6.3. *Quarterly employment index: 1990(1) to 1997(2)*

poverty in Cuyahoga County, which is the county that contains the city of Cleveland.

George Zeller, of the Greater Cleveland Council for Economic Opportunities, estimates the number of people with incomes below the poverty line and the percent of the population with incomes below the poverty line for Cuyahoga County. Figure 6.4 reproduces Zeller's estimates from 1980 to 1995. The poverty estimates roughly track the employment index that was displayed in figure 6.2. The estimated number of poor individuals climbed rapidly from 1980 to 1983. The number continued to increase but at a much slower rate until 1989, when it dipped a bit. The number of poor climbed once again with the recession of the early 1990s and began to drop in absolute numbers in 1993. The percent of the county's population that is poor closely tracked the number of poor individuals. It is clear from these data that the incidence of poverty is closely connected to job formation.

Beyond the Glitz: Structural Economic Challenges

Leadership Cleveland's 1996 class titled its economic study day: "Cleveland—Beyond the Glitz." The title was an acknowledgment of the reality of the region's recovery and transition. It also was a clear sign of emotional

Number and percent of the population poor in Cuyahoga County

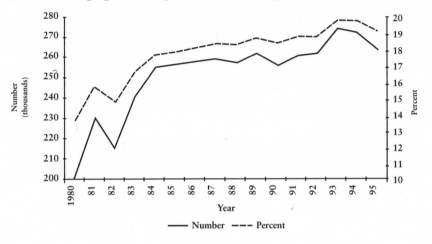

	Cuyahoga County	
Year	Number	Percent
1980	200,218	13.6
1981	230,267	15.7
1982	215,788	14.8
1983	240,654	16.6
1984	255,127	17.7
1985	256,874	17.9
1986	258,740	18.2
1987	259,772	18.4
1988	258,342	18.4
1989	262,898	18.8
1990	257,047	18.5
1991	261,793	18.9
1992	262,774	18.9
1993	275,295	19.9
1994	273,907	19.9
1995	265,725	19.3

Figure 6.4. *Number and percent of the population poor in Cuyahoga County*

security because it marked the start of an honest evaluation of the state of the region. A title that indicated an incomplete comeback would have been unthinkable by civic boosters a few years earlier.

An honest evaluation was aided by three reports made available in 1994: one by the Citizens League of Greater Cleveland, one by researchers at Wayne State and Cleveland State Universities, and the third by consultants to the Greater Cleveland Growth Association. All indicate that the economic transition has had uneven impacts on the region.

The Citizens League measured the region's progress in five broad areas—amenities, people, education, government, and economic performance—against thirteen benchmark regions. Three of these regions were chosen because they are similar to Cleveland (Detroit, Pittsburgh, and St. Louis), seven were seen as national role models (Atlanta, Charlotte, Cincinnati, Indianapolis, Minneapolis, Phoenix, and Seattle), and three were viewed as stable regional centers (Boston, Chicago, and San Francisco). Compared to these other regions, Greater Cleveland's efforts at revitalization have been mixed. Greater Cleveland ranked:

- First in amenities—measures of cultural opportunities and leisure activities.

- Seventh in people—measures of poverty, crime, health, environmental quality, and racial integration.

- Eighth in education—measures of educational opportunities and workforce preparedness.

- Ninth in government—measures of political participation and accountability of leadership.

- Next to last in economic performance—measures of productivity, fiscal disparities, and employment growth.

In the second study, Wayne State University's Harold Wolman and Coit Ford, along with the author, examined the economic performance of the residents of central cities and their metropolitan areas that were economically distressed in 1980 and 1990. We used a panel of experts to identify those places that were distressed in 1980 and had a reputation of having revitalized over the following decade. We then measured the economic well-being of their residents using the 1990 Census of Population and compared the performance of those places that reportedly had successfully revitalized with those that did not have this reputation but were distressed in 1980.

Cleveland was one of the cities reputed to have revitalized, but it did not perform well. The unemployment rate in the city of Cleveland increased by 3.9 percentage points over the decade, versus an average increase of 1.3 percentage points for the "unsuccessful cities"; median household income in Cleveland (unadjusted for inflation) increased by 45.2 percent, compared to 76.8 percent for the "unsuccessful" group; the percentage change in per capita income was 60.5 percent in Cleveland, compared to 87.6 percent for the comparison group; the percentage of the population below the poverty line increased by 6.6 percentage points, compared to 2.9 percentage points for the reference group; and the labor force participation rate increased by 0.3 percentage points in Cleveland, compared to an average increase of 2.7 percentage points for the "unsuccessful" cities. The results for the metropolitan area were similar. We concluded that, with the exceptions of Atlanta, Baltimore, and Boston, the reportedly revitalized cities performed no better, and in many cases performed much worse, than cities that were equally distressed in 1980.

Finally, the Greater Cleveland Growth Association reviewed approximately one hundred studies prepared on various aspects of the regional economy since the early 1980s and interviewed more than fifty Cleveland leaders to assess the progress of the community. It concluded that there have been marked "gains in physical infrastructure, 'livability,' and civic image/attitude during the 1980s," and that "while the local economy bottomed out in 1983, more growth is needed . . . notably: economic performance remains below average, but the gap has narrowed, manufacturing concentration heightened the region's vulnerability, but service sector slowness has been as damaging as a manufacturing decline, [and] the urban center has underperformed the region." This is a notably honest evaluation of the state of the region, and of the city's position within the region.

The three reports indicate that the economic benefits from the restructuring of the regional economy have been unequally earned or distributed. Much of this disparity reflects national patterns in the income distribution, rates of return to educational attainment, and the industrial composition of the regional economy. There are two ways of viewing the major development problem that Greater Cleveland faces—from the demand and supply sides of the labor market.

Slow-growth Industries

The most important measure of the health of a local economy is its ability to increase the number of jobs, an area where Greater Cleveland has fallen behind the state and nation. The Cleveland-Akron metropolitan area did not generate a large number of net new jobs over the fifteen-year period from 1979 to 1994. The problem does not lie in the behavior of the economy during the 1990 recession; it lies partially with the impact of the restructuring of the economy from 1979 to the mid-1980s and also with the region's industrial base. It is important to remember that it took ten years, from 1979 to 1989, for the region to regenerate the number of jobs lost in the restructuring that occurred from 1979 to 1983. However, the composition of the economy is very different than it was in the late 1970s.

The gap in employment generation occurred from 1983 to 1988, as the nation recovered from the earlier recession. From 1983 to 1988 the fast growing industries in the nation were non-bank financial services, electronics and software industries connected to defense and microelectronics, and health care. Greater Cleveland is relatively weak in all of these sectors, with the exception of health care. The core of the region's industrial base is made up of mature manufacturing industries and their headquarters operations. The region's service sector primarily services manufacturing. Therefore, as manufacturing is slow growing, so is demand for labor in the region. While the nation was expanding employment in newer service industries, firms in this region were investing in capital and restructuring their operations to increase productivity. Productivity increased; employment did not.

The region's economy is built upon a foundation of steel, automobiles, paints, plastics, and chemicals. Development in the region depends not just on entrepreneurs but on the economic vitality of these central activities and the relationship of other industries to this core. In addition, there are two other components of the region's industrial core: industries that have either corporate or divisional headquarters and production activities in the region (greeting cards, petroleum refining, blast furnaces and basic steel products, electric lighting and wiring, paints and allied products, non-plastic plumbing and heating products, drugstores and proprietary stores, and automobile parking); and metal-working industries, which depend on the presence of competitive integrated steel mills as sources of supply and durable goods manufacturers as customers.

The supply-side view of the performance of the regional labor market rests on the observation that the region has a level of educational attainment that lags behind both its competitor and benchmark regions. The level of educational attainment is unacceptably low compared to its competitor regions, in part because Northeast Ohio's economy remains rooted in sectors of the economy that have traditionally been a haven for people with relatively low levels of educational attainment.

Northeast Ohio's economy is a slow-growth economy with little population increase, yet the amount of land that the economy is consuming has increased markedly over the past twenty years. Does the economy have to grow more jobs to remain healthy and viable? Or is there another route to take to a prosperous future? The answer consists of two parts and one is not exclusive of the other.

In the mid- to late 1990s, the economy has reached near the effective capacity of the labor force. By this I mean that all those with skills that make them easy to employ are employed. The economy does have people who are not working, but either they live in the parts of the region where low-skilled jobs are not increasing at a rapid rate and are cut off from information networks that can inform them of more distant, though appropriate, jobs or else these more distant, appropriately skilled jobs pay too little to justify the commute. To increase economic well-being further, the economy has to engage in three sets of practices:

1. Improve job matching across the metropolitan area and find cost-effective ways of transporting people to more distant work sites.

2. Import workers from elsewhere.

3. Improve the quality of the workforce to the point where employers can change the mix of capital and labor and increase productivity at a faster rate than has been experienced.

The most important development strategy is the last one because increasing productivity is the only way to increase standards of living over the long term. However, Northeast Ohio faces a major educational challenge.

Blue-collar Educational Legacy

The Greater Cleveland region is saddled with a blue-collar legacy in terms of educational attainment. High performance blue-collar workplaces are looking for better educated and skilled workers who possess what has become known as the "extended basics" of manual dexterity, reasoning, ability to work as a team member, and familiarity with information systems. Differences in rates of return to different levels of education are solid indicators of what labor markets judge to be educational characteristics that are either surplus or in short supply. During the 1980s rates of return increased for those who went beyond secondary school and declined for those who did not.

Nearly one out of four adults in the Greater Cleveland CMSA terminated their education before they graduated from high school, which puts the CMSA just above the median metropolitan area in the nation on this score (table 6.2). The region is also far above the median in terms of the share of the population that stopped education at the secondary school level. These are the two groups that lost ground in terms of real income over the past decade and a half. Nearly one out of five adults in Cleveland's CMSA has a college degree. This is below the national metropolitan average but above the median.

Table 6.2

Percent distribution of educational attainment
ages 25 years and older

Terminal attainment	CALE		Metropolitan	
	%dist.	Rank*	Average** (percent)	Median (percent)
College degree	19.0	134	22.5	18.8
Some college	23.9	184	25.9	25.6
High school	33.4	84	28.6	30.6
Dropout	23.7	144	23.0	23.8

Source: 1990 Census of Population, PUMS
* Among 284 metropolitan areas
** Weighted average of all metropolitan areas

Of greatest importance to a region that specializes in production and aspires to create high performance workplaces is the percent of adults who have gone beyond secondary school but do not have four-year college degrees. The national median is 25.6 percent of the adult population and the weighted average is 25.9 percent. Cleveland is two full percentage points behind the average, with 23.9 percent, and sits in 184th place out of 284 metropolitan areas. The reason Cleveland lags is due to the proportions of adults who either drop out of school or are satisfied with the returns from a secondary school degree.

How then does educational attainment in the Greater Cleveland region compare with levels of both its benchmark regions and its competitors? Table 6.3 lists all of the metropolitan regions that were used by the Citizens League as benchmarks and also includes metropolitan regions in adjoining states that can be viewed as competitors. There are four groups of metropolitan regions in the list: three regions are international economic centers (Boston, Chicago, and San Francisco), seven are regional economic capitals (Atlanta, Charlotte, Dallas, Denver, Minneapolis, Phoenix, and Seattle), two are similar industrial metropolitan areas (Detroit and St. Louis), and seven are regional competitors to Cleveland (Buffalo, Cincinnati, Columbus, Dayton, Indianapolis, Louisville, and Pittsburgh). Detroit could also be viewed as a regional competitor.

Table 6.3 contains an index of educational attainment of the adult (age twenty-five and above) population. Each of the 284 metropolitan areas in the nation was ranked according to the percentage of the population that held a college degree in 1990. Then, a similar rank order was created based on the percentage of the population that had some college education but had not completed college. Two-thirds of the index weight was given to the rank ordering of the percentage of the population that has some postsecondary education but did not complete college, and one-third of the weight was given to the percentage that graduated from college. The metropolitan areas in the table are listed according to their index score.

The Cleveland CMSA is third from the bottom, trailed only by Louisville and Pittsburgh. All of the metropolitan areas in the surrounding Rust Belt region are at the bottom of this group of twenty regions, with the exception of Detroit. (Detroit is an interesting case because its region contains fast-growing suburban Oakland County, which is capturing large numbers of auto-related factories and headquarters that are fleeing the city of Detroit. Yet this same region ranked last in the Citizens League's multi-dimensional index of economic growth. Clearly educational attainment is not the only indicator of economic growth and development, but it is an important factor.)

It is also clear from table 6.3 that the international economic centers and the regional economic capitals have much better educated workforces than do the Rust Belt metropolitan areas. We have no information about cause and effect; we do not know if these places are attracting people who have been educated elsewhere, and we do not know if these deeper pools of educated talent are the result of homegrown human capital investments. What is clear is that the Cleveland CMSA has a low level of educational attainment among its resident adult population compared to its competitors.

Table 6.3

Educated labor supply index
(Population age 25 years or greater in 1990, ranked among 284 metro areas)

Metro Area	Index
Seattle	6
Denver	15
San Francisco	16
Phoenix	18
Minneapolis	28
Dallas	35
Atlanta	79
Detroit	92
Chicago	113
Charlotte	116
St. Louis	133
Boston	145
Dayton	148
Columbus	152
Indianapolis	163
Buffalo	164
Cincinnati	179
Cleveland	183
Louisville	191
Pittsburgh	233

Uneven Recovery

Greater Cleveland has indeed recovered from the economic restructuring of the late 1970s, as evidenced by the physical rebuilding of the downtown, the renewed competitiveness of its industrial base, and the marked improvement in the region's unemployment rate. However, the recovery has been, and continues to be, uneven. Poverty increased over most of this period, as those without education that went beyond secondary school were left behind by an economy that increasingly does not value those with limited skills. The region also lags in job creation. Whether or not this is due to a skills shortage among the population—thereby leaving jobs unfilled—is not known. The lack of job creation is more likely due to the region's manufacturing base (the sector where productivity is increasing the fastest) and downtown Cleveland's dependence on firms in industries that are either consolidating, such as finance and advertising, or on firms in industries that are under increasing competitive pressure as they are deregulated, such as telecommunications and utility services. Most troubling is the low level of educational attainment among the adult population compared to the region's competitors. This will become a drag on the region's attempts to improve economic well-being.

Summary

What is to be concluded about Northeast Ohio's economy since its great crash in 1979? First, Cleveland's downtown has been revitalized by a series of large "gorilla" projects that have taken a large amount of civic energy but have also served as a symbol for a new beginning for the region. The challenge that remains is to move from a transactional, deal-oriented approach to downtown and to concentrate on building an urban fabric that ties together the new icons in a coherent manner. At the same time, the competitive position of downtown Cleveland and Akron as sites for office development needs to be better understood and the explicit and implicit subsidies for suburban and exurban office development need to be reconsidered.

Second, the low levels of unemployment that the region has experienced in the mid-1990s marks a victory and presents both a challenge and an opportunity. The victory is the recovery of Northeast Ohio's regional economy from the restructuring of 1979. The challenge is to move those who are not part of the labor force into the labor force and to provide them with the educational and "people" skills required for success in the world of work.

Third, the region is generating jobs at roughly the pace of the national economy, but it is falling behind the rate of job growth experienced in the rest of Ohio. What can be done to increase the economic well-being of the region's residents? There are three sets of actions:

1. Undertake aggressive job-matching activities for the underemployed.

2. Strengthen the clusters of industries where the region has a competitive advantage and encourage new firm formation and product development within those clusters.

3. Over the long term, strengthen the quality of the workforce through improved educational outcomes at the secondary and postsecondary levels of the public educational system.

Chapter 7

Race Relations in Cleveland

People Are Talking

Mittie Olion Chandler

Consciously or not, intentionally or not, the issue of race underlies most other issues in Greater Cleveland. More than thirty years after the Civil Rights Act the metropolitan area is still overwhelmingly segregated. Blacks and whites have sharply different perceptions of the state of race relations. One bright sign is the development of programs that promote dialogue about this vexing problem.

Mittie Olion Chandler is associate professor and director of the Master of Science in Urban Studies Program and the Master of Urban Planning, Design and Development Program at Cleveland State University's Levin College of Urban Affairs.

The backdrop for the consideration of race relations is precarious, given the troubled racial history of the United States. Chattel slavery, employment discrimination, housing segregation, and civil disturbances stand out as indicators of race-related problems that span time and space. Few people would argue that this country has experienced turmoil rooted in racial difference and racial separation, although the intensity of discord has varied over time. Today, optimists and pessimists can perceive the state of race relations quite differently. The realists may be those who acknowledge that problems exist but are hopeful that they can be ameliorated through deliberate efforts.

The city of Cleveland is home to one of the country's most racially and ethnically diverse populations. In Cleveland and most other major cities of the Midwest and Northeast, however, discussions of race relations have focused on interactions between blacks and whites living in metropolitan areas. This continues to be the case despite the growing numbers of Hispanics and Asians. The emphasis stems from the unique, interwoven histories of blacks and whites in the United States and the racial divide between blacks and whites, which is greater than for any other two groups.

The city of Cleveland has experienced notable breakthroughs in race and ethnic relations—the first African American mayor of a major city (Carl B. Stokes), the first African American player on an American League baseball team (Larry Doby), and one of the first renowned African American inventors (Garrett Morgan). The significance of these individual achievements is masked, however, by evidence of more widespread and continued difficulties on the racial front.

The Study of Race Relations

In Greater Cleveland, issues of race permeate many aspects of life—matters of residence, mortgage lending, health care, employment, education, and other areas that span the public, private, and nonprofit sectors. Therefore, a comprehensive assessment of race relations should acknowledge the cross-cutting nature of this issue and consider conditions in a variety of areas.

Two approaches are commonly used to consider race relations in the United States. The first is to survey public opinion and attitudes about whether race relations have improved or deteriorated. Often this approach compares data using different independent variables such as race, age, or place of residence. Attitudinal surveys compile responses on racially sensitive topics such as affirmative action, school desegregation, and housing integration. Typically, whites have a more optimistic outlook about race relations and perceive fewer racial problems than do African Americans.

The second approach involves compiling quantitative indicators of

well-being, including such variables as the extent of residential segregation, the number of racially or ethnically motivated incidents, and socioeconomic conditions. Indexes of dissimilarity or segregation measure the
degree of residential separation between blacks, whites, and others within
a given community. Observers infer trends in intergroup tension from
racial and ethnic incidence numbers. Socioeconomic data (such as median
income and years of school) indicate the relative status of racial and ethnic groups. In turn, group comparisons allow the examination of disparities among groups and their causes.[1]

A third, more speculative look at the state of race relations assesses
the impact of efforts to better interactions across racial and ethnic lines.
Organized efforts to promote racial harmony exist throughout urban
America. While communities cannot deny the benefits of taking a proactive approach, it is virtually impossible to quantify the outcomes of such
programs in a scientific manner. Perhaps the emergence of programs is a
sign of progress even if such evidence is inconclusive.

This chapter provides an overview and interpretations of recent data
regarding racial matters in the Cleveland area. The activities of four organizations that pursue race relations programming are then described. The
chapter concludes with a prognosis for the future in this perplexing area
of human affairs. Although limited in scope, this overview of race relations should serve as a guide for further exploration of how a city can
cope with an ongoing social dilemma.

Opinions of Race Relations in Cleveland

Differing perceptions are at the root of dissension between blacks, whites,
and other racial/ethnic groups with regard to racial issues. A survey commissioned by the *Plain Dealer* in 1992, for example, found that blacks are
more likely than whites to believe that race affects work conditions and
opportunities. The survey found that 28 percent of blacks said that blacks
are treated worse at their workplace; just 3 percent of whites held this
belief. Blacks were also more likely to favor laws protecting minorities
from discrimination in hiring and promotion.

According to the survey, blacks were more likely to sense disparate
treatment in media coverage of minorities. Seventy-nine percent of blacks
and 41 percent of whites responded that the media give too much cover-

age to crimes by blacks and other minorities; meanwhile, 60 percent of whites and 24 percent of blacks responded that the media cover news about whites and minorities the same way.

Blacks were almost twice as likely as whites (37 to 20 percent) to believe that race relations in Cleveland had deteriorated in the previous year. The remainder of both races thought race relations had stayed the same or improved. Improvement was noted by 22 percent of whites and 19 percent of blacks. When asked about their own communities, blacks were three times more likely than whites (21 to 7 percent) to believe race relations had deteriorated.

On a more hopeful note, blacks and whites were more optimistic about race relations in the upcoming five years than in the previous year, both in Greater Cleveland and in their own communities. Forty-four percent of whites and 35 percent of blacks expected race relations to improve in Cleveland during the next five years; 34 percent of whites and 25 percent of blacks expected race relations in their community to improve in the same period.

These data point out the differential reality that exists for black and white Americans. The growing opposition to affirmative action largely among, though not limited to, whites reflects a sense that such policies are no longer needed or are not resulting in the changes desired by the majority population. Former Gen. Colin Powell reflected the other American reality when he said recently, "The notion that affirmative action should be completely stripped away [is] ridiculous. Anyone who would suggest that racism is a thing of the past is wrong. People are still being denied access to jobs because of the color of their skin."[2]

A 1991 survey of race relations by the Citizens League Research Institute of Cleveland considered city/suburban differences as well as racial differences among respondents. This survey also revealed differing perceptions about the existence of bias in the reporting by Cleveland media. Blacks were more likely than whites or Hispanics to perceive overall media bias among radio/television as well as newspapers and magazines (see figure 7.1).

According to the Citizens League survey, similar percentages of blacks, whites, and Hispanics believed that race relations had gotten better during the previous year, although Hispanics were more likely to say that race relations remained the same. Clevelanders were more likely than subur-

Bias in Cleveland media

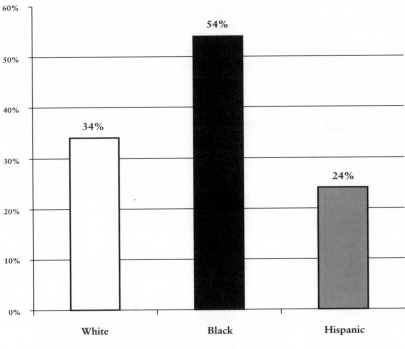

Overall media bias

Source: The Citizens League Research Institute (1991)

Figure 7.1. *Bias in Cleveland media*

banites to say that race relations were better. Suburbanites more frequently reported no change or a worsening of race relations (see figure 7.2).

The Citizens League survey was also informative on the topic of personal prejudicial attitudes toward persons of other races. Half of Greater Clevelanders reported no prejudice against people of other races, ethnic backgrounds, or religions; one-third reported just a little prejudice. Hispanic persons reported no prejudice more often than blacks or whites. Blacks said the subjects of their prejudice most frequently were whites, and vice versa.

In 1982 the Greater Cleveland Roundtable (described in greater detail below) commissioned a study on race and ethnic relations that

Status of race relations: Cleveland/suburbs
(Compared to previous year)

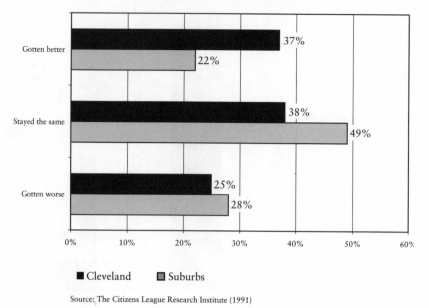

■ Cleveland   □ Suburbs

Source: The Citizens League Research Institute (1991)

Figure 7.2. *Status of race relations: Cleveland/suburbs (compared to previous year)*

included a survey component with responses from Greater Cleveland residents and community leaders and census data measurements of socioeconomic variables. The study reported evidence of racial disparity in terms of income, poverty, education, and unemployment; that separation of the races is the norm in neighborhoods (although less so for Hispanics), in schools, and in employment; and that racial tension is front-page news.[3]

The survey revealed that a majority of Cleveland residents of all races reported an improvement in race relations during the prior five years, although a larger majority felt that more progress was needed. Race relations were more of a concern to Cleveland's black and Hispanic populations, and 80 percent of persons identified as "leaders" viewed race relations as at least a moderate problem. Seventy-five percent of residents responded that they were not satisfied with race relations either in the city of Cleveland or in the metropolitan area.

School integration efforts, specifically busing, were viewed less favorably than the notion that black and white children should attend the same schools. Ninety-seven percent of blacks and 86 percent of whites agreed that black and white children should attend the same schools; 76 percent of blacks, 57 percent of Hispanics, and 50 percent of whites thought that school integration efforts were a good idea.

The Roundtable study also included data about residential segregation. One-third of whites believed that neighborhood integration was a bad idea—in stark contrast to what 74 percent of blacks, 50 percent of Hispanics, and many community leaders thought. Almost a third of whites thought that whites have the right to keep blacks out of their neighborhoods, and just 14 percent of whites supported government intervention to achieve neighborhood integration (versus 59 percent of blacks and 47 percent of Hispanics). Among the Cleveland leaders responding, 42 percent of whites were supportive of strong government intervention.

From a regional perspective, race relations are more salient in the city than the suburbs. White suburbanites expressed far higher levels of satisfaction and lower levels of concern about most aspects of Cleveland life, including race relations. The concerns of black suburban residents differed little from those of black city residents. Further, people still live and interact primarily with persons of their own race.

Specifically, the study reported:

- Different racial groups reveal varying levels of satisfaction with life in the Cleveland area—74 percent of whites satisfied, 39 percent of blacks satisfied, and 67 percent of Hispanics satisfied.
- Seventy-five percent of whites and 41 percent of blacks considered Cleveland a good place to raise a family.
- Sixteen percent of blacks and 35 percent of whites viewed police protection in Cleveland as good.
- Blacks and Hispanics are more affected by hard times as reflected in their concerns about life in Cleveland. Over half of employed blacks and two-thirds of Hispanics, as compared to one-third of whites, expressed worry about losing their jobs.

Socioeconomic Differences

The 1980 census data included in the Greater Cleveland Roundtable study exposed differences in the socioeconomic status of different groups in the Cleveland metropolitan area. The 1990 data are included here to permit comparisons regarding changes in these conditions. Disparities in mean family income in 1980 were noted and continued in 1990:

	1980	1990
Whites	27,943	40,862
Blacks	16,070 (57%)	24,069 (59%)
Hispanics	19,477 (70%)	26,941 (66%)

(numbers in dollars, with percentage of white income given for blacks and Hispanics)

The Asian population was not included in the 1980 study, but it is worth noting that the Asian mean family income in 1990 was $55,833.

Differences noted in poverty rates in 1980 persisted in 1990 as well:

	1980	1990
Whites	6.3%	7.5%
Blacks	29.6%	31.2%
Hispanics	15.3%	31.6%

The average educational level of blacks and Hispanics lags below the level of whites, as indicated by the percentage of high school graduates:

	1980	1990
Whites	72%	77.6%
Blacks	53%	62.2%
Hispanics	49%	55.6%

Unemployment rates also showed substantial variance as figures for blacks and Hispanics exceeded those for whites:

	1980*	1990**
Whites	7.0%	5.0%
Blacks	20.7%	16.3%
Hispanics	n.r.	13.7%

n.r.: not reported
* 1980 for persons 20+
**1990 for persons 16+

Between 1980 and 1990 modest gains were revealed for blacks in some areas when compared to white, such as mean family income, poverty rate, and educational level; however, unemployment declined more for whites and remained at one-third the level for blacks. Conditions for Hispanics worsened when contrasted to whites in terms of mean income and poverty. More significant change is needed to achieve parity among racial and ethnic groups in Greater Cleveland.

Residential Segregation/Separation and Living Patterns

For many years Cleveland has been one of the most segregated cities/metropolitan areas in the country. One recent study ranked Greater Cleveland as the fourth most segregated metropolitan area behind Gary, Detroit, and Chicago. The findings were reported in *Population Today* by Reynolds Farley of the University of Michigan and were based upon Census Bureau housing reports on communities that had at least 3 percent black population or at least twenty thousand blacks. The Cleveland area segregation index declined from 90 in 1980 to 86 in 1990, indicating a slight improvement.

Some observers object to the use of segregation indices, saying that they are obsolete and not reflective of more recent trends in neighborhood change. In Cleveland, for example, some white households are moving into predominantly black areas of the central city in response to economic incentives and the conveniences of inner-city living. Further, there is evidence of more racial and ethnic diversity on Cleveland's west side, which formerly was all white. Nevertheless, the amount of housing integration required to reverse decades of patterns and policies remains daunting.

Questions about the causes of residential segregation—whether housing patterns are related more to economic standing (also subject to racial impacts), informed or uninformed choice, or other factors—also lead some to object to the use of segregation indices. Researchers have debated these issues, and housing discrimination surfaces as a major factor.

If the validity and conclusions of segregation studies are accepted, the high level of segregation in Greater Cleveland is a cause of concern. Other studies suggest that patterns of racial segregation perpetuate differences in the overall quality of life, including education, environment, and employment opportunities. A series on race in the *Plain Dealer* in 1992 documented the extent of racial separation in housing in the seven-county Greater Cleveland area: 60 percent of blacks lived in a mostly black neighborhood and 25 percent in a racially mixed neighborhood; 82 percent of whites lived in a mostly white neighborhood and 14 percent in a racially mixed neighborhood.

The degree to which people are divided into identifiable racial/ethnic neighborhoods could suggest something positive, such as racial solidarity or neighborhood stability, but more often it is a sign of racial intolerance and tension. The extent to which blacks and whites live in separate communities also has become a proxy indicator for the extent to which fair housing legislation has failed (the existence of housing discrimination), the economic status of African Americans (attainment of economic parity with whites), as well as the desire of the races to live in closer proximity. Regardless of why they exist, segregated neighborhoods prevent socializing across racial lines in neighborhoods and institutions.

A significant change in racial living patterns in the metropolitan area is the ongoing suburbanization of the black community. Increasingly, African Americans have moved into predominantly white suburbs without major incident. Two Cleveland suburbs, Cleveland Heights and Shaker Heights, are known nationally for relatively successful efforts to maintain racial heterogeneity. With persistent and sometimes contentious work of the cities and nonprofit organizations, the most pernicious, sudden effects of white flight, blockbusting, and steering have been avoided.

Nonetheless, gradual changes in racial composition over a thirty-year period are shown in table 7.1.

Table 7.1

Surburban population change, 1960–90

City	1960 Population/Percent				1970 Population/Percent			
	Total	White	Black	Other	Total	White	Black	Other
Bedford Heights	15,223 100	15,201 99.9	2 .013	20 .13	13,063 100	12,856 98.4	113 .87	94 .73
Cleveland Heights	61,813 100	61,399 99.3	251 0.4	163 0.3	60,767 100	58,798 96.8	1,508 2.5	461 0.7
Maple Heights	31,667 100	31,388 99.1	255 0.8	24 0.1	34,093 100	33,332 97.8	698 2.0	63 0.2
Shaker Heights	36,460 100	36,079 99	357 .98	24 0.7	36,378 100	30,880 84.9	5,227 14.4	271 .74
Warrensville Heights	10,609 100	10,580 99.7	20 0.2	9 <0.1	18,925 100	14,689 77.6	4,007 21.2	229 1.2

City	1980 Population/Percent				1990 Population/Percent			
	Total	White	Black	Other	Total	White	Black	Other
Bedford Heights	13,214 100	9,214 71.2	3,523 26.7	279 2.1	12,131 100	5,469 45.1	6,379 52.6	283 2.3
Cleveland Heights	54,438 100	41,192 73.0	14,061 24.9	1,185 2.1	54,052 100	32,534 60.2	20,054 37.1	1,464 2.7
Maple Heights	12,949 100	12,676 97.9	140 1.1	133 1.0	27,089 100	22,691 83.8	3,987 14.7	411 1.5
Shaker Heights	32,487 100	24,164 74.4	7,917 24.4	406 1.2	30,831 100	20,633 66.9	9,543 30.7	745 2.4
Warrensville Heights	16,565 100	3,870 23.4	12,416 74.9	279 1.7	15,745 100	1,498 9.5	14,011 89.0	236 1.5

Overall population figures, and even segregation indices, only tell a partial story. Within Shaker and Cleveland Heights, racial divides can be observed among individual neighborhoods. Further, the experiences of these two cities demonstrate that the challenges of racial integration go far beyond the composition of communities and who lives on what property. The public school systems in both cities have been a source of contention. The African American population constitutes a much larger proportion of the public school populations than of the city populations as a whole. Issues of educational quality and fair treatment of students challenge the school system administrators, teachers, and parents, as well as the students themselves. In early 1997 a Shaker Heights High School student newspaper article created a furor by reporting on disparities in Scholastic Aptitude Test scores obtained by black and white students. Among the concerns raised were how administrators handled the issue and what, if anything, could be done to raise the scores of black students.

In other Cleveland-area suburbs some whites are resisting the trend of black suburbanization by moving out when the number of blacks reaches a certain point of personal discomfort. Some blacks moving into such areas report that white neighbors are unfriendly and not welcoming.

The percentage of African Americans in Maple Heights, for example, grew from 3 percent in 1980 to 14.7 percent in 1990. Enrollment of blacks in the Maple Heights schools surged from 27 percent in 1990 to 67 percent in 1997. Despite the increases, the school board remains all white, and parents have complained that the schools are unresponsive to the needs of black students.

Tensions often surface when groups of people who have interacted little come into close contact. But there is the peculiar context of black-white engagement where people sometimes collaborate on some basis (work, sports, organizations) but do not become closely associated within each other's primary circle of friends and colleagues. Thus, racial anxiety remains beneath the surface of many placid settings. Diversity training initiatives established at some workplaces may enhance the quality of the work setting for all employees in this regard. Heightened awareness of diversity issues at work may spawn more dialogue that extends into neighborhoods, churches, and other places.

Ethnoviolence in Cleveland

Ethnoviolence describes violent acts in which the race of the victim motivates the perpetrator. The number of incidents of ethnoviolence in Cleveland suggests that positive change is occurring along this dimension of racial/ethnic interaction. The number of incidents reported has declined since their peak in 1987, as reported by the City's Community Relations Board (CRB):

Year	Number of incidents
1984	25
1985	50
1986	70
1987	90
1988	87
1989	86
1990	55
1991	43
1992	48
1993	31
1994	42
1995	24
1996	25
1997	22

The overall drop in the city's population may have affected the number of reported incidents, and the enhanced visibility and outreach activities of the CRB after the death of Mabel Gant in 1985 may explain the increased number of reported incidents during the period. Gant was an elderly African American woman killed in the white ethnic neighborhood of Slavic Village after moving into a single-family house rented to her family by the local public housing authority. After 1985, therefore, victims may have been more willing to come forward. More recently, the number of reported incidents has returned to the 1984 level, which may still be considered problematic.

Organizational Efforts to Improve Race Relations

Community Relations Board

Cleveland's Community Relations Board (CRB) was established in 1945 by Mayor Thomas Burke and the City Council "to promote amicable relations among the racial and cultural groups within the community." It followed a recommendation of the Postwar Planning Council, which advised action on interracial relations, among other matters, in anticipation of the difficulties surrounding the return of servicemen from World War II. Potential sources of tension included expected unemployment resulting from closing of war plants, competition over jobs and housing between whites returning from the war and blacks, and severe overcrowding among blacks who migrated from the South. The panel recommended permanent administrative machinery in the mayor's office to deal with racial problems when or, if possible, before they arose. The early days of the CRB met with some objection due to controversial stances taken early on.[4]

In recent years, the CRB has been mainly involved with police activities, neighborhood issues, and race and ethnic programming. To foster neighborhood unity, the CRB has established ongoing multicultural dialogue groups between African Americans, Italians, Arab Americans, and other ethnic communities. Under Mayor George Voinovich the board began providing human relations training to the Cleveland police academy and effective police-citizen community relations committees were established in the city's six police districts. In addition, an autonomous Civilian Review Board was established in 1982 in response to complaints regarding police misconduct.[5]

Expanded CRB activities since 1990 under Mayor Michael White have made further inroads against racial incidents. According to the 1992 *Plain Dealer* survey, about three-fourths of both blacks and whites believed that Mayor White had improved race relations. White has been perceived as racially conciliatory, and he campaigned on a promise of bringing blacks and whites on both the east and west sides of town together. He further insisted that the CRB become more proactive in investigating even minor disputes between neighbors. He expanded the role of the district police-community relations committees. He visited victims of racial incidents to express the city's support, and he insisted that those arrested for ethnic intimidation be prosecuted. Police in the Repeat Offenders Enforcement Program (ROEP) unit use their training and expertise to pursue perpetrators of hate crimes. Between 1990 and 1995 two hundred arrests were made of individuals charged with hate crimes.[6] Moreover, the city began an ambitious community policing program in 1994, which is viewed as having a favorable impact on neighborhood crime and attitudes toward police. The city also initiated an annual Unity Day in 1992 as a way to promote the acceptance of cultural and racial differences.

While Cleveland seems to have weathered potential storms around racial tension, occasionally an incident reminds us that this is still a factor in urban life. The death of an African American male, Michael Pipkens, while in police custody in December 1993 (in the wake of the Rodney King beating and the death of a Detroit man in an incident involving police) was a potentially volatile incident. It is perhaps a testament to the mayor, the CRB, and others in the community that the investigation and settlement of this unfortunate situation occurred with less rancor and confrontation than similar situations in other cities.

Greater Cleveland Roundtable

The Greater Cleveland Roundtable is a coalition of sixty community leaders from business, labor, education, government, religious, ethnic, and civic organizations. When established in 1982, it was expected to encourage the revitalization of Greater Cleveland in a manner consistent with the needs and aspirations of all area residents. The Roundtable was mandated to foster racial harmony, cooperation, and the empowerment of all segments of Cleveland's diverse population in an effort to improve the quality of life of every resident. While its emphasis on race relations issues has been more prominent at some times than others, the interplay of race with the range of activities undertaken by the organization has been evident from the start.

Recent undertakings of the Roundtable that relate to diversity and race relations include the following:

- Race relations forums to provide opportunities for community groups to discuss mutual concerns and explore opportunities for dialogue
- The Diversity Institute to enable metropolitan Cleveland employers to effectively work with the region's diverse population
- The Inter-Cultural Community Council to promote cultural under-standing and harmony
- The Residential Housing and Mortgage Credit Project, established amid concerns about discrimination in housing, with task forces

working on improved access to mortgage credit and to available housing choices, property insurance, mortgage insurance, and credit bureaus

The involvement of community leaders in diversity dialogue and workshops is an important first step toward integrating such training into business. Other activities address challenges facing racially changing neighborhoods, housing diversity, minority business development, the need for minority educators, and multicultural and diversity training for outside groups.

Young Women's Christian Association

The work of the YWCA of Cleveland is noteworthy because its mission is to empower women and eliminate racism. The local organization dates back to 1868. The national imperative of the YWCA for the past twenty-five years has been the elimination of racism. Recently, through its Empowerment and Racial Justice Department, the local organization has instituted ethnic and diversity workshops and study circle dialogues on racism and race relations that encourage people of different racial and ethnic backgrounds to discuss their feelings about racism openly and honestly. YWCA officials report that hundreds of individuals have been reached through its initiatives.

National Conference

The National Conference was founded in 1927 as the National Conference of Christians and Jews. The northern Ohio office was founded in 1936 and initially focused on combating the anti-Semitism and anti-Catholicism rampant in the early 1930s. It is now described as a human relations organization dedicated to fighting bias, bigotry, and racism in America. It employs advocacy, conflict resolution, and education as tools to promote understanding among all races. The organization's representation of religious groups is now much broader as well.

The National Conference facilitates programs that address bias and prejudice for a number of audiences, including businesses, schools, and community groups. It develops customized programs to provide diversity training in workplace settings. The organization also sponsors Honest

Conversations involving small groups of individuals from various sectors of business, educational institutions, government, religious, and community organizations to share experiences about racism and race relations. In the fall of 1996, the group reported that forty groups were in place or in the planning stage.

Conclusion

Based on traditional indicators of attitudes, opinions, socioeconomic data, ethnoviolence, and residential separation, Cleveland continues to experience difficulty in the area of race relations. The key to conflict management—in Cleveland and throughout the rest of America—is to recognize the reality of racial tension and to work toward its amelioration with appropriate and innovative strategies.

It is further obvious that no one approach to dealing with racial tension will be the answer to all problems. The private sector—through the work of groups like the Roundtable—can promote diversity awareness and discussions of racial issues. Elected officials must continually speak out strongly for racial harmony, even when the political climate is shifting against programs like affirmative action.

The fact that many groups are concerned with issues of diversity and race relations is a positive sign. The introduction to a report prepared by the Race Relations Forum, convened by the Greater Cleveland Roundtable in 1988, describes the participants as representing forty-seven Cleveland area organizations identified as having a stake in improving race relations in our community. The fact that many of these persons had never met or worked together previously was telling, and the need for collaboration and coordination emerged as an often repeated theme.

A promising result of the Citizens League survey was that the vast majority of respondents, regardless of race or ethnicity, thinks that improving race relations is very important. Respondents indicated support for various ways of improving race relations with community involvement, treating people as individuals, better education on race relations, and more understanding rated highest. (See figure 7.3.) Unfortunately, only a quarter of Greater Clevelanders responded that they were aware of programs and agencies that foster better race relations, and only one-tenth could name one. (Those named most frequently were National Association for the Advancement of Colored People, National Conference [of Christians and Jews], and churches/church groups.)

Ways of improving race relations

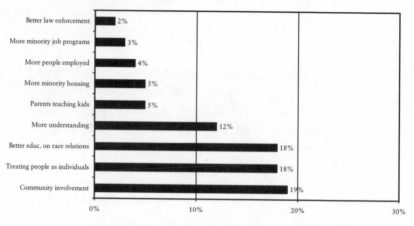

Source: The Citizens League Research Institute (1991)

Figure 7.3. *Ways of improving race relations*

A telephone survey conducted by the Greater Cleveland Roundtable found that sixteen organizations in the Greater Cleveland area offer ongoing programming that includes conflict resolution, human relations training, dialogue groups, speakers bureaus, special events, and other diversity activities. The groups range from the American Jewish Committee to the Spanish American Committee; others without ongoing programming but which are active on the issue of race relations include the NAACP, the Organization of Chinese Americans, and the Arab American Community Center.

Besides Cleveland Mayor Michael White, many other elected officials and community leaders can affect race relations. In fact, the 1988 Roundtable study indicated that the general public had greatest confidence in their minister/priest/rabbi to influence race/ethnic relations. Other key actors noted were the *Plain Dealer,* local television stations, and the Roman Catholic bishop of Cleveland, Anthony M. Pilla, who has been very outspoken about policy issues related to race, such as urban sprawl.

President Bill Clinton engaged the federal government on the issue of race when he announced in 1997 "One America in the 21ˢᵗ Century," an initiative on race. In doing so, he asked Americans to engage in open and honest discussions on the subject. The dialogue has included two major national town hall sessions on race—in Akron, Ohio, and Houston, Texas. While the president's venture has additional legislative and programmatic components, it highlights the importance of communication as a starting point in confronting race-related issues.

Ultimately, the attitudes and actions of each individual, regardless of station in life, will affect the status of race relations in Cleveland and beyond. Diversity and race relations programming, therefore, should be expanded and made available to a larger segment opf the community. While there are risks in approaching the complex and sensitive issues around race relations, the alternative—ignoring the situation—would only contribute to denial, lack of awareness, and inaction.

Yes, people are talking about race relations in Greater Cleveland. The next step is to motivate every individual to take the actions, large and small, needed for change.

Notes

1. The index determines how much population movement would be necessary for racial representation within all census tracts to reflect racial composition in the entire metropolitan area.

2. Cited in *Tragic Failure* by Tom Wicker (New York: Morrow, 1996).

3. Pertinent news stories of the time were the city of Parma's loss of a suit alleging racially discriminatory housing practices; busing Cleveland school district children to achieve integration; a court order directing the Cleveland Police Department to hire and promote more black officers; controversy over the race of a public housing director; and contention over the killing of Michael Woods, a black man, by a Cleveland police officer.

4. Fred McGunagle, *Accepting the Challenge: The Cleveland Community Relations Board, 1945-1995* (City of Cleveland, Community Relations Board, 1995).

5. Ibid.

6. Ibid.

Chapter 8

Neighborhood Leadership Today for Cleveland's Future

Philip Star and Julie Rittenhouse

Rather than being viewed as collections of daunting problems, urban neighborhoods are increasingly being seen as reservoirs of talent and assets that can be building blocks of a better future. New styles of collaborative leadership can mobilize these latent talents and assets where previous neighborhood organizing efforts have failed.

Philip Star is director of the Center for Neighborhood Development, Levin College of Urban Affairs, Cleveland State University. Julie Rittenhouse was project manager for Neighborhood Leadership Cleveland at the Center for Neighborhood Development during its development.

Futurists have a tantalizing way of describing the year 2001 as though being there has little to do with getting there. The future simply arrives full-blown. But it is the succession of days and years between now and then that will determine what life will be like — and what we will do with each of those days and years.

—John Goodlad, *Teachers for Our Nation's Schools*

Community Leadership for the Twenty-first Century

We need to be concerned about the decisions and actions taken in the succession of days and years as we look to our future. And, just as important, we must look to *who* is involved in deciding and implementing what that future will look like, since who is involved on a daily basis will be the strongest determinant of arriving at a better future embraced by the whole community.

Cleveland, like other older urban industrial cities, has seen that the future is not always better. We have learned that progress is not inevitable and that a community without vision and consensus can be adrift. The way in which leadership has expressed itself in the past—the concentration of power narrowly held—has not always led to community betterment and revitalization. Varied interests in community have learned how to block things from happening, and the results of conflict are evident all around. To overcome this civic gridlock, new forms of action have emerged—collaborative processes or public-private partnerships—and these require new forms of leadership.

To achieve a future guided by partnerships, citizens today need training for these new leadership roles. They also need opportunities for inclusiveness so that the entire community can define its own visions for the future.

After all, our democratic system assumes an involved citizenry. Today there is mounting concern over low voter turnout, lack of civic involvement, and the breakdown of community. This concern has been expressed in the naming of the "Me Generation" and a call to alarm by a new Communitarian movement, which has diagnosed a society that puts all its emphasis on individual rights and little on individual responsibility. Writers such as Robert Bellah in *Habits of the Heart: Individualism and Commitment in American Life* and Amitai Etzioni in *The Spirit of Community: Rights, Responsibilities, and the Communitarian Agenda* harken back to an America described by Alexis de Tocqueville in *Democracy in America* in which people came together in mutual association and worked together to solve problems rather than relying on government or the aristocracy. De Tocqueville saw this as unique to this country and the principal reason why America would prosper. (He also warned that slavery and racism were the major factors that threatened the future of the country.)

As many are concerned today over the loss of involvement and lack of responsibility, so too are there questions about the loss of community.

In the cities of America it is commonly believed that neighborhoods have declined in large part because of this lack of resident involvement, a lack of leadership, a lack of community. The loss of population from many of these neighborhoods, the declining economic status of those left behind, and the loss of "role-models" and people with skills who have moved to the suburbs are all cited as major causes for the decline and inability of these areas to be revitalized. There's often not much hope for recovery.

Until very recently this view of urban America, with its underlying racist implications, was the easy explanation for the failure of urban programs. However, as anybody knows who has traveled recently through Cleveland's neighborhoods or is aware of the transformation of the South Bronx or parts of Newark or Baltimore, the same areas that have been written off for the past twenty years are showing signs of rebirth and revitalization. The same people live there today as after the shock waves of suburbanization hit these neighborhoods; the economics impacting these neighborhoods have not improved, and many of these neighborhoods have become even poorer. The one noticeable change is the increase in involvement of the residents and, in most cases, the existence of a community-based organization that has been able to focus the interests of the community into development efforts—first in housing and later in commercial revitalization—that have begun to re-create the market in these neighborhoods. The interest and involvement were always present, but they needed to be focused and connected to strategies to bring about change.

No new massive government program has brought about this change. In fact, most of these efforts have come about in a time of declining federal resources, and much of what has occurred is in response to the loss of governmental programs and private disinvestment. Community-based and community-controlled efforts are helping neighborhood residents take responsibility for the future of their neighborhood. Citizens themselves are beginning to have success by forming mutual associations, developing their own visions for their neighborhoods, and enlisting local governments and professionals to assist them in revitalization projects. Locally grown development corporations have rehabilitated housing, built new housing, assisted business expansion, and improved the quality of life in their neighborhood. Those most involved are those who were so often left out of the process in the past—individuals traditionally seen as the problem because of lack of skills, wisdom, or ability to help rebuild the community. In sum, the big difference from past efforts at revitalization is that people in communities are seeking the resources to solve their problems rather than relying on someone else or allowing a solution to be imposed that may neither fit the circumstances nor respond to the most pressing needs.

Evolution of Citizen Participation

These new efforts are in response to experiences with three other organizational models that have failed to revitalize neighborhoods: government-initiated citizen participation; top-down, large-scale, government efforts; and bottom-up, grassroots efforts. While all of these efforts have recognized the importance of citizen involvement, each had significant limitations. In many ways, the more recent successes are based on a synthesis of these experiences in a new community rebuilding model.

Citizen participation requirements in federal programs often require that citizens be given the opportunity to comment on proposed government actions. The Community Development Block Grant (CDBG) program merged the experience of the federal government in both the Urban Renewal program and Model Cities to create a local government citizen participation process that balanced the need for local review but protected local government decision making. Such an approach safeguards against violation of the statutory purpose of the funds but provides little assurance that a neighborhood will be directly involved in the actual decision making about priorities and projects. Very few communities make citizen participation part of the decision-making process. One exception is Dayton, where Citizen Priority Boards determine how CDBG funding will be spent. To be on the board, a resident must complete a leadership development course and be elected by the community. In most other places, however, the concept of participation is narrowed to a citizen's superficial right to attend a meeting and respond to a proposal or fill out a survey about how he or she wants funds to be spent. While the federal government upholds the concept of and suggests the need for resident involvement, it has neither found nor legislated ways in which such involvement really takes place. Citizen involvement at this level often does not inspire citizens to be involved, nor does it give them a sense that they are being heard. The result is a low level of satisfaction when issues are addressed by government, since there is little personal investment in the decision or outcome. Government officials, in turn, often become frustrated since a significant "public involvement" effort is met with little positive response.

A greater degree of involvement provides more ownership in both the process and the outcome. Many citizens have learned to work with the CDBG process by learning the regulations and reviewing performance reports and proposals. This level of involvement has demonstrated that average citizens can fully participate. Such participation requires time, effort, and an enhancement of knowledge. National organizations like the Center for Community Change have helped neighborhood residents integrate their neighborhood knowledge with an understanding of the federal rules of the game. Neighborhood residents have also learned that real involvement does carry responsibility. If people really do want to participate, they must be willing to spend the time to understand the issues and program objectives and to work with diverse interests to find a mutually acceptable approach.

At the other end of the spectrum, grassroots organizations emerged in the 1970s to challenge governmental indifference to neighborhood conditions. From these grassroots efforts, three major lessons have been incorporated into present-day successful community revitalization efforts. First, the community must identify the problem and own the solution. That does not mean they have all the resources or all the answers, but community members must guide the process. In many cases of community organizing, grassroots advocacy organizations simply demanded that government solve a problem. The organizations often were not involved in developing the solution, and sometimes the solution picked created other problems. In addition, the capacity of the community to solve its problems was not enhanced.

Second, many of the things that impact a neighborhood are beyond the control of the neighborhood. From this, grassroots organizations learned to form partnerships and coalitions. For example, the loss of a bank branch was a much bigger issue than one neighborhood could address. In fact, a solution that would solve the problem in one neighborhood might hurt another, which might see their branch closed instead. This led to the understanding that some issues needed to be addressed either citywide or even nationally. In the case of financial institution disinvestment, it lead to the development of a national coalition organized by National People in Action, which successfully lobbied for the passage of the Community Reinvestment Act (CRA).

Third, and most significant, grassroots organizations affirmed the importance of the people who lived in the neighborhood and enhanced their leadership skills. While the prevailing view was that little was left in these neighborhoods, these organizations proved there was a reservoir of talent and commitment.

Such efforts provided the impetus for John L. McKnight, director of community studies at the Center for Urban Affairs and Policy Research at Northwestern University, to reconsider how we look at community and neighborhoods. McKnight had his students go out into the city and do a neighborhood inventory—a traditional needs analysis. They would document all of the community problems, as well as needs and deficiencies of individuals. McKnight came to realize, however, that he and his students were thinking about inner-city neighborhoods as a collection of problems. It's easy for universities and the government to take this approach, since they are experienced in counting, measuring, and evaluating problems. But, as McKnight has written, this approach makes the people in the neighborhood "think of themselves and their neighbors as fundamentally deficient, victims incapable of taking charge of their lives and of their community's future." Relying on such a needs map ensures the deepening of the cycle of dependence. Indeed, problems must always appear worse than last year to justify continued or increased funding for neighborhood programs. According to McKnight:

> Providing resources on the basis of the needs map underlines the perception that only outside experts can provide real help. Therefore, the relationships that count most for local residents are no longer those inside the community, those neighbor-to-neighbor links of mutual support and problem solving. Rather, the most important relationships are those that involve the expert, the social worker, the health provider, the funder. Once again, the glue that binds communities together is weakened.[1]

This analysis has led to a new approach with three key elements:

- A combination of the top-down and bottom-up approaches in establishing partnerships between all stakeholders

- A recognition of and the building on the existing assets of a community

- The affirmation of leadership and building on the skills of existing residents

Any hope for the future of our cities must include adequate preparation of neighborhood residents to be full participants in collaborative processes and be active leaders. Without that, the result will be a return to professional, top-down solutions such as Urban Renewal and Model Cities or the eventual decline of effective, community-based organizations.

Collaborative Leadership

This concept of leadership for the future is grounded in the democratic belief that people have the capacity to create their own visions and solve their own problems when the appropriate people are brought together and the stakeholders of a community (government, business, institutions, and citizens) take action in constructive ways through an open process that is inclusive and credible. Such a process requires the availability of good information that leads to a shared understanding of problems and concerns. The outcome will be the creation of authentic visions and strategies for addressing the shared concerns of the community. For this to happen, there must be leadership that convenes, energizes, facilitates, and sustains this process.[2] Such leadership must be understood and practiced by all of the stakeholders.

This new form of leadership has been called collaborative leadership in recognition that, in our society, the complexity of issues and the ability of interest groups to block any action requires new methods to bring about change. No longer is one person in a position to forge a solution and control the outcome. Even the historically iron-willed leadership in Congress has had to yield to more inclusiveness in order to move legislation. In areas where we face especially complex challenges, such as education, crime, drugs, and poverty—where there often is no agreement on the problems themselves, much less on possible solutions—there must be community consensus and a new form of leadership to bring about solutions. Such efforts require that participants have knowledge of these approaches and possess enough skills so that all parties can participate on an equal playing field.

Two dominant forms of leadership are well established in our culture. Chrislip and Larson define these as tactical leadership (heroic) and positional leadership. A tactical leader, like a military commander, coach, or surgeon, has a clear goal or objective (win the game, arrest the outlaw). He or she explains the plan, organizes and coordinates all of the activity, motivates, and implements. We all grew up watching films with such heroes (real and imaginary) that take care of the enemy or beat the criminals.

According to Chrislip, "Positional leadership is associated with being at the top of a functional structure. For many people, including the media, leadership and position are synonymous."[3] The CEO of a corporation, the president of a college, curator of a museum, or head of government are such leaders and are recognized for their ability to set and achieve goals. A greater sense of ability is required to be a positional leader than a heroic leader, and there is an ongoing process that provides an opportunity for the development of leadership skills as one moves through the organization. Those who inspire and energize us have become well known and sometimes well rewarded for many worthwhile and noble endeavors. This type of success often inspires people to want to be that type of leader or, conversely, scares people away from leadership since they do not see themselves in that role or having the necessary type of knowledge, power, or solutions. However, without the functional structure (which does not exist when dealing with problems that present challenges to the future of a community), these leaders, or any community leader who wants to emulate them, cannot mandate or develop a solution that will work. People often retreat from leadership roles in the community because they do not see a leadership model that fits them or which they believe will work. Thus, while these two leadership models have provided great success, neither has been effective in the community context.

Because of these limitations and the need to bring all stakeholders together, a new form of leadership has emerged from the frustration of urban decay. In Newark, New Jersey, in 1984 Prudential Insurance made a commitment to stay and try to figure out what the company could do to help the city solve the problems that had made it a national symbol for inner-city decay. A study by the company of how other cities had worked to solve common problems yielded the following result:

> One clear lesson emerged: most city partnerships were between government and business and excluded community groups, non-

profits, educational representatives, and other key stakeholders. In many cases, these excluded groups were able to block initiatives of the "public/private" partnerships. By leaving out key perspectives and interests, the authors of these initiatives were unable to create a powerful enough constituency to implement their recommendations.[4]

The recommendation was to support a communitywide, collaborative effort that involved not only the financial support from the company but also the president's personal participation. This new model of collaboration also yielded a new form of leadership, which has been called facilitative, or collaborative, leadership.

Chrislip and Larson have identified four aspects of this leadership that make it a successful model for resolving community problems.

1. Inspire commitment and action: Leadership requires that something be accomplished, that goals are met. The idea of collaboration and consensus building often is misinterpreted as leading to inaction. A collaborative leader brings about change. The action, however, involves convincing people that something can be done, "not telling them what to do or doing the work for them."[5]

2. Lead as peer problem solver: Collaborative leaders help groups create visions and solve problems. By creating an inclusive process where ownership is shared, stakeholders have confidence in the credibility and effectiveness of the process. In the end, the collaborative leader's role is to serve the group and the broader purposes for which it exists.

3. Build broad-based involvement: Success is only achieved when all interests are represented. One of the greatest challenges for collaborative leadership is to include all the relevant community of interests, regardless of diversity. Leadership comes from understanding the issues and being able to identify all the stakeholders who are necessary to define the problem, determine solutions, and obtain results.

4. Sustain hope and participation: Finally, as the process unfolds, people may tend to fall back on previous relationship and old ways of getting things done. Leaders help groups do hard work when it would be easier to quit, and they sustain commitment and confidence in the process.

What this means on the community level is that organizations do not always have to be responding to the latest crisis. By bringing together all of the stakeholders in a community, a shared vision can emerge that will become the blueprint for community action. Rather than bring people together around negatives and problems, a positive focus can be achieved that must respond to and remove barriers. Rather than focusing on the smaller organizational issues and conflicts that often lead to turf battles, organizations can see themselves in the context of broader goals.

In order for this to happen, three things are needed. First, community residents must have the opportunity to be trained in these new skills. Second, there must be community acceptance of a collaborative model (that is, people need to see that this can work and that there is broad-based support for a new method). Third, there must be a willingness to allow neighborhood residents into the decision-making process at the earliest possible time. When positions have been taken and interests defined, it is almost impossible to use the collaborative model effectively; the only response is to block action. Thus, efforts have to be made to bring the community in and have leadership in place to build the collaborative effort. The result will not be that every concern of every resident is addressed, but that the best possible solution to meet the needs of the community will be developed.

The community, to be successful, needs a much better understanding of the role of leaders. Leaders need to understand this new model, be affirmed as leaders, and build a new set of skills on their assets. Watching John Wayne movies will no longer provide the necessary curriculum, nor will leadership training programs that guide leaders to move beyond management to a leadership role within a defined structure. In many cases, this new definition and role of leader opens up leadership opportunities to a much larger community, since people no longer need to climb to the top of an organization, engage in heroic acts, or solve all the problems.

There is a set of facilitative skills that need to be learned. While all stakeholders should learn these skills, the greatest need is at the community level. Too often, significant time is spent in frustration over problems, in tedious meetings where little is accomplished, and in arguing to be heard or being part of failed solutions. A collaborative approach provides the opportunity to work in partnership to bring about positive change.

Many of the concepts of collaborative leadership have begun to be integrated into both business and government with the concepts of team building and total quality management. The use of focus groups and facilitators has become more common in recent years in regular business practices. In addition, the concept of public/private partnerships is well entrenched in Cleveland. The stage for the increased use of collaborative leadership has clearly been set.

Future success and sustained progress in Cleveland requires that the collaborative process includes all of the stakeholders, particularly community organizations and community leaders, in this new partnership in order to mold the future of the community. Great strides have been made over the past ten years through the work of community development corporations in physical redevelopment. As the success of downtown and these neighborhood development projects increases, we will have an opportunity to develop a new vision for Cleveland's neighborhoods. The residents of the neighborhoods must be ready to participate.

Two efforts are presently under way to build the capacity of residents to participate in such a collaborative visioning. The Cleveland Community Building Initiative (CCBI) is using the asset model in four neighborhoods of Cleveland to build the capacity of local residents to set an agenda for their neighborhood. And the Neighborhood Leadership Cleveland program, designed and developed by the Center for Neighborhood Development at Cleveland State University and the Greater Cleveland Neighborhood Centers Association, is an effort to affirm the leaders of Cleveland's neighborhoods and provide new skills in collaborative leadership. These two approaches are described in more detail below.

Cleveland Community Building Initiative

In 1990 the Cleveland Foundation Commission on Poverty was formed to develop a strategy to combat the rising level of poverty in Cleveland's neighborhoods. A group of thirty community and business leaders met for almost three years to develop an action plan. The plan, CCBI, included five guiding principles, which stated that to reverse persistent poverty, strategies must be (1) comprehensive and integrated; (2) tailored to individual neighborhoods; (3) based on a neighborhood's assets, not its deficits; (4) resident driven; and (5) tested in pilot "villages" and carefully evaluated before attempts are made to implement them in other neighborhoods.

The selection criteria for the pilot neighborhoods included sufficient local assets to build upon, interest within the community for such an effort, and overall potential for success. The four areas chosen were East-Fairfax, Central-King Kennedy, Mt. Pleasant, and Near West Side-Ohio City. A village council made up of residents and other village stakeholders has been established in each neighborhood. The purpose of the village council is to involve residents in forming village-based collaborations and partners, setting priorities, and generating strategies to improve the quality of life and opportunities for self-sufficiency in their community.

Today, CCBI is chartered as a not-for-profit organization and is governed by a board comprised of eighteen trustees. Each board member is assigned to one of the four villages and is expected to participate with the respective village council. Additionally, each village council has a seat on the board.

The Central Village Council is involved in a school-to-work project, a juvenile justice project, and a church-based economic summit. The East Village Council has developed its strategic plan and asset directory, and it has representation on the advisory committee of Cleveland's federal Empowerment Zone to plan for labor-force development and community-building issues. In Mt. Pleasant, a village council is in the process of implementing its strategic plan and is supporting a community school concept at Alexander Hamilton Middle School, one of the fast-track schools of the Cleveland Public School System. The West Village Council has recently been formed and is in the process of developing task forces to address a broad range of community issues.

At the same time the Poverty Commission was studying ways to reverse conditions that lead to and maintain poverty, the Greater Cleveland Neighborhood Centers Association (NCA) was developing a community-building approach of its own for member agencies. In its 1991–92 annual report, entitled "Rebuilding the Second City," NCA argued that Cleveland was a story of two cities. "The first city . . . is a tribute to collective vision and action. Strengths are identified, then enhanced through long-term financial commitment. The language spoken is the language of development. In the shadow . . . lies a second city. In this city change is reactive, triggered by crisis. The language spoken is the language of rescue."[6]

Similarly, Phillip Clay, Albert A. Levin Professor of urban studies and public service at Cleveland State University in 1987–88, after a yearlong strategic assessment of Cleveland concluded that downtown development initiatives, "while substantial, are still insufficient to reverse the serious problems the city already faces and will face by the turn of the century."[7] In his 1988 report, "Transforming Cleveland's Future: Issues and Strategies for a Heartland City," Clay suggested goals and strategies that will prompt broad-based community discussion and education, building a strong base of support for change. To stimulate transformation, the report emphasized the need for Cleveland "to redefine and expand its leadership base."

In response to the challenges of rebuilding Cleveland's "second city," NCA developed a strategic plan that proposed a comprehensive, community-building approach for strengthening Cleveland's families and neighborhoods. Called the "Kellogg Initiative" because of a multiyear grant from the Kellogg Foundation, it is a plan to restructure NCA's twenty-one neighborhood centers and develop a neighborhood-based, citywide leadership development training program. A holistic model, focusing on the strengths of families and neighborhoods, would direct this process.

Neighborhood Leadership Cleveland

Community change demands leadership. Planning for a leadership training program for both Cleveland's seasoned and emergent neighborhood leaders was initiated in 1992. Like so many initiatives in Cleveland, a partnership was formed, in this case between NCA and the Center for Neighborhood Development (CND), a program of the Urban Center, Maxine Goodman Levin College of Urban Affairs, Cleveland State University. Both partners were joined by NCA's network of twenty-one neighborhood centers and settlement houses. These centers are neighborhood-based, nonprofit organizations that provide an array of social services in Greater Cleveland, many since the turn of the century.

The goal for both partners was to develop a leadership development model that would bring neighborhood leaders citywide together in a supportive environment, leading to collaborative action and community-building activities. In designing the leadership training program, the partners agreed that a new approach focusing on capabilities, skills, and resources was necessary. Early in the planning process, however, it became evident that there were few examples that matched NCA's vision for asset-based family and community development. Indeed, most family and community development activities are still rooted in needs, deficiencies, and problems. Traditionally, programs are developed in reaction to a crisis, and trainers work in isolation, developing curriculum and training materials without input from program constituents or community stakeholders. From the inception of Neighborhood Leadership Cleveland, the resources in the community were tapped to ensure that the training met the goals of NCA and community leaders.

Neighborhood Leadership Cleveland is designed to increase the participation and effectiveness of neighborhood residents in determining the future of their communities. The twelve-week program offers information about issues and resources that affect neighborhoods, new leadership skills, and contacts that will assist leaders in furthering their community goals. The program takes a two-tiered approach to leadership training, consisting of an introductory course and a specialized level of training, including instruction, technical assistance, and community forums. Program participants explore such topics as the different definitions of leadership and leadership styles, decision-making analysis, neighborhood goal setting, and conflict resolution. Simulations, group presentations, a retreat, and neighborhood tours ensure that the class has a hands-on experience with practical applications.

Since the fall of 1994, more than three hundred community leaders representing neighborhoods throughout Cleveland and adjacent suburbs, such as East Cleveland, Garfield Heights, Cleveland Heights, and Shaker Heights, have graduated from Neighborhood Leadership Cleveland. Beginning with the second NLC class, graduates formed the Greater Cleveland Neighborhood Forum. This group meets monthly to exchange information about their community activities and to participate in issue seminars and training in such skills as public speaking, proposal writing, fundraising for nonprofit boards, school governance, labor force development strategies, and alternative community building models.

Outcome studies have been conducted for Neighborhood Leadership Cleveland to measure its impacts on participating community leaders. The survey results and focus group findings confirm that there is a demand for leadership development training and technical assistance at the grassroots level. Of great significance is the recognition by most participants that leadership development is a process not conducted in isolation and that it is achieved in stages. Neighborhood leaders are interested in additional training that would enable them to continue to enhance their leadership skills, strengthen their relationships with one another, and increase capacity building opportunities for their organizations and institutions. The evaluation findings also indicate that collaboration among program participants crosses neighborhood and racial boundaries, as suggested by those leaders who actively participate in the Greater Cleveland Neighborhood Forum.

In addition, the program has helped open doors to both human and capital resources in the community. One graduate engaged in a political campaign and was elected to East Cleveland City Council. Another graduate with a long history of supporting school reform was selected to serve on the Cleveland Public Schools' watchdog panel, known as the Levy Accountability Committee.

Challenges to Neighborhood Leadership Cleveland

Neighborhood Leadership Cleveland (NLC) is at a turning point. The challenges are to position community leaders in key institutions, develop strategies for specific initiatives, and institutionalize the training program. Community mobilization is difficult to generate and sustain over a long period. It requires both capacity and trust across all sectors of the community.

Shortly after the NLC program began in 1994, the Center for Neighborhood Development at Cleveland State University, in partnership with the Center on Urban Poverty and Social Change and the Center for Community Development at Case Western Reserve University, were awarded a Community Outreach Partnership Center (COPC) grant from the U.S. Department of Housing and Urban Development (HUD). The COPC program is part of a broader effort by HUD to harness the intellectual and financial resources of colleges and universities "to create communities of opportunity," enabling schools to become forces for positive changes in their communities. "With this funding," former HUD Secretary Henry Cisneros said, "universities will help to reshape cities to become, once again, driving forces in the economic, social and cultural life of this nation."

Cleveland's COPC is a partnership with the city of Cleveland and the two universities to provide technical assistance in implementing the city's Empowerment Zone strategies. It is the intent also to remove obstacles so that residents can use the resources and educational opportunities at the two institutions. This grant supported four additional classes of Neighborhood Leadership Cleveland beyond the seed funding.

It is rare that nonprofits or the public sector ask universities to solve "real" problems. Beyond the data files and analytical tools, universities can have a unique role in contributing to community development. An illustration of this is Ohio's Urban University Program (UUP). The UUP is a model of collaboration between urban universities and the community, as well as collaboration within its own structure. The UUP enables Ohio's eight urban universities to link research, outreach, training, and technical resources to the community and state legislature.

The university-community concept is relatively new, and there are obstacles to address in securing long-term institutional support. There is evidence, however, that these partnerships can be a tool in leveraging innovative and existing resources. Both HUD's COPC program and Ohio's UUP have supported linkages for community development and outreach activities in Cleveland and other metropolitan areas in Ohio. In turn, the NLC program and its graduates are contributing to this discussion and, in some cases, providing innovative ideas on neighborhood issues.

Training and capacity building activities, such as NLC and the Cleveland Community Building Initiative, can help alter decision-making patterns and increase Cleveland's capacity to find common ground among diverse stakeholders. For communities that are initiating and supporting similar leadership development programs, there are important lessons from the Cleveland experience:

- Provide institutional support: The Neighborhood Centers Association, in partnership with the Center for Neighborhood Development, shepherded this neighborhood leadership initiative and, in the process, increased the skills of a small but growing number of neighborhood leaders. It also raised the level of discussion about the future of Cleveland's neighborhoods, moving it beyond isolated individuals and neighborhood organizations.

- Foster a broader dialogue: The discussions among NLC participants and the network of graduates demonstrate the concern that neighborhood leaders and organizational leadership alike have for the future of the entire city of Cleveland. Building leadership that reflects the community's breadth of interest, commonalities, and commitment to change is an important first step.

- Build community commitment: The continuation of this community conversation depends on the leadership of the public, private, and civic sectors, including local foundations. Such support allows for the exploration of a common vision for Cleveland's neighborhoods and also strengthens programs like Neighborhood Leadership Cleveland.

- Reach out to civic and business leaders: Civic and business leaders can play an important role by donating expertise and financially supporting leadership development programs. Their involvement will help create an environment that advances opportunities and access for Cleveland's neighborhood leaders and, in the process, elevates the status of community leadership.

Leadership development programs can make a major contribution to the future viability of communities. The multiple issues that neighborhood leaders are attempting to address in their communities are visible reminders that will alone is not enough. Success is dependent on the continuous development of leadership skills and collaboration with others for coalition building and, ultimately, change.

Conclusion

Cleveland is in an uncommon position as it celebrates its accomplishments of the past two hundred years. In the last decade, significant changes have occurred in Cleveland because of the leadership that brought corporate interests together to develop a vision of downtown. Cleveland also has been successful in creating and using public-private partnerships to implement a downtown revitalization agenda and identifying new ways to assist neighborhood development. Now there exists an opportunity to take another step forward by expanding the existing partnerships to include those who have the most intimate knowledge of the city—the residents of Cleveland's neighborhoods. The process of forming this new civic agenda should also include partnerships with the inner-ring suburbs that are dependent on the future of Cleveland and its neighborhoods. There are no simple solutions or cure for urban decline, but experience suggests that those who are most vulnerable and are most directly affected should, at the very least, be at the table.

Consensus building requires a different kind of participation and involvement by the residents of Cleveland's neighborhoods. While there has been an extraordinary amount of residential involvement, there has been a lack of coordination and relationship building between people within and among neighborhoods. Today's active residents and community leaders could, with appropriate assistance and capacity building opportunities, shape a process that will create a vision for the neighborhoods similar to the one for downtown—a vision that will revitalize each neighborhood in the context of the larger community. If people are allowed to dream, to enhance their skills, and to build the necessary relationships to fulfill their dreams, the future of the city can only be brighter.

As we approach the twenty-first century, cooperation and commitments from the public, business, and civic sectors are critical for a more equitable balance of community resources and power. Clearly, full citizen participation in the democratic process will not become a reality without a strong commitment from all partners. Many future leaders are counting on them.

Notes

1. John P. Kretzmann and John L. McKnight, *Building Communities from the Inside Out: A Path Toward Finding and Mobilizing Community Assets* (Chicago: ACTA Publications, 3d printing, 1993), 4.

2. David D. Chrislip and Carl E. Larson, *Collaborative Leadership: How Citizens and Civic Leaders Can Make A Difference* (San Francisco: Jossey-Bass Publishers, 1994); Robert Mier with Robert P. Giloth, "Cooperative Leadership for Community Problem Solving" in *Social Justice and Local Development Policy*, ed. Robert Mier (Newbury Park, Calif.: Sage Publications, 1993).

3. Chrislip and Larson, 128.

4. Ibid., 133.

5. Ibid., 139.

6. "Rebuilding the Second City," Neighborhood Centers Association Annual Report 1991–92 (Greater Cleveland Neighborhood Centers Association, 1992).

7. Phillip A. Clay, "Transforming Cleveland's Future: Issues and Strategies for a Heartland City," Maxine Goodman Levin College of Urban Affairs, Levin Chair Report, 1988, viii.

Chapter 9

Youth, Citizenship, and Cleveland's Future

Gina Zipkin Weisblat,
Wendy Slone, and Susan Petrone

Anecdotal and statistical evidence indicate that today's youth are disconnected from their communities; this attitude negatively influences their relationships with adults and is symptomatic of the decline in many neighborhoods. Communities need to reclaim and take responsibility for their youth. Traditional methods of community building, such as extended family involvement, organized neighborhood activities, and well-defined roles for individuals of all ages, no longer exist within communities. Youth need real opportunities to take part in constructive change within their neighborhoods.

Gina Zipkin Weisblat and Wendy Slone are doctoral students at the Levin College of Urban Affairs. Susan Petrone is the editor at the Levin College's Urban Center and a freelance fiction writer, playwright, and editor.

Youth at a Glance

One of the most difficult and often unnoticed challenges facing the revitalization of Cleveland and its neighborhoods is the disengagement of youth. In reshaping the role of young people within our communities, their current role within their families, neighborhoods, and communities at large must be examined. Additionally, the needs and wants of these youth must be identified and programs must be implemented to offer youth an opportunity to become full participants in making decisions, implementing ideas, and creating change in their communities.

Since the early 1970s the United States has seen vast changes in the way in which young people are raised and find their place in society. What has traditionally been perceived as the typical American family— a middle-class, two-parent phenomenon—has changed. The support and guidance once found within the family unit and in the community are available less frequently, or sometimes not at all. It is not an overexaggeration to say that youth are in crisis. Statistical evidence bears out this claim.

The 1994 annual report of the Cuyahoga County Juvenile Court reported 11,611 complaints lodged against juveniles, which averages out to thirty-two complaints against youth a day in Cuyahoga County. The most heinous of those crimes reported included 60 cases of arson, 178 cases of sex offenses, 1,047 cases of burglary and robbery, 1,214 cases of drug charges, and 33 cases of homicide.[1]

Violence is a constant threat to youth. What is disturbing is that the potential for violence is not concentrated only in schools or at home; it is a pervasive part of growing up in America in the late twentieth century. In a recent article in the *Journal of the American Medical Association,* entitled "Adolescent Exposure to Violence and Associated Symptoms of Psychological Trauma," researchers studied the percentage of students victimized by violence within the Central neighborhood of the city of Cleveland. They found that 25.4 percent of female and 23.7 percent of male youths had been threatened at home; 30.5 percent of female and 34.8 percent of male youths had been threatened at school; 29.1 percent of female and 42.9 percent of male youths had been threatened in their neighborhood; 8.8 percent of female and 22.4 percent of male youths had been beaten or mugged in their neighborhood; 3.6 percent of female and 9.1 percent of male youths had been beaten or mugged at school; 16.3 percent of female and 7.0 percent male youths had been sexually abused/assaulted; 9.1 percent of female and 16.0 percent of male youths had been attacked with a knife or involved in a stabbing; and 10.1 percent of female and 33.4 percent of male youths had been shot at or actually shot.

In addition to the threat of violence, youth are threatening their own future by disregarding their education. The Cleveland Public Schools' 1992 year-end review showed that 39.0 percent of ninth graders, 31.0 percent of tenth graders, 22.0 percent of eleventh graders, and 17.0 percent of seniors failed their current grade. Additionally, 10.5 percent of the youth in the Cleveland Public Schools voluntarily dropped out. Each year within the Cleveland Public Schools approximately 1,300 elementary students, 4,250 intermediate students, and 5,250 high school students are suspended and approximately 135 students expelled. More ominous is the fact that over three hundred weapons are confiscated from Cleveland Public School children each year.[2]

In the early 1990s, the Children's Defense Fund Greater Cleveland Project released startling statistics testifying to the difficulties and dangers faced by young people in Cleveland and similar urban areas. According to these statistics, one in five babies born in the city of Cleveland was born to a teenage mother and 91 percent of these births were to unmarried teens. Fifty percent of these mothers, aged eighteen and nineteen, had no high school diploma. Finally, at the time these statistics were released, 26 percent of all children living in Cuyahoga County were on Aid to Families with Dependent Children.[3]

A day in the life of America's youth

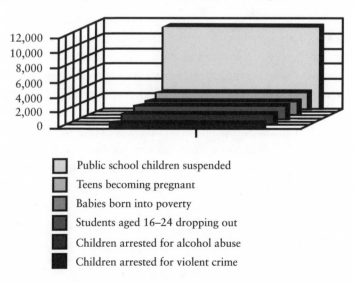

12,000
10,000
8,000
6,000
4,000
2,000
0

☐ Public school children suspended
☐ Teens becoming pregnant
☐ Babies born into poverty
■ Students aged 16–24 dropping out
■ Children arrested for alcohol abuse
■ Children arrested for violent crime

Figure 9.1. *A day in the life of America's youth*

Also in 1990, the national Children's Defense Fund profiled a life in the day of America's youth and found that, on any given day, 2,756 teens become pregnant, 2,685 babies are born into poverty, 248 children are arrested for violent crimes, 176 children are arrested for drug abuse, 427 children are arrested for alcohol abuse or drunk driving, 10,988 public school children are suspended, and 2,250 students aged sixteen to twenty-four drop out of school.[4]

This barrage of statistics reflects a war of attrition taking place in our neighborhoods and communities and an increasing sense of despair, fear, and apathy. In spite of this seemingly irrevocable trend, changes can be made and revitalization is possible. The process must begin with a reexamination of the role of youth within our society.

The teenage years are a time for cognitive, emotional, social, and moral development. During this time, it is crucial that young people have opportunities to explore their new roles, develop independence through personal discovery, and discover how their identities are perceived within the community. Adolescence, much like young childhood, requires exploration of newly developed skills, such as coping and communication skills, the establishment of personal values systems, and more meaningful relationships with others. Judging from the aforementioned statistics, many young people do not feel valued in their communities and are not being given a positive and supportive atmosphere in which to grow and develop. Instead of being presented with tools to expand their abilities and role models to guide them, many youth are left to themselves or an unsupervised peer group.

The Carnegie Corporation (of New York) Task Force on Youth Development conducted a national survey and evaluation of youth programs, from which emerged a number of consistent themes. Youth would like programs that allow them to increase and test their personal and social skills and that they can participate in on non-school time. Low-income and minority youth and those from single-parent families reported the highest amount of benefit and satisfaction from such programming; most notably, such programming appears to reduce high-risk behavior and increase positive behavior.

Society's Perception of Youth

Only 2 students allowed at a time.

—Dairymart

This statement typifies the insensitivity to young people and the lack of confidence the adult community has in our youth. Young people are very sensitive to adult apprehension, whether it is covert disregard or overt suspicion, such as this notice placed in a convenience store entrance. Youth internalize these signals and, in turn, react in a negative manner toward themselves and society at large. Ruthanne Kurth-Schai, in her paper "The Roles of Youth in Society: A Reconceptualization," asserts that as perceptions cause adults to prize the opposite qualities in children that are respected in adults, we deny youth the opportunity to test out their individuality in safe situations and develop needed adult traits.

Kurth-Schai also reports on the traditional approach that adults have taken toward youth programming. She contends that most youth-oriented programs of today address adult-identified perceptions of youth issues, that these programs offer limited leadership roles and decision-making opportunities for the youth involved, and that the standard for success in the program is solely in judging personal growth instead of looking at the youths' contribution to society. Lastly, she points out that many programs are inaccessible to the majority of youth in this country.[5]

Youth programs need to be accessible to the widest possible range of students, but programming must also challenge them emotionally and intellectually while providing opportunities to develop leadership, communication, and social skills. It seems clear that it is necessary to evolve new mechanisms for youth acceptance and advancement—ones that could also lead to neighborhood revitalization. One potential mechanism for youth and neighborhood revitalization is the concept of citizenship.

Citizenship: An Overview

Citizenship is a part of the decision-making process that emphasizes rights and privileges within a formal society. Citizenship increases the level of responsibility of individuals and provides an outlet for community and individual empowerment. When examining today's youth it is evident that many young people have not been taught, formally or informally, their role within a thriving society. One means of educating youth in citizenship and all it entails is through youth-driven, youth-organized, and youth-implemented organizations.

In the United States, citizenship was traditionally a concept taught through community-centered schools and reinforced within the family.

Civic education programs were used as a tool to prepare students for the political responsibilities of citizenship. Students were also actively exposed to the civic responsibilities of citizenship through extracurricular activities, such as student government, athletics, or school-based drama, music, and other special interest clubs.

The concept of citizenship that existed up through the mid-1960s has eroded as the structures and institutions that perpetuated its future have died out. Instead of neighborhood grocery stores, drugstores, and restaurants we have Stop-N-Shops, Wal-Marts, and McDonalds. Instead of neighborhood block parties, impromptu community evening activities, or a local " gathering spot" such as a coffee shop or bar where informal politics are discussed, we have chat rooms and e-mail. Technology and the information age have changed the way in which people interact and view personal responsibility. Neighborhoods have become transient in nature and are no longer the lifelines to needed supplies or to social activities. With such a rapidly changing social structure, it is small wonder that young people no longer find the conventional concepts of citizenship to be relevant to their lives.

In order to engage youth as citizens and as an essential element of our social fabric, Americans need to rethink the way they operate youth programming and youth involvement within the community. Traditional service learning programs, such as Boy Scouts, Girl Scouts, and school student council programs, arm students with some of the tools required for active citizenship. These programs provide a common language and atmosphere for student-led events and challenges. They also provide an opportunity for young people to explore the world of responsibility via the safety of a prestructured environment. However, such programs also eliminate choices by virtue of their precreated structure, thus limiting the ability to negotiate power within issues that the young people choose to explore. Further, there is little reflection on how the chosen activities affect either the youths' private self-interest or the community as a whole.

Methods for encouraging youth participation in the future must be driven by youth interest. Young people are aware of the issues that impact their communities, but they need to have confidence in their peers and in the adult community. Solutions to community problems will only come from a process of understanding neighborhood structure, networks, dynamics, influences, and resources. Through an effective youth/adult partnership, youth can take ownership of community problems and work toward enacting their solutions.

Tools for Teaching Youth Citizenship

There are three important aspects to teaching the tools of youth citizenship: power structures, communication skills, and historical context. The literature is full of concrete examples which show that, given the proper tools, youth can effect change in their communities. The first of these tools, power structures, can be defined in the context of three subareas: use of direct democracy for neighborhoods, power distribution, and reactionary power.

Direct democracy is one of the most basic methods for an individual or group to assert its voice in the political arena. Robert Woodson's 1989 speech, "Stabilizing and Revitalizing Urban Neighborhoods" claims that direct democracy is a necessity for the transformation and revitalization of neighborhoods. He furthers states that collective and individual responsibility is fundamental to making change, saying: "We believe the poor should be empowered to become not only recipients of services, but also the providers and deliverers of these services."[6]

Power structures also include the concept of power distribution, specifically the distribution of knowledge, resources, and rights to all individuals in an equal manner. This process can start at the state, local, or federal level with dissemination of information, funds, and mandatory acceptance of local input. Power is distributed in the neighborhood by individuals sharing information, creating local networks, and becoming more inclusive. Lastly, redistribution of power can be affected by a lack of community renewal.

The last major ingredient that makes power structures so important is the effect of reaction. The literature makes a strong case for individual involvement once he or she has reached the point of direct reaction (a by-product of individual self-interest). Woodson most succinctly summarizes the underlying concept here, saying, "Nobody will do more for us than we are willing to do for ourselves."[7]

The second clearly defined variable that has a bearing on teaching youth citizenship is communication skills. The literature points to an array of issues that may impede or improve communication skills on the local level. The broader concept of communication skills can be broken down into four main points: (1) voice equals power; (2) false perceptions can endanger community development; (3) communication networks are a direct link to the availability of potential power; and (4) individuals and organizations must use their ability to collect, filter, and use information that directly affects their community.

In relevant literature, the concept that voice equals power is quite prevalent. Data collected from a variety of studies strongly support the idea that neighborhood mobilization is directly linked to a community's ability to effectively communicate.[8] Specifically, Jeffres and Dobos state that self-definition and community growth are direct links that occur as a result of communication, using the example of community- and neighborhood-based newspapers as one means by which residents can define their own situation in their own words.

Communication can have both positive and negative effects on a community. False perceptions can damage a community's ability to mobilize and garner strength from within. The literature points out strong support for the negative impact and damage this type of communication can cause to community effort. Crenshaw and St. John discovered this as a factor while researching organizationally dependent communities, stating, "People who fear their neighborhoods might soon be in decline are less committed to them than others."[9] As part of revitalization, they found a strong need for communities to have "attachment" and "commitment." They further state that individuals must feel they are a meaningful asset and resource to their community in order to be effective.

Another major facet of communication skills is the way information and motivation are linked to informal and formal community networks. Jeffres and Dobos conducted a formal study on how communication and neighborhood mobilization link. They found that community communication networks formed around interpersonal issues. They concluded that such networks were often a method through which widespread community attention may be paid to community self-help projects, stating: "Clearly, the ties that bind people together as neighborhood residents also increase the likelihood of interpersonal communication and potential involvement in neighborhood mobilization projects."[10]

The last aspect of communication skills in mobilization is the individual's and organization's ability to collect, filter, and use information that directly affects their neighborhood. The literature makes a clear case that information and important resources are often unavailable to communities. In addition, some communities are not aware of what information is available and lack the experience to find alternative information sources or to effectively process the information if they do have it. Specifically, Jeffres and Dobos explain Davis and Baran's theory of "framing" — essentially how individuals process and learn from everyday situations. They state, "Frames are sets of cues that people use to organize experiences of situations, which can then be used to organize action in those situations."[11] Without a set of "frames" for analysis and application of information, communities often find themselves handicapped and at the mercy of local, state, and federal governments.

The last tool for teaching youth citizenship is the historical context in which a community has developed. Neighborhoods bear signs of the past generations and culture that are the blocks upon which they were built. Specifically, each neighborhood did not start with the goal that one day it would be revitalized. Rather, each community began with a clean slate, and its founders helped shape it as parents help shape a child's development. Influences such as cultural background and government economic and social policy played a part in the values and choices made in the shaping and developing of each neighborhood. Youth need to be aware of and learn from the history of their neighborhoods and the neighborhoods of others in order to find effective solutions to current problems.

Effective Youth Programs—Some Examples

The last section of this chapter examines how local groups in Cleveland are currently approaching the challenge of promoting youth citizenship within the community. These programs include the BRICK (Brotherhood, Respect, Intelligence, Conduct, and Knowledge) at Martin Luther King and Franklin D. Roosevelt Middle and Senior High Schools, City Year of Cleveland Youth Corps, and SGORR (Student Group on Race Relations) at Shaker Heights High School. Each of these programs features many of the components outlined as ideal for teaching youth citizenship via a process of civic renewal.

The BRICK program began in 1996 at Martin Luther King Middle School as a faculty-initiated program. Since then, it has expanded as a student-run organization to include older students not only at MLK but also at Franklin D. Roosevelt Middle and High Schools. The mission of the program is to encourage youth to participate in citizenship development, individual emotional growth, and community enhancement by interacting in constructive activities. Many of the youth who come to the BRICK program lack strong, positive adult role models from whom they can learn socially responsible adult behavior, and much of their contact with mainstream adults is through school classroom learning or the juvenile corrections system. BRICK offers positive male role models and activities that speak to community engagement and is designed to be an alternative to illegal activities, drug abuse, gangs, and teenage fatherhood.

Young people in the group identify the issues that affect their community in a variety of ways. After examining, discussing, and understanding these issues, they then develop workable solutions that can make a difference. The program also provides a format for evaluation and creates a new language of communication for students to understand how to use the tools they have and their community resources to change the inner workings of their communities. BRICK provides an opportunity for young people to work with others to improve their community. Its members also learn responsibility, good communication skills, leadership skills, role modeling, and how to make positive life choices. These all-important nontangible skills can then be transferred into home, school, and work life.

BRICK members meet weekly, and participation includes community service projects as well as a variety of workshops, conferences, and public events. Between the two schools there are currently more than 225 African American young men between the ages of eleven and nineteen in the program.

The second program, the City Year of Cleveland Youth Corps, is a national organization that provides an opportunity for young people between the ages of seventeen and twenty-four years to volunteer for nine months working a variety of areas within the community. Youth who are involved in the program vary in age, race, and socioeconomic backgrounds. Young people in this program receive a weekly stipend and an educational bonus upon completion of the program requirements. City Year provides young people with an opportunity to serve others. Through this service, young people learn how to better take care of a neighborhood, responsibility, how to solve problems that at first appear impossible, how to work with others, how to step forward or step down at the appropriate time, and the importance of respect.

City Year members work in teams of ten to twelve in a variety of communities and projects. For example, they assist teachers in a classroom, tutor students, help a nonprofit agency renovate their offices, or clean a trash-filled area. Through their community service work the young adults learn how to identify issues, map out their environments, work within existing power structures, and evaluate their work and interaction within the community. City Year Corps members work a full day Monday through Thursday on community projects and undergo in-service training on Fridays. Here, the youth learn how to better serve the communities that they are in, evaluate their work, and train in areas valuable to adult development, such as how to write a resume or fill in a tax return.

In addition to the regular weekly projects, youth corps members may also assist in special projects such as Young Heroes, City Heroes, Citzgy, or the Serve-a-thon. Young Heroes is a program that the City Year Corps members run on Saturdays for middle schoolers. It is essentially a mini-City Year, allowing middle school–aged students to volunteer and undertake projects at various nonprofit agencies throughout the city. City Heroes is a similar program geared toward high school students. Citzgy is a City Year Corps member conference held in different City Year sites each year. The conference focuses on sharing information, learning formal community-building techniques, and educating corps members on how to best serve their communities. Serve-a-thon is a day of service involving the community at large.

The last program, the Student Group on Race Relations (SGORR), is an organization of high school students in the Shaker Heights schools that promotes good social relations among racially diverse children. SGORR was initiated in 1983 by a group of concerned students who had noticed that the good relationships enjoyed by blacks and whites in elementary school often did not survive the transition to middle school. The focus of the group was to work with students before those relationships were lost.

SGORR is unique because it was initiated by students in a true expression of citizenship. Because SGORR is student organized and student run it embodies many aspects of youth citizenship. It provides an open format for learning how to negotiate within a structure to make changes and places much of the responsibility on the youth for organizing, implementing, operating, and evaluating the program. The result of these direct tasks of responsibility is a greater understanding of the tools necessary to practice youth citizenship.

The basic program consists of three days spaced throughout the school year. Concepts such as trust, deferred judgment, prejudice, discrimination, and polarization are covered using the techniques of role-playing, story telling, group discussion, film, and structured exercises. SGORR creates an awareness of race issues, how to identify the problems of peer pressure, and how to utilize particular problem-solving strategies to make decisions when faced with value conflicts.

The goal of the first day's session is to build an atmosphere of trust and support among participants. The second day is devoted to helping them understand the roles that peer pressure and self-image play in influencing behaviors that lead to racial discrimination and social polarization. On the third day, problem-solving methods are taught and are applied to racial, social, and academic issues. Between SGORR visits, classroom teachers use a packet of follow-up activities designed by the high school students to reinforce the classroom lessons.

SGORR members facilitate the sessions and the sixth graders readily accept those older students as leaders and teachers. Anecdotal evidence suggests that high school students can often have a greater impact on younger students than adults. One indication of how deeply the SGORR resonates with middle school students is the increasing number of high school students (nearly 150 a year) who volunteer as SGORR members when they reach high school age.

SGORR is organized into a board (known as the "core") and teams. The board comprises approximately ten to twenty students who serve as team leaders. The leaders and assistants work with six to eight other students as a team throughout the school year. A faculty adviser serves as a consultant and facilitator.

Core members meet with the SGORR adviser to lead their team in preparing presentations for the sixth graders as well as with the sixth grade teachers to discuss a variety of presentation options. The leaders have four meetings with their teams before each workshop to teach and model for them the concepts and strategies offered through the program.

After the teams have made presentations to the sixth grade classes, the teachers meet with the teams for one-on-one feedback. The adviser and the core evaluate their experiences with the sixth graders and begin preparing for the next session. Through the process, which is repeated after each session, SGORR members continually rewrite and improve the curriculum. Consequently, each new group of SGORR members becomes invested in the program and is encouraged to assume ownership of the results.

The success of the SGORR program in the Shaker Heights schools demonstrates the importance of racial harmony and good human relations to elementary and high school students. SGORR has been asked to make many presentations to numerous outside organizations and has gained outstanding support as a result of their efforts. In addition, the program has been shared with and adopted by school districts both statewide and nationally.

SGORR helps students focus on interpersonal relationships, which are at a critical developmental point during adolescence. The group has often brought up issues that might not have been talked about but are certainly on students' minds. Having high school students facilitate the sessions enables younger students to discuss their thoughts and feelings more openly and honestly than they might have were a teacher or other adult leading the discussion.

Recommendations

Youth participation in the discussion of community issues is vital to neighborhood revitalization in the twenty-first century because the very future of neighborhood revitalization is rooted in the youth of the community. In order to make changes and increase the level of youth who practice youth citizenship we must change the way we look at the role of youth within the community as well as the role of our current institutions. As a society, we must make a commitment to provide youth with a strong understanding of what citizenship is as well as practical experience in exercising the ingredients of youth citizenship. Institutions need to rethink the way they interact with youth and, when possible, provide more opportunities for young people to understand their environment, explore potential opportunities, and make decisions which can help others and ultimately improve the well-being of our society.

Since the early 1970s the United States has seen a tremendous decline in the average citizen's level of trust in government, institutions, and the political process. Citizenship, the practice of rights and responsibilities, has become an institution of rights with few taking responsibility. One social construct that measures citizenship and civic responsibility is voting. Fourteen percent of the country's adult population is made up of young Americans aged eighteen to twenty-four; however, of this population, only 6 percent vote. This trend among young people toward voluntary disfranchisement reflects a lack of education and understanding in civic responsibility. Learning civic responsibility is a process best understood through action. As today's youth take civic courses and must pass civic proficiency tests, they must also have an opportunity to enact the skills and the systems they learn through this process. By not teaching youth citizenship within our communities, we are depriving young people of the tools necessary to take full advantage of all their rights and responsibilities as citizens. As young people become the leaders of tomorrow, an incomplete understanding of citizenship will surely have a negative effect on the progress and success of our country.

Notes

1. Cuyahoga County Juvenile Court, Annual Report, 1994, unpublished.

2. M. I. Singer, T. M. Anglin, L. Y. Song, and L. Lunghofer, "Adolescents' Exposure to Violence and Associated Symptoms of Psychological Trauma," *JAMA* 273, no. 6 (February 1995): 477–82.

3. Lolita McDavid, "One in Four Children Extremely Poor," Children's Defense Fund Greater Cleveland Project, 1992.

4. Children's Defense Fund, *An Opinion Maker's Guide to Children in Election Year 1992* (Washington, D.C.: Children's Defense Fund, 1991).

5. Ruthanne Kurth-Schai, "The Roles of Youth in Society: A Reconceptualization," *The Educational Forum* 52, no. 2 (winter 1988).

6. Robert Woodson, "Stabilizing and Revitalizing Urban Neighborhoods," *Journal of Negro Education* 58, no. 3 (1989): 403.

7. Ibid., 404.

8. See Bruce Anthony Jones, "Collaboration: The Case for Indigenous Community Based Organization Support of Dropout Prevention Programming and Implementation," *Journal of Negro Education* 61, no. 4 (1992): 496–507; Leo W. Jeffres and Jean A. Dobos, "Communication and Neighborhood Mobilization," *Urban Affairs Quarterly* 20, no. 1 (September 1984): 97–112; Edward Crenshaw and Craig St. John, "The Organizationally Dependent Community: A

Comparative Study of Neighborhood Attachment," *Urban Affairs Quarterly* 24, no. 3 (March 1989): 412-34.

9. Crenshaw and St. John, "The Organizationally Dependent Community," 145.

10. Jeffres and Dobos, "Communication and Neighborhood Mobilization," 110.

11. Ibid.

Chapter 10

Corporate Regionalism

Collaboration Efforts among Business
Leaders in Northeast Ohio

William H. Bryant

In a time of scarce financial resources in both the public and private sectors, regional collaboration can be an important tool for increasing an area's competitive edge—especially as metropolitan regions become increasingly prominent as the basic units of the global economy. This chapter chronicles regional collaboration efforts of Northeast Ohio's business community over the past twenty-five years, evaluates these efforts, and offers recommendations for moving to a higher level of accomplishment. The forms of collaboration discussed here do not blur or remove municipal boundaries; instead, they offer methods of voluntary collaboration in which each municipality maintains its own identity while working cooperatively toward a shared vision.

William H. Bryant wrote this chapter as a monograph during his tenure as executive in residence at the Levin College of Urban Affairs at Cleveland State University (1996–97). Prior to that he served as executive director of the Greater Cleveland Growth Association, the chamber of commerce for the greater Cleveland area.

An emphasis on regional cooperation is not new in the field of economic development. Significant regional collaboration efforts in the United States date back at least four decades. Government and business leaders in Chicago, for instance, placed special emphasis on this type of initiative as early as the mid-1950s. Urban areas such as Atlanta, Boston, and Pittsburgh were not far behind.

What is new about regional collaboration is the increased awareness of its advantages and the growing recognition for the necessity of combining strengths to compete effectively. Development experts agree that city boundaries are no longer the drivers of location decisions. Instead, business decision makers evaluate the strengths and weakness of a region as a whole—including the level of public and private cooperation within that region.

The benefits of thinking as a region are being recognized by development officials throughout the nation. Individuals concerned with economic growth and community betterment have become increasingly aware of the advantages of cooperating in such areas as transportation and infrastructure development, visitor attraction, image building, governmental influences, preservation of the natural environment, land use, and facility planning. Leaders from regions such as Dallas–Fort Worth and Minneapolis–St. Paul are working together in formal compacts or councils to assure that high priority, mutual objectives are achieved. In Seattle and Tampa, regional collaborations are addressing transportation improvements and overall economic development. Some regions are moving away from the "my-place-or-no-place" philosophy when competing for development; the greater Cincinnati tristate region, for instance, has embraced the idea that investment anywhere within the region—regardless of the city or suburb—is better than investment elsewhere.

Characteristics of Regional Collaboration

The characteristics of regional collaboration efforts throughout the country vary widely, although nearly all—including those in Northeast Ohio—can be grouped into one or more of the following five areas: (1) communications and fact-based discussions; (2) coordination to achieve sharply focused objectives; (3) coordination of ongoing major programs; (4) delivery of public services; and (5) governance. It is helpful to understand how these five components contribute to regional coordination.

Communications and Fact-based Discussions

This is the most fundamental form of regional coordination. It involves leaders meeting on a regular basis to discuss issues of mutual concern, and it is clearly the most common form of regional collaboration in the United States today. This phase is relatively easy to get started and equally easy to manage in its early stages. The downside is that, unless this component is translated into action in reasonably short order, top leaders tend to lose interest and drift away from the process.

The entire regional communications process must include a wide variety of functions and representation—including such individuals as community leadership program directors, educators, and community and area planners meeting with their counterparts on a regular basis. However, one constant above and beyond this staff-level involvement characterizes successful regional communication efforts: top level leaders, especially business CEOs, must have ownership in the regional collaboration effort and meet regularly to drive the process. These CEOs have the ability to bring government and institutional leaders to the table, creating a priority and a sharp focus for high impact, collaborative work. Most importantly, these individuals will send a signal to program and project leaders throughout the region that collaboration is the right road to travel.

In almost every situation where recurrent regionwide communication is taking place, participants quickly develop a set of mutually accepted facts or "realities" that apply to the region as a whole. The development of these facts—which can reflect data gathered on population, employment, service delivery, or any of a number of issues—is critical to the communication process. They provide an early framework to achieve a common understanding and frequently form the cornerstone for virtually all early communications.

Coordination to Achieve Sharply Focused Objectives

The birth of regional cooperation is most commonly found in this area. The threatened loss of a major federal facility or sports franchise, the possible location of a major headquarters operation or large manufacturing facility, the clear need for improved air transportation, or a forecast for economic decline are all issues that have cleared the minds of regional leaders and stimulated regional collaboration. In the truest sense, issues like these tend to make local leaders aware of the fact that by combining their strengths they have greater political leverage, enhanced assets, and a greater ability to compete successfully against other areas. International competition has clearly provided an additional stimulus for coordinating and leveraging regional resources.

The rewards for success with this component of regionalism are substantial. Unfortunately, failure—or even perceived failure—can deal regionalism a severe blow or even introduce a collaboration "death spiral."

Coordination of Major Programs

The next logical component of regional collaboration is to coordinate important, high impact programs; research and leadership development, infrastructure (especially surface transportation), area image building, visitor attractions, and increased influence at the state and federal government levels characterize many existing efforts. Increased emphasis is also starting to be placed on coordinating regionally based programs in such areas as higher education, workforce readiness, international trade, air service development, tax and business incentives policy, and direct economic development work.

The intensity of efforts aimed at coordinating programs appears to be growing dramatically in urban regions throughout the nation. Philadelphia's Call to Action Conference in 1995 brought nearly two thousand individuals from across metropolitan Philadelphia to search for what they referred to as "win-win" approaches to regional problem solving. Leaders from the conference noted that "the defining event of the late twentieth century is the emergence of the global economy" and that "regions will be the key units of economic competition." They noted further that strategies of regional cooperation are essential to metropolitan growth.

In Chicago, the Metropolitan Planning Council (MPC), through the Regional Cooperation Initiative (RCI), has developed an understanding of regional issues and ideas designed to achieve a healthy future for a six-county region. The RCI helps solve specific problems important to the region, providing models for further regional cooperation. MPC has noted that many interrelated actions are needed to create a workable region and to achieve a sense of regional community. The organization has further explained that they do not recommend the creation of a general purpose regional government to impose approaches to regional issues. Rather, MPC believes that cooperation is possible to achieve clear objectives that are beneficial to all parts of the region. Nine such objectives have been identified:

1   Create a tax system that enhances regional cooperation.

2. Strengthen regional transit.

3. Price auto use in the region closer to its full cost.

4. Take an integrated regional approach to transportation land use.

5. Assure affordable housing across the region.

6. Implement a regional growth strategy.

7. Make the core of the region attractive for living and working.

8. Enhance the role of state government in strengthening the region.

9. Develop a leadership group whose goal is to foster a widely held sense of regional citizenship.

The catalyst for coordination of this type is frequently a perceived crisis or special opportunity with the potential to affect an entire region. It also must be recognized that, if program coordination is to become widespread and have staying power, leadership must provide a substantial measure of inspiration on a sustained basis. The "big picture view" of business leadership is particularly important. Unlike elected public officials, who are constrained by jurisdictional boundaries, CEOs can cross geographic boundaries and provide a much needed voice of neutrality in the collaboration process. By demonstrating a solid understanding of the benefits of regional cooperation—as well as a deeply felt commitment to regional growth—business leaders can serve as forceful and effective drivers to the process.

Public Services

Historically, urban regions have found it difficult to coordinate their efforts to provide public services over a broad geographic area. Perhaps the most obvious reason is the difficulty in getting leaders to agree on need and on a funding formula. Reaching agreement between municipalities within a county is difficult. Attempting to obtain agreement over a multi-county area is adventuresome at best. Yet progress is being made in some urban regions to address important public service issues, such as housing, transit, water resources, brownfields, infrastructure development and maintenance, and air service planning and development.

The Metropolitan Council, which represents a wide area that includes Minneapolis and St. Paul, is a strong example of regional collaboration in the public service area. The Metro Council was established by the Minnesota Legislature in 1967 to plan and coordinate the "orderly and economic development" of the Twin Cities, seven counties, and a 140-jurisdiction region. The council has seventeen members, each of whom is appointed by the governor of the state of Minnesota. The chair serves at the pleasure of the governor. The remaining sixteen members serve four-year terms representing districts of equal population. The council conducts its business through four standing committees on development, metro systems, environmental resources, and management.

In carrying out their mission, council officials note that their style of leadership has changed over the past few years, emphasizing collaboration and partnerships rather than regulation. This change seems to characterize other regionwide public service efforts throughout the United States.

Metropolitan Portland has a long history of taking a regional approach to providing a number of public services. In the July 1995 issue of *Urban Land*, Douglas R. Porter points out that Portland is a metropolitan area that works. Porter observes that urban leaders who question many of the development practices of twentieth-century America view Portland's regional approach to guiding urban development as sensible, competitive, and exemplary. The area's new 2040 regional plan takes strong steps to further assist in regional solutions to public service issues such as transportation and housing.

Although there are a few additional examples of public services being coordinated over multicounty areas, true success stories are limited and the future of these approaches is clearly uncertain.

Governance

There are very few examples in the United States of successful initiatives that have regional government as their base. The city of Toronto, however, was mandated by law to form a cost-saving, metrowide system of coordinating regional delivery of several programs and services, including police, public transportation, sewage treatment, regional parks, public housing, regional planning, and related initiatives. Although launched by the electorate with considerable enthusiasm, the effort has failed to live up to expectations. The majority of present population growth, as well as that which is projected for the future, is taking place outside the metro area. This has placed substantial strain on public services such as the regional rail system. As a consequence, the federated system of government itself is coming under increased attacks from both elected officials and citizens alike.

While multicounty governance of the delivery of services is an interesting form of regional collaboration, it does not seem to have useful application in Northeast Ohio at this time.

Examples of Regional Collaboration in Northeast Ohio

The history of business-led regional collaboration efforts in Northeast Ohio began more recently than in Chicago and certain other U.S. urban regions. It does, however, date back a quarter of a century and is rich in commitment and content.

It is interesting and perhaps revealing to note that no two comprehensive collaboration attempts have considered the same cluster of counties. In this chapter, Northeast Ohio is defined to include the following twelve counties: Ashtabula, Trumbull, Mahoning, Lake, Geauga, Portage, Stark, Cuyahoga, Summit, Lorain, Medina, and Wayne. (See Figure 10.1).

Northern Ohio Urban System Research Project

The first significant commitment to a regional approach to problem solving and opportunity development in Northeast Ohio was the Northern Ohio Urban System Research Project (NOUS), which began in the summer of 1970.

The NOUS project was sponsored by the East Ohio Gas Company, Ohio Bell, and the Higbee department store company. The effort had four major objectives:

1. Collect and analyze demographic, economic, physical, investment, environmental, and institutional data for a total of thirty-five counties (thirty in Northeast Ohio and five in Northwest Pennsylvania).

Northeast Ohio

Prepared by

Northern Ohio Data & Information Service (NODIS)
  a member of Ohio GIS-Net
The Urban Center
Maxine Goodman Levin College of Urban Affairs
Cleveland State University

March 1999 mjs

Figure 10.1. *Northeast Ohio*

2. Test, analyze, and project these data to show their evident and poten-
    tial trends for the mid-1970s as well as through the year 2000.

3. Summarize the specific problems, potentials, and opportunities sug-
    gested by these trends for the NOUS area.

4. Study alternative patterns for the future development of the NOUS
    area. Identify patterns that will minimize the area's problems in the

future while taking full advantage of its potential for growth. Recommend a series of action plans that would suggest ways of implementing this alternative pattern.

The project resulted in a series of reports, including "A Concept Plan for Future Development," which was released in January 1973. The series is still being used by serious students of regionalism and by those whose interests have area-wide impact.

The NOUS exercise clearly illustrated that the destinies of the units that comprise our region are deeply intertwined and that these units were, even at that time, moving together in measurable ways. Constantinos Doxiadis, who served as the managing consultant for the project, drew a vivid picture of just how "regional" the area was becoming by estimating that the Cleveland urban cluster expands outward in every direction at the rate of one and a half yards each day. Akron, he stated, was growing in similar fashion—moving northward at the rate of about one yard each day. Twenty-three years after this view was presented, we see that he was almost uncannily accurate in his observations.

In addition to drawing attention to the importance of a regional approach to development and providing baseline data for the region, the NOUS project generated positive momentum for regional collaboration. Significantly, it created a core group of business and institutional leaders who were committed to thinking regionwide as they considered local priorities and programs. Perhaps most importantly, the father of modern regionalism in Northeast Ohio surfaced from the effort. Herbert E. Strawbridge, then chairman of the Higbee Company, emerged as the spokesperson for regionalism in Northeast Ohio and inspired others to focus on the value of regional collaboration.

By the time the final NOUS report was presented, Cleveland, Akron, Canton, Youngstown, and, indeed, the entire Northeast Ohio area had come under substantial economic stress. During the next few years, most areas throughout the region experienced decline or only very slow economic growth. The city of Cleveland itself experienced a variety of reverses, including the highly publicized "default." In short, during this extended period of economic stress, regional collaboration was perhaps the last thing on the minds of those attempting to stem the tide of decline.

Ironically, however, it is during such periods of distress that a regional approach is most needed. And in Northeast Ohio clear evidence indicated that a regional collaborative effort was required if the area's decline was to be reversed. This evidence was provided by the economic downturn itself, which affected not just Cleveland, as many believed, but virtually all of Northeast Ohio.

Those who doubt the regionwide impact of the downturn need only review a Chase Econometrics report published in 1979. The report, which ranked 107 U.S. cities according to ten-year projected growth rates, predicted a bleak future for the entire Northeast Ohio area. Of the 107 cities they ranked, Cleveland was 105th, Akron was 103rd, Youngstown was 101st, and Canton was 98th. Clearly, Northeast Ohio's economic slowdown of the 1970s—and its predicted decline throughout the 1980s— were problems that demanded regional attention.

In a time of crisis, leaders understandably address the most doable issues that appear to offer a quick return on investment. In Northeast Ohio, regional collaboration did not qualify for major attention or allocation of resources during the late 1970s or early 1980s. This does not imply that there was no regional coordination during this period. Throughout the early- and mid-1980s, the presidents of the Greater Cleveland Growth Association and the Akron Regional Development Board met on a quarterly basis. This "presidents' roundtable" proved to be a highly effective vehicle for exchanging information on local development initiatives and coordinating high-priority program activities, and soon the president of the Stark County Development Board joined the meetings. Within just a few years, this group grew significantly and became formalized under the name Northeast Ohio Development Council.

Northeast Ohio Development Council

By 1986 the presidents' roundtable had expanded to include all full-time institutional development specialists representing multicounty areas in Northeast Ohio. This new body, the Northeast Ohio Development Council (NEO-DC), comprised approximately twenty representatives from public utilities, chambers of commerce, and related development institutions.

The Northeast Ohio Development Council has three central objectives:

1. To serve as a forum where development professionals from Northeast Ohio come together to share information, opportunities, and concerns.

2. To undertake a limited number of initiatives deemed important to every organization represented, such as the development of uniform information on labor costs in Northeast Ohio.

3. To direct action to influence Ohio's economic development program, such as tax impact analysis and economic development recommendation reports presented to gubernatorial candidates.

Since the beginning of the Northeast Ohio Development Council in 1986, three large-scale, comprehensive, regional collaboration efforts— as well as a number of special purpose initiatives—have been put into place in Northeast Ohio. These efforts include the Western Reserve Economic Development Council, the Akron-Cleveland Business Summit, and the Ohio Task Force on Regional Competitiveness and Cooperation. Each of these three programs is detailed on the following pages.

Western Reserve Economic Development Council

In 1987 Gordon Heffern, then chairman of Society National Bank, and Robert Broadbent, then chairman of the Higbee Company, concluded that they were listening to similar problems from one end of Northeast Ohio to the other and recognized a need for regional problem solving. Their central objective was to create a unified region to produce additional opportunities to market the resources of Northeast Ohio. With these thoughts in mind, the Western Reserve Economic Development Council was created. Today, the council embraces seventeen counties: Ashland, Ashtabula, Columbiana, Cuyahoga, Erie, Geauga, Huron, Lake, Lorain, Mahoning, Medina, Portage, Richland, Stark, Summit, Trumbull, and Wayne.

The council's mission is to help coordinate the plans of the region's economic development agencies. It works to increase the economic and spiritual health and vitality of the region, identify and build upon the resources of the region, and assist in the strengthening of area employers and add new ones to the region.

To focus its efforts, the council targeted eleven areas: arts, chamber of commerce, colleges and universities, foundations, health care, infrastructure, labor management, media, recreation, religious groups, and United Way and other social agencies. Over the past few years, the council's most active project has been its effort to assure that an international airport is developed in Northeast Ohio.

Akron-Cleveland Business Summit

A second major collaboration effort began more out of crisis than opportunity. In 1990, as the reality of Cleveland's Gateway stadium/arena project became apparent, so too did the understanding that the Richfield Coliseum (located in a rural area between Cleveland and Akron and, at that time, home of the Cleveland Cavaliers basketball team) would no longer serve as the home for professional basketball and related activities. This issue threatened to become divisive and presented a potentially serious obstacle to further regional progress, especially between Akron and Cleveland.

In an effort to minimize the impact and duration of this tension, Akron-area Congressman Thomas C. Sawyer contacted the president of the Greater Cleveland Growth Association in the summer of 1990, suggesting a meeting between top business leaders from Akron and Cleveland. Sawyer explained that the purpose of the meeting would be to discuss the coliseum situation openly and to see if progress might be made on this and other common issues facing the two cities.

This meeting was held at a location midway between Akron and Cleveland. A number of substantial agreements and decisions were reached:

1. There was a need for a group of top level business people to work together to address common problems and opportunities.
2. This group would concentrate on areas of opportunity but would not back away from more difficult issues, such as the use of the coliseum.
3. Issues important to Northeast Ohio would be considered, yet the clear focus would be placed on Greater Akron and Greater Cleveland. (In arriving at this decision the participants felt that they must demonstrate that two cities could work together before undertaking broader regionwide geography and concerns.)
4. The group would continue to meet on a quarterly basis and a chairman would be appointed.

This group has championed a number of initiatives. Most prominent of these has been joint Akron-Cleveland actions in Washington, D.C.; joint action on the state of Ohio's capital budget; and transportation issues such as the widening of I-77 and funding for the Cuyahoga Valley Railroad to assure a link between downtown Cleveland and downtown Akron.

The group now has six goals:

- Akron and Cleveland will become the core of a true, well-defined urban region where each city maintains its own identify, yet works cooperatively toward a shared regional vision and impact.

- In the years ahead, Northeast Ohio will become, and will be perceived as, the dominant business area on the lower Great Lakes between New York and Chicago.

- A world-class transportation network will be established in Northeast Ohio, led by first-class air service that facilitates business development on a global scale.

- Northeast Ohio will be "internationalized" in thought and action.

- Northeast Ohio will be a visitor destination region, taking full advantage of the Rock and Roll Hall of Fame, Inventure Place (inventors hall of fame), and the Pro Football Hall of Fame.

- Harmony and pride will be developed and promoted in Northeast Ohio.

Ohio Task Force on Regional Competitiveness and Cooperation

Recognizing the need for broad-based regional cooperation, Sen. Grace Drake and Rep. Patrick A. Sweeney (with assistance from the Maxine Goodman Levin College of Urban Affairs at Cleveland State University) sponsored a summit of leaders in Northeast Ohio. The meeting, which took place in 1992, was intended to define regional competitiveness and to identify the factors that make a region competitive. Leaders from both government and the private sector were included in this eight-county summit meeting.

Based on the summit's success, a second meeting was held in 1993. State Sen. Roy L. Ray from Akron joined as the third sponsor. From this session came the call for the creation of the Ohio Task Force on Regional Competitiveness and Cooperation, an organization formally launched by a vote of the Ohio General Assembly in 1993.

The task force was charged to study current efforts to encourage or facilitate regional competitiveness in the nation, with special emphasis on Northeast Ohio; conduct a survey of business leaders and public officials to identify perceptions of regional competitiveness and cooperation in

Northeast Ohio; and prepare a report to outline the findings of the task force and its recommendations to improve regional competitiveness.

The task force comprised thirty citizens representing the entire region, including both the public and private sectors. In addition, a cross section of top leadership in the region served as advisers to the project. The task force developed recommendations in five major areas: education, workforce, and retraining; infrastructure and environment; tax policy and finance; markets and marketing; charting a new course.

In the "charting a new course" recommendations, the task force listed four specific actions for regional collaboration in Northeast Ohio:

- Create a "regional council" to assist in the identification of a vision for Northeast Ohio.

- Develop a strategy to communicate the vision.

- Secure funding from a diverse coalition of stakeholders.

- Encourage the Ohio Legislature to identify and review state laws and regulations that impede regional collaboration and governance.

In addition to the recommendations they provided, the Ohio Task Force on Regional Competitiveness and Cooperation also documented that Northeast Ohio is ripe for regional collaboration. More than 72 percent of those surveyed responded "yes" when asked if they believe greater regional cooperation could increase the competitiveness of Northeast Ohio business. This effort has presented regional proponents with a "flagship" document and positive momentum for action.

Other Regional Organizations

While the Western Reserve Economic Development Council, the Akron-Cleveland Business Summit, and the Ohio Task Force on Regional Competitiveness have been tackling comprehensive regional collaboration efforts, the leaders of a number of organizations have also recognized the value of regional collaboration and are moving in that direction with strong programs of their own. Some of the most effective of these organizations are the following.

Work in Northeast Ohio Council (WINOC) was created in 1981 by a group of business, labor, and professional leaders to strengthen the overall economy in Northeast Ohio. WINOC serves business, labor, government, and academia throughout Northeast Ohio by providing education, training, and best practices for improving quality and productivity through employee involvement.

Edison Polymer Innovation Corporation (EPIC) serves the entire state of Ohio. It has added greatly to regionalism in Northeast Ohio with its success in promoting the reality and image of the area as "Polymer Valley."

The Cleveland Advanced Manufacturing Program (CAMP) fosters innovation in manufacturing enterprises through research, development, technology deployment, and training. In its first five years, CAMP centered its work in Cuyahoga, Geauga, Lake, and Summit Counties, but it has more recently expanded to cover all of Northeast Ohio.

The Urban University Program's Northeast Ohio Research Consortium comprises the University of Akron, Cleveland State University, Kent State University, and Youngstown State University. The consortium is part of the Ohio Urban University Program. Its mission, which is carried out by the urban research and public service center located on each campus, is to help identify the problems of Northeast Ohio (the state's most urbanized and challenged economic region) and to propose alternative solutions designed to enhance the region's viability. The consortium published a series of twelve monographs on regional competitiveness and cooperation and is considering additional monographs and study to assist Northeast Ohio competitiveness.

The Northeast Ohio Council on Higher Education, formerly known as the Cleveland Commission on Higher Education, has become involved in a number of collaborative education programs in Northeast Ohio. It includes eighteen collegiate member institutions and serves as an effective advocacy and coordinating organization for higher education in the region. The organization primarily operates through the following types of programs:

- Timely assessments of issues critical to the educational needs of the region, with strategies that address these issues and needs

- Demographic studies from which connections can be made between campus workforce training programs and the needs of area businesses and organizations

- Leadership and issue-oriented forums enhancing communication and coordination

- Programs to increase understanding of the crucial role played by colleges and universities in enhancing community values and quality of life

Other Coordination Programs

In addition to the comprehensive regional collaboration efforts and organizations that are successfully incorporating a regional focus in their program agendas, three regionwide initiatives are worthy of special mention: the coordination of regional infrastructure needs, community-based leadership programs, and workforce preparation efforts.

Infrastructure coordination: A recent joint effort between three public-private partnerships—the Akron Regional Infrastructure Alliance, Build Up Greater Cleveland, and the Stark County Infrastructure Committee—has resulted in the publication of two important documents: "The Face of Northeast Ohio in 2010," which contains an overview of surface transportation plans for an eight-county area, and "Infrastructure Priorities, 1995," which outlines high-priority infrastructure needs for the Northeast Ohio interurban corridor.

Leadership programs coordination: For the past ten years, leadership programs have been developed and conducted in cities and counties throughout Northeast Ohio. The purpose of these programs is to enhance the knowledge and awareness of local leaders in the areas of planning and economic development, health, business, human services, government, and education. At a meeting of area program directors and alumni presidents in 1995 it was determined that regionalism needs to be a part of the curriculum of each leadership program. The desired result is to generate and maintain a cadre of informed citizen leaders at the regional level.

Workforce preparation: A number of workforce preparation initiatives are under way in Northeast Ohio. Leaders of these programs meet regularly under the working title of the Regional Workforce Development Coordinating Committee. The committee identifies common concerns of workforce education and training and promotes collaboration on workforce development efforts to limit duplication of efforts.

The Status of Regional Cooperation
in Northeast Ohio, 1970–95

Now that an understanding of the initiatives, programs, and organizations involved in regional collaboration has been reached, it may prove useful to examine each of the five characteristics of regionalism to "score" the level of progress in each. Following, then, is an evaluation of the status of regional cooperation in Northeast Ohio.

Communications and Fact-based Discussions

The NOUS project created a strong general database and facilitated communications throughout the region in the mid-1970s. While some efforts were made during the following ten to twelve years, it was not until the late 1980s that this component of regionalism began to recover from the long period of neglect brought on by the economic decline of the late 1970s and early 1980s.

Today, communications vehicles are in place and a wealth of current regional data is being generated. The Urban Policy Monograph Series on Regional Competitiveness and Cooperation alone developed twelve monographs on Northeast Ohio. The Citizens League of Greater Cleveland has published their "Rating the Region" analysis, and the research department of the Greater Cleveland Growth Association and the College of Urban Affairs at Cleveland State University have published a major "Economic and Social Profile" of Northeast Ohio.

Thus, the trends are positive and the grade is "good" when critiquing this component of collaboration.

TRENDS   Fact-based communication between program areas is growing at a very healthy pace.

Communication vehicles involving top business CEOs are at a fork in the road and in fact have slowed over the past twelve to eighteen months.

NEEDS   Clearly the need is for a strong regional council, comprised of top private and public sector leaders, to be formed and become the flagship vehicle for the entire collaboration effort.

Without CEO leadership, communications will not continue to progress.

GRADE   Good! (Yet future is uncertain.) Grade: B+

We have the ability to achieve a national-class rating in this phase of collaboration within the next three to five years.

Coordination to Achieve Sharply Focused Objectives

Nationally, this component most frequently causes the first interest in regional collaboration. This has not been the case, however, in Northeast Ohio. Certain high-level objectives, such as assuring quality use of the Coliseum and various transportation projects, have commanded serious attention among regional leaders. Yet more fundamental concerns and objectives appear to be driving present collaboration efforts. This is especially apparent when comparing the slow progress in this component with the rapid pace of program coordination over the past few years.

With limited exceptions, regional leaders to this point have not been able to agree on one or two clear projects and to collaborate to achieve implementation. Unless top business CEOs and government leaders meet on a regular basis, it will be almost impossible to discuss key regional needs and opportunities, much less agree on specific initiatives and priorities for action.

TRENDS   With limited exceptions, collaboration has been designed to achieve objectives in special areas, such as higher education, infrastructure, database gathering, and purchasing.

NEEDS   Clear need for a vision of Northeast Ohio for the next ten to twenty years.

Need to select one to three major target objectives that top leaders agree to (e.g., workforce readiness, visitor destination, marketing).

GRADE   Poor! Grade: C–

Well below average of national class regional collaboration programs.

Coordination of Ongoing Major Programs

In recent years, this component has been the clear strength of regional collaboration activity in Northeast Ohio. Regional cooperation efforts in higher education and infrastructure have been noted. In addition, planning commission programs, leadership programs, database work, workforce training, and economic development efforts have cooperated in strong and meaningful ways.

Regional leaders need to understand the depth of coordination that now exists in program collaboration in Northeast Ohio, as well as its enormous long-term benefits. Information and knowledge is expanded and shared, resources are leveraged and conserved, and, as a result, programs become more effective at a lower cost to individual communities. Top level leadership in all sectors must encourage this type of coordination in the strongest ways whenever possible.

CHARACTERISTICS OF SUCCESSFUL EFFORTS	Top leaders serve as inspiration to institutions, especially program leaders. Leaders of programs cooperate on a wide range of initiatives, including leadership, infrastructure, labor-management, transportation, higher education, and workforce training.
ADVANTAGES	Formal processes or organization not required Quick way of exchanging information and best practices Long-term benefits are substantial
SPECIAL CHALLENGES	Difficult to get top leaders to focus on this component. They want a clearer payoff Difficult to get program leaders to allocate enough time for this function Difficult to quantify values

Public Services

While some progress has been made in delivering public services on a multicounty basis, and significant discussion continues to surround such issues as transportation, waste disposal, and water delivery, most public service initiatives are being dealt with (in accordance with standard federal and state mandates) by area planning commissions. In terms of actual delivery of public services, virtually all, including those that have the term *regional* in their title, are delivered on a municipal basis, or, at their most far-reaching, on a countywide basis. It is commendable that there is substantial communication and coordination taking place between area-wide planning commissions in Northeast Ohio.

Governance

In terms of regional decision making, the Citizens League noted in a recent publication that "locally, the growing disparity in wealth and population between the central city and the suburbs increases the need for strategic regional decision making." While no consideration of actual regional government in Northeast Ohio is offered here, it should be understood that, if public officials and other leaders do not find ways to cooperate on the delivery of public services, there will be increased demands from taxpayers to consolidate the vehicles that deliver the services.

Status Summary

When the status of all of the components of regional collaboration presented in this document are considered, it becomes clear that the trend is positive in Northeast Ohio. National leaders have, in fact, come to view the region as one of the most important in the country. Despite its relatively compact size, Northeast Ohio's socioeconomic importance is enormous. If Northeast Ohio were a state, its standard economic measures would exceed more than half of the states in the nation.

Working together, Northeast Ohio has the population and resource base to become both a powerful lobbying and marketing force—a force with the strength to compete against other regions throughout the world. Working independently, no single political jurisdiction in the region has this ability. According to a recent survey by the Center for Urban Studies of the University of Akron, the residents of Northeast Ohio recognize this fact and support the regionalism concept.

Northeast Ohio stands today at a crossroads. Either this region moves aggressively to drive the collaboration process forward or it will most certainly pale in comparison to other, more forward-thinking areas. To remain competitive, Northeast Ohio must rise to the challenge being presented by its competitors: "Thinking globally, and acting regionally."

The importance of decisive, committed, and effective leadership simply cannot be overemphasized. A new generation of chief executive officers and government leaders must join with those who have moved regionalism in Northeast Ohio to its present level. The alternatives, after this area fought so hard to rise from economic disaster, are simply unthinkable.

Almost instinctively we know that collaboration is the right course to chart and follow. Yet creating and executing clear initiatives that promote individual as well as regional progress is a more difficult process. In an effort to stimulate thought and action, the following recommendations are offered to assist in facilitating realistic regional collaboration.

Recommendations

Recommendations in this report have been positioned into two broad divisions, or tiers. Tier 1 recommendations are those that are clearly achievable and yet have enormous impact. The objectives in this tier should be considered as the first order of business in moving regional collaboration to the next level. Tier 2 recommendations are "facilitating objectives" to assure that a successful regional collaboration effort is in place. Short-term and long-term action steps to accomplish each recommendation are offered in each case.

Tier 1: Priority Recommendations

Think of regional collaboration as a component of a program, not as a program itself. Don't be afraid of regional cooperation or think of it as an academic or theoretical exercise, and assiduously avoid thinking of regionalism as an end objective. Simply by applying regional input and a regional thought process to existing programs, tremendous progress can be made. For example, the Greater Cleveland Growth Association conducts a meeting each year for local leaders to meet with the Northeast Ohio congressional delegation. The meeting provides an opportunity for discussion on Northeast Ohio's federal legislative priorities. Years ago, the meeting consisted solely of Cleveland leaders. Shortly thereafter, Akron's leadership was included. In 1996, Lorain and Canton participated as well. This is an excellent example of how an inclusive regional twist can enhance an already well-established program.

Short-term Action

Examine major programs to determine if any of the following initiatives will enhance existing efforts:

- Conduct regional briefing sessions to explain the intentions, advantages, and needs of the program or initiative. Provide periodic written follow-up with regional leaders.

- Bring new people to the table—as in the Growth Association example given above.

- Build key regional institutions directly into initiatives.

- Involve high impact individuals who are strong supporters of regional cooperation. The Urban Center at Cleveland State's College of Urban Affairs can assist in this area.

- Initiate direct and regular communication with state government leaders who are taking a leadership position in regional cooperation.

- Consider the resources of the entire region when developing a programmatic implementation plan.

Long-term Action

- Use these and other regional considerations collectively to form a de facto regional collaboration policy and program for major development/improvement organizations in Northeast Ohio.

Assure ongoing, organized advocacy for regional collaboration. Even the simple act of building a regional component into existing and future programs will wind down if there is not encouragement from some key source. Regional leaders must understand that regional collaboration is an ongoing process that is never accomplished "once and for all."

The "big three" of broad-based collaboration initiatives (Akron-Cleveland Business Summit, Western Reserve Economic Development Council, and the Ohio Task Force on Regional Competitiveness) are in various stages of winding down—either by design or due to light activity. Now is the right time to combine the best of the three efforts and move to the next level.

Short-term Actions

- Conduct a meeting of the chairpersons and leaders of the "big three" initiatives to reenergize the regionalism effort. It seems logical that a single regional initiative, combining the best of all three programs, would be most effective at this time.

- Select the proper individuals to chair and co-chair the effort. A leader with proven regional experience and credibility must be attracted to the chair. Co-chairs should include an emerging business CEO as well as a top government leader with a regional base. With proper encouragement from key individuals and institutions from both the public and private sectors, this critical step is achievable.

- Reenergize the CEO and government leaders component of regional collaboration. The officers of the combined effort should concentrate early efforts on this priority. State government, as well as key Northeast Ohio General Assembly members, can play an important role here.

- Begin to meet again, on a quarterly basis, with the first priority being to learn about the current significant collaboration initiatives and to show CEO and government appreciation and support for these initiatives.

Long-term Actions

- Create the "regional council" called for in the Ohio Task Force report. This can clearly be accomplished without creating a new, free-standing organization with separate staff and associated costs. This function can be managed from one of the major universities or development institutions in the region.

- Establish a means of encouraging the collaboration efforts of program and institutional leaders throughout the region.

Tier 2: Facilitating Recommendations

Place a high priority on regional collaboration. The major development organizations throughout the region must place this objective on their priority list—or at least on their "radar screen."

Short-term Actions

- Develop agreement among major development organizations in Akron, Canton, Cleveland, Lorain, and Youngstown to list regional collaboration as a priority.

- Provide regular (perhaps semiannual) activity and progress reports to the boards of the organizations involved, as well as to each other.

Long-term Action

- Provide activity and progress coverage in annual reports and at annual meetings.

Get the right people and organizations involved. James A. Norton, former director of the Cleveland Foundation, was one of the first individuals to recognize the importance of private sector involvement to the regionalization process. Government officials, Norton said, are elected to serve their own constituents—not constituents of an entire region. And those that look too far beyond their own jurisdictional boundaries may soon feel the voters' wrath.

Although Norton's thoughts are still relevant today, many elected public officials have taken firm stands in support of regionalism. Former Gov. George Voinovich and Lt. Gov. Nancy Hollister, general assembly leaders such as Grace Drake, Patrick Sweeney, and Roy Ray—as well as U.S. congressional members representing the Greater Akron, Canton, Cleveland, and Lorain areas—have all been vocal champions of the regional cause.

It is imperative, however, that these "regional pioneers" in public office be strongly supported by key CEOs and institutions with the regional interests and objectivity discussed earlier. Institutions that serve the entire region, such as banks and utilities, seem to be natural candidates for this leadership role.

Short-term Actions

- CEOs in Cleveland and Akron, especially the volunteer leaders of the major economic development institutions, must work with the "big three" to identify one CEO to take the lead and to give this individual strong support. Ideally, the individual should have a direct interest in both Akron and Cleveland and a substantial interest in Northeast Ohio. Additional representation should come from top contemporary leaders in business, government, higher education, foundations, organized labor, development, and related institutions. Minorities and neighborhood interests must be well represented from the outset.

- Get state government involved. Many statewide programs are now taking a regional approach to delivery. Executive and legislative branch leaders have demonstrated support. The state's Department of Development and the governor's regional office directors can and will provide support.

Long-term Actions

- Develop strong, top level regional advocates in key geographic areas throughout Northeast Ohio.
- Get high level local government officials to participate in the same manner that they have with broad-based infrastructure programs.

Select the right objectives. The proper balance must be reached between doable initiatives and impactive objectives. Fortunately, much groundwork has been accomplished to assist these decisions. The priorities of the "big three" organizations, along with priorities of other special-purpose organizations, are shining examples in this area.

Short-term Actions

- Select a limited number of highly achievable objectives that have regionwide impact. While many initiatives are possible, three appear to have special support: workforce readiness on a regional basis, making Northeast Ohio an international-class visitor destination, and marketing and promoting investment in Northeast Ohio.
- Provide strong support for existing regionally based organizations and initiatives.
- Link directly with the state of Ohio's current and planned regional efforts.

- Actively encourage state government to provide incentives that promote regional cooperation.

Once more, it should be kept in mind that it is not imperative that we build a regional program.

We must, however, build a regional component into key local objectives. Collectively, these components will provide the base for strong and lasting regional collaboration and a regional "will," or mindset.

Long-term Actions

A shared vision for Northeast Ohio may now be within reach. A set of specific objectives, such as those developed in Chicago, would be a logical follow-up phase. Special attention should be given to issues where regional cooperation is clearly in the best interest of everyone.

- Give strong consideration to special-purpose efforts (such as infrastructure development) that are already experiencing a strong measure of regional cooperation and coordination.
- Develop and market a shared vision for the future development of Northeast Ohio that emphasizes full participation and world-class objectives and results.

Select the right geography. The big three collaboration initiatives cover different geographical areas. Western Reserve includes seventeen counties, the Ohio Task Force includes twelve counties, and the Akron-Cleveland Business Summit has focused on Greater Akron and Greater Cleveland. The geography selected for future work should include the best features of each of these initiatives.

Short-term Actions

- Focus intense efforts on collaboration along the inter-urban corridor of the Cleveland-Akron-Canton area. Transportation links, common media markets, and visitor attractions provide special momentum for this concentration. Lorain County should also be included since key leaders are knowledgeable and supportive of regional coordination.

- Demonstrate that collaboration can be achieved in this corridor with sharply focused mutual interest efforts (e.g., widening of I-77, full development of the Cuyahoga Valley National Recreation Area, completion of the Cuyahoga Valley Railroad, promotion of the museums and halls of fame in each area).

Long-term Actions

- For certain initiatives, a larger geographic definition is appropriate (e.g., regional air service). Find ways of involving the larger region with the philosophy "if you feel you're in the region, you're in the region."
- Promote the identification of the larger geography as well as the urban centers of Akron, Canton, Cleveland, Lorain, and Youngstown.

Summary

Since the concept of regionalism was first introduced in Northeast Ohio more than twenty-five years ago, considerable progress has been made in developing a true regional approach to development and problem solving. It is clear, however, that this area is truly at a crossroads. While coordination on ongoing major regional programs is outstanding, and communications between governments and institutions within the region is good, additional efforts are needed to bring about the true "regional state of mind" that will herald success.

Demonstrated success has not occurred by accident. An enormous effort by dedicated individuals has taken Northeast Ohio to its current level of regional maturity. A great danger, however, lies in resting on this success and settling back into complacency. It is imperative that the new generation of leaders understands the need for and the value of cooperating on a regional basis and takes a lead role in continuing the journey. Only in this way can Northeast Ohio capitalize on the benefits of regional cooperation and successfully compete in the national and global marketplace.

Part 3

Toward a Civic Dialogue

The seventeen county area of Northeast Ohio must come together more cohesively as a single economic region. Cleveland can be a linchpin but it must work cooperatively in a give-and-take mode with the other municipalities and counties within the region.

—Richard Pogue, co-chair, Cleveland Bicentennial Commission and senior advisor, Dix & Eaton, Cleveland

Chapter 11

Regional Benchmarking

A Framework to Encourage
Dialogue on Community Issues

Janis Purdy and Michael A. Eugene

How does the Cleveland metropolitan region compare with other regions with which it must compete? Using a methodology called "benchmarking," the Citizens League of Greater Cleveland and its research arm, the Citizens League Research Institute, have been analyzing the performance of Greater Cleveland on measures ranging from health care to infrastructure. The League's Rating the Region study suggests that good information on strengths and weaknesses, coupled with honest dialogue among citizens and community leaders, can lead to smart regional solutions.

The following selection was written by Janis Purdy during her tenure as executive director of the Citizens League of Greater Cleveland, and by Michael Eugene during his tenure as project director at the Citizens League Research Institute.

Government and civic leaders across the country are talking about "the region" and the need to "think regionally." In Greater Cleveland, community leaders talk regularly about the importance of regional approaches to our future. Why is regionalism becoming such an important issue? Because our economic and social—and therefore political—problems, along with our population, are rapidly growing beyond traditional political boundaries.

Fifty years ago major problems such as air pollution, inadequate transportation systems, and lingering poverty would be addressed by one central city or county. Today, the dispersion of our urban populations means that many problems migrate across city, county, and sometimes state boundaries. Faced with increasingly complex problems, citizens of Greater Cleveland and other metropolitan areas are discovering that coordinated regional solutions are, in many cases, the only solutions.

The Citizens League of Greater Cleveland and the Citizens League Research Institute (CLRI) have been concerned with government and community governance since their founding in 1896. During the past decade we concluded that a regional focus is crucial to the future quality of life and economic competitiveness of our community. We believed we could contribute with the kind of useful, objective information that has been our hallmark for more than a century. CLRI's *Rating the Region* project was designed to accomplish this objective through an open, communitywide effort to identify actions that citizens and government leaders could take to improve our region's future.

Sound Decisions Need Good Information

Movement of people from the central city to the suburbs—outward migration—is a phenomenon occurring in many regions across the country. This dynamic has a significant impact on the physical, social, and economic character of a region, as well as on the connections citizens feel toward each other. In Northeast Ohio the 1990 U.S. Census documented the continuation of a forty-year decline in the city of Cleveland's population, from nearly one million to about five hundred thousand. Most of Cleveland's suburbs lost population as well. Cuyahoga County lost nearly 6 percent of its population during the 1980s, with almost eighty-seven thousand people moving to one of the six surrounding counties. Not only are people moving toward the outer edge of the region, many have left the region entirely. In fact, the region lost 3 percent of its population during the same time.

Citizens of Greater Cleveland are increasingly aware of the need to make decisions together if the region is to remain livable and to thrive. During the past six years, CLRI public opinion polls have found that a growing number of Greater Clevelanders are interested in finding regional solutions to our problems. In the 1996 CLRI Survey of Community Attitudes, residents were asked how decisions should be made by their local government leaders. Nearly three-quarters, 73 percent, of Cuyahoga County residents said that decisions should be based on "what is best for the entire Greater Cleveland area," as opposed to only 22 percent who wanted decisions based on "what is best for their city." Favoring cooperative solutions to regional problems grew as a favored approach since 1990, from 71 percent to 81 percent. Eighty-one percent of Cuyahoga County residents believed there should be "more opportunities for citizen involvement in problem-solving," up from 69 percent in 1990.

Citizens seem to recognize that, as people move out of the central city and suburbs incorporated earlier in this century, problems increasingly are not matched with political jurisdictions. It may be decades, if ever, before a regional political jurisdiction is created that is smaller than the state and larger than one county (although some regional services already have been "assigned" to special-purpose regional entities). Without a formal political structure to mandate responsibility for solving multijurisdictional problems, civic leaders and public officials in Northeast Ohio and elsewhere must tackle regional problems in creative and cooperative ways.

Social and economic problems and community priorities will differ from region to region. Because of this, solutions to problems must differ from region to region. Fortunately, ideas about programmatic solutions to regional problems are being shared through professional networks and national publications. The Portland, Oregon, region has become a model for effective regional land use planning. Minneapolis's use of tax-base sharing is frequently held out as an example of an innovative regional tax policy with an ability to draw economic resources back to the central core. But is Greater Cleveland ready for those approaches? In Cleveland the moral dimension of central city poverty is being addressed by the Catholic diocese through the efforts of Bishop Anthony Pilla. But would this approach work in another region without Pilla's dynamic leadership style?

Deciding what problems to tackle requires a thorough knowledge of where you are as a region and where you want to go as a community. Before regional leaders and citizens can import solutions from elsewhere they need to know if a solution fits the context of their region. But whatever the problem or approach, policymakers and civic leaders must start with good information.

A Case for Benchmarking the Region

When CLRI started its regional initiative in early 1993, we believed relevant performance measures and a system to monitor them would provide sound information with which to confront the issues facing Northeast Ohio. Performance measures provide facts to support a constructive dialogue about public policy goals and can be used to set common expectations among elected officials, government policymakers, civic leaders, and citizens about the steps required to meet agreed-upon objectives.

The project methodology for *Rating the Region* was modeled on the corporate management technique called "benchmarking." The goal of benchmarking is to determine why your competitors are ahead and then to learn how to improve your own performance by studying their circumstances and approaches. According to benchmarking advocates at the management consulting firm McKinsey and Company, "Competitive analysis is a powerful tool in formulating strategy. But while it can spot gaps between you and your competitor in cost, quality and timeliness, it usually does not provide a deep understanding of the processes and skills that create superior performance. Benchmarking, on the other hand, is a way to go backstage and watch a competitor's performance from the wings, where all the stage tricks and hurried realignments are visible. If the performance you choose to benchmark is world class, you will learn a lot about the art of management from this inside angle."

Applying this corporate approach to the social and economic problems of a metropolitan region proved to be a challenging task. It was a task bigger than just comparing Greater Cleveland to one or two other regions on a few randomly selected factors. In fact, one of our objectives was to counteract the dizzying array of one-factor studies of communities that declare someplace as "best place to live," with "most days of sunshine" or "least depressed people." Finding useful, comparative regional data was another factor that proved to be more difficult than expected. Conducting a community process—"bringing in the managers"—was time consuming, too. And the performance results were not all good news; our public presentation of negative indicators drew some heavy fire. However, corporate experience with thorough benchmarking prepared us for the work to be done and kept us focused and patient.

The four major steps in the benchmarking process adapted to our regional analysis were the following:

1. Selecting and compiling data to compare our region with our competitors

2. Identifying factors in which our region's performance leads and lags

3. Studying the gaps between our region and the "best-in-class" region to determine why it might be ahead

4. Developing recommendations and proposing changes for actions to "close the gap" between our region and the best-in-class performer

Benchmarking is a very useful tool for closing performance gaps. Benchmarking requires you to learn as much as possible about your competition and forces you to admit your true position relative to your competitors—even when it is not a pretty picture. Benchmarking reveals areas where you can improve and exposes areas where you can't, or shouldn't, try. For example, the unusually high number of winter freeze and thaw cycles on the shores of Lake Erie will always make pothole repair more expensive in Northeast Ohio than in other regions.

Benchmarking also forces you to measure outcomes—real results— rather than just taking the safer measure of inputs and convincing yourself that resources alone, like more staff or increased taxes, will get the job done. Finally, as a consensus process, benchmarking unifies expectations and builds buy-in among decision makers and managers responsible for future performance. It gives those with vested interests a common roadmap to follow.

Our benchmarking index contains indicators organized into nine issue topics. Rather than using single indicators or indices, we used several indicators to illuminate an issue. Using a cluster of indicators to measure an issue like health, for example, allows us to make a better assessment of the dynamics of that community issue. A cluster of measures gives a clearer picture than any one measure and makes it possible to examine their relationships.

In the health section, for example, the data shows that Greater Cleveland performs well on the availability of doctors. However, by using several indicators of health, we show that, while our region ranks comparatively high on the number of medical specialists, it ranks low on the number of general and family practitioners. Some experts express a concern about the lack of general practitioners, which can result in longer waiting periods for medical care or untreated illness, leading to costly advanced treatment.

An illustration from the 1997 report demonstrates how our data might be useful to policymakers and community leaders for establishing goals and deciding how resources should be spent. Education is one of the best predictors of future economic prosperity. Therefore the relatively low education attainment rate among Greater Clevelanders is a cause for concern. The Greater Cleveland region has one of the lowest college education attainment levels among the regions we studied. Only 19 percent of the area's adults have a four-year degree or higher, compared to 32 percent in best-in-class Austin, Texas. Experts explain that, since Greater Cleveland has an abundant supply of colleges and universities, the region must be exporting educated workers.

There is good news to be found upon further analysis, however. Examining one-year comparisons does not indicate the regional trends. Are we closing the gap, holding our own, or getting worse compared to the best-in-class performing region? By using benchmark trends for college education, we see that our region has made significant improvement since 1980. In Greater Cleveland the college-educated population has increased by 25 percent since 1980, while in Austin it only increased 14 percent. This suggests that the gap is closing.

Analysis of the data within each region produces additional interesting facts and suggests strategies appropriate for communities within the region. In Greater Cleveland we see that the highest concentration of adults with college degrees is in Geauga County. Lorain County is far below Austin or the regional median. But Lorain County community leaders should be pleased to note that their strategy to secure four-year degree programs for Lorain Community College is right on target. It will be interesting to see if future *Rating the Region* reports show Lorain County improving on this measure due to strategic planning and action by policymakers.

Regions differ in demographics, geographic size and location, culture, political systems, requirements of state law, government spending priorities, and more. Because of these differences, it may not be feasible for our region to close the gap with a best-in-class region in certain cases.

Educational attainment by region: 1990 census
(Percent of population with a four-year degree or higher)

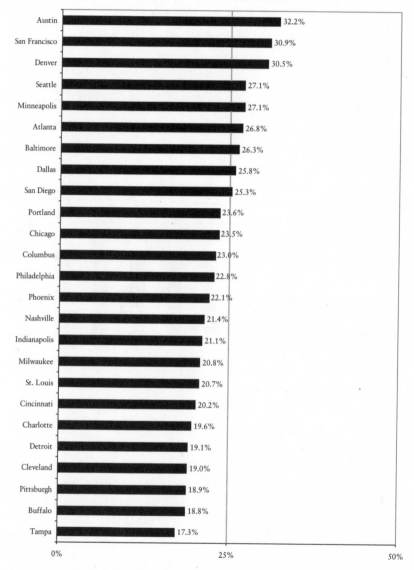

Region	Percent
Austin	32.2%
San Francisco	30.9%
Denver	30.5%
Seattle	27.1%
Minneapolis	27.1%
Atlanta	26.8%
Baltimore	26.3%
Dallas	25.8%
San Diego	25.3%
Portland	23.6%
Chicago	23.5%
Columbus	23.0%
Philadelphia	22.8%
Phoenix	22.1%
Nashville	21.4%
Indianapolis	21.1%
Milwaukee	20.8%
St. Louis	20.7%
Cincinnati	20.2%
Charlotte	19.6%
Detroit	19.1%
Cleveland	19.0%
Pittsburgh	18.9%
Buffalo	18.8%
Tampa	17.3%

Source: The Citizens League Research Institute (1991)

Figure 11.1. *Educational attainment by region: 1990 census*

For instance, there is a sizable gap between Cleveland and Chicago in the number of hotel rooms each region has available. During the five-year period from 1987 to 1992, Chicago built 13,340 new hotel rooms, for a total of 70,217, nearly as many as Cleveland had to begin with (13,462). The reason for this difference is the sheer size of Chicago's regional economy compared to our own.

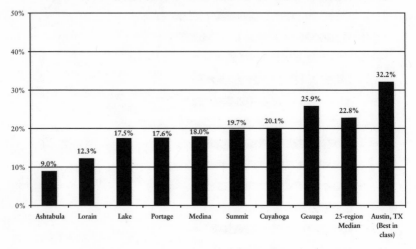

Educational attainment by county: 1990 census
(Percent of population with a four year degree or higher)

Figure 11.2. *Educational attainment by county: 1990 census*

Does this mean that we shouldn't make such comparisons? Some have argued that we shouldn't. But the fact that we'll never have as many hotel rooms as Chicago doesn't mean that Chicago has nothing to teach us about the development of a strong tourist industry.

Where Do We Go from Here?

It is a reality that regions compete for business investment and people. We constructed our *Rating the Region* index to show how the Greater Cleveland region compares to the regions with which we compete. Benchmarking is an evolving, fluid process. To do it right takes time, patience, and significant resources to collect data that will be meaningful. But bench-marking is about more than data. It is a process. And, the process part, the dialogue among citizens and community leaders, is as important as the data itself. Honest, open dialogue must be supported by good infor-mation and can yield the kind of strategies needed for communities to move forward.

There is new national attention being given to regional benchmark-ing and performance measurement. As a result, there is a greater willing-ness in many regions to share information. Data collection is becoming easier too. This side-by-side analysis with other metropolitan areas illu-minates the comparative peaks and valleys in our economic competitive-ness and quality of life and shows where efforts must be concentrated to address potential problem areas.

The Citizens League Research Institute intends to implement the final step in the benchmarking process, namely "proposing changes so we can take actions to close the gaps." CLRI will asses the potential problem areas that may call for further investigation and then perform a county-by-county analysis to learn the facts needed for good decision making. Only when we examine the region from the inside out can we truly under-stand what initiatives are needed, where resources must be focused, and how to convene local partners to collaborate on regional problem solving.

Urban affairs expert Neal Peirce wrote about our regional bench-marking project in one of his nationally syndicated columns. He stated, "to play the game, players need to know what their smart counterparts are doing across the continent. They need to have some notion of where they stand, where they're lagging, and where they want to go." More important, Peirce notes that American cities willing to undertake similar analysis move beyond mere competition and create a win-win situation as "more wealth and competence are built and the cumulative strength of American citistates rises in the global economy."

Chapter 12

Into the Future

Visions of Cleveland 2046

Sanda Kaufman and Wendy Kellogg*

A clear and broadly shared vision can be a powerful force for shaping a region's future. As part of Cleveland's bicentennial activites, a project began collecting vision statements from citizens about desired futures and strategies for achieving the desired outcomes. The diversity of responses illuminates the challenge of forging regional consensus, as well as the need for a common base of information about problems, solutions, and decision-making processes.

Sandra Kaufman is a professor and Wendy Kellogg is an associate professor at Cleveland State University's Levin College of Urban Affairs. Kaufman's research focuses on decision making and conflict management. Kellogg's current research investigates the role of community-based organizations and the use of information technologies in environmental problem solving.

We of today reach forth our hands across the gulf of a hundred years to clasp your hands. We make you heirs to all we have, and

* The authors thank Kathryn Wertheim Hexter and Allison Bach for assistance with this chapter.

enjoin you to improve your heritage. We bequeath to you a city of a century; prosperous and beautiful and yet far from our ideal.

—Mrs. Elroy M. Avery, chairman of the executive committee, Women's Department of Cleveland's First Centennial Commission

In recent years collective visioning has increasingly become part of community planning processes.[1] In all its variations, visioning is essentially the joint crafting of a scenario that participants find desirable for some specified space at some future time. It is used as a first step, especially in planning processes that actively involve those likely to be affected by the plans.[2]

One purpose of visioning is to fashion a common image for the future, behind which participants feel they can all rally. A shared vision can link residents with local government and other institutions, effectively joining disparate efforts in order to improve the community in a synergistic fashion.[3] For example, while urban sprawl has become a concern for the Cleveland region, numerous current initiatives to counter sprawl were operating almost independently, in some cases even duplicating efforts at great cost. Following a participatory project that forged a vision for the region, those involved in formerly disjointed efforts have begun to join forces, support each other, and avoid duplication.[4]

Another aim of visioning is to involve participants in setting long-range goals that meet the needs of all citizens in a community.[5] Forging such a public consensus, when possible, provides an incentive for politicians and bureaucrats to make decisions consistent with this consensus and implement them. These decision makers are otherwise frequently paralyzed into inaction by conflicting constituent demands. For example, Cleveland watched with dismay for some years as its downtown declined while decision makers hesitated between various showcase projects and investment in inner-city neighborhoods. A clear public mandate regarding the citizenry's attitude toward its least fortunate members living in the older neighborhoods might galvanize decision makers into action, knowing that the public stands behind them.

Some see visioning exercises as a revival of direct citizen participation in governance, according to a model where citizens become a deliberative body "created through a process of discussion, debate, and dialogue about current affairs."[6] This ongoing dialogue can be a vehicle enabling citizens to develop knowledge of each other's values and priorities. Some Remedial Action Plans (RAPs) addressing water quality problems around the Great Lakes have used visioning to such purposes.[7] If, according to Hansell, "Whether conscious of it or not, every community has a vision of its future," then, over time, such a dialogue might enable this vision to surface.[8]

When decision making by consensus is sought in public arenas, visioning helps begin an exchange of views among participants. However, this exchange needs to be developed and nurtured throughout the planning process, as choices become more specific, short-range, and likely to bring out differences. Again, RAPs offer examples: their implementation has proven quite a bit more difficult than the beginning stages, not least because short-range interests may have been affected in ways that long-range visions did not reflect.[9]

Visioning has become a common component of change initiatives, where the stakeholders affected by the change can be identified and invited to participate, and the spatial scope of the change can also be defined and incorporated into the vision. The ensuing participatory process poses numerous challenges, such as recruiting participants in a manner that represents the whole range of diverse interests affected, sustaining the participation in time, and adopting consensus-seeking processes that work for the resulting group. The wider the scope of change, the larger the core group of participants and the more difficult these challenges become. When, however, the physical scale of the affected space is that of a fairly large metropolitan area, such as Cleveland, or when instead of a specific change initiative the future itself is under consideration, visioning has to be adapted to these special circumstances.

In this chapter, we describe just such a special visioning effort for Cleveland. Its purpose was to elicit from citizens their expectations for the future, identifying shared interests as well as differences. The initiative also sought to encourage citizen participation in the shaping of a common future. However, in this case a key component of visioning—the active dialogue—is missing, because this project was of an exploratory rather than initiative-oriented nature. It sought to probe the level of consensus rather than foster it. Our strategy was to work toward the development of a metropolitan vision in steps that take into account the scale and complexity of this area. While an active, directly participatory process from the outset might be difficult to achieve, the information we have begun to collect can form the basis for the design of such a process in the future. We propose that such a strategy of visioning in stages can contribute to the implementation of a successful, fully participatory process of developing a vision for Cleveland and, more generally, for an area of similar scale. The vision statements and their analysis will constitute the beginning of building a record to the present for future generations who may look back at the path taken by the region. Thus the individual visions may become a valuable source of information for future reference and research.

Vision Quest 2046

The Cleveland Vision Quest 2046 took place in 1996 as part of the city's bicentennial celebration. It was an important part of the Bicentennial Symposium, a program organized through a partnership between the Levin College of Urban Affairs at Cleveland State University, the Citizens League, and the City Club.

What We Asked

Following Bishop Pilla's inspirational address (chap. 1), individuals from across the Cleveland metropolitan area were invited to respond to a survey in which they described their vision for Cleveland in the year 2046. The questions were designed to elicit information about the respondents' perceptions, values, and goals for the future. They also assessed the level of consensus among respondents regarding the following:

- The range of desirable futures, with their underlying core values and priorities
- Strategies and mechanisms for achieving the visions, reflecting the respondents' level of knowledge about the region's current issues
- Beliefs about who is responsible for the changes needed to attain the visions and about local public decision processes

    The vision survey was mailed to symposium attendees, planners, environmentalists, Citizens League members, Cooperative Extension agents in the region, members of the Catholic Commission on Community Action, and members of the Cleveland Bicentennial Commission. Vision surveys were also distributed to the Cleveland Public Libraries and were printed in local newspapers. Levin College students also had the opportunity to respond. All vision statements received are archived at the Western Reserve Historical Society.

The survey asked three open-ended questions:

1. What is your vision for the future of the city and the region?
2. What are the most critical actions that could be taken now to bring your vision to life?
3. Who must act and how?

The first question asked respondents to be dreamers, and the very words they would choose to describe Cleveland in 2046 could tell us what they value. The second question required respondents to connect their visions with the present, even if for the first question they took flights of fancy. It reminded them that they are contributors to the road from today to 2046, with the added difficulty that many may not be around to experience the outcomes they hoped to promote. The third question, atypical for visioning exercises in general, was posed to enable understanding of how respondents view themselves in the quagmire of present big and small decisions that will shape the Cleveland of 2046. Responses to each of the three visioning questions were analyzed.

Analysis of Responses

Fifty-five vision statements were received. A respondent profile was developed tabulating self-defined occupations, average age, and places of residence within the Cleveland area. The content of the responses to the three vision questions was analyzed to derive key ideas, areas of broad consensus or divergence, as well as the respondents' perceptions regarding public decision processes. For this purpose the handwritten responses were entered into a text database and searched by key words to gain an overall view of the participants' emphases. This initial search was followed with a round of content analysis of each complete statement to ascertain its tenor and to capture details. What follows is a summary of findings regarding respondents and their vision statements.

Who Answered: Respondent Characteristics

Visionaries, whose median age was about forty-two, were somewhat older than the general American population and the population living in the Cleveland metropolitan area (whose median age is thirty-four).[10] The group drew even numbers from the pool of represented occupations (table 12.2) as well as from the four key metropolitan locations—center, inner suburbs, outer suburbs, and exurban region (table 12.1).[11] Since respondents chose to participate rather than being selected to form a random sample, this even locational representation is surprising. In fact, the percentage of exurban respondents in our group is double the actual (10 percent rural) distribution of residences in greater Cleveland.

Table 12.1

Respondent place of residence

Location	Number
Cleveland	13
Inner suburb	16
Outer-ring suburb	9
Exurban region	11

The same cannot be said, however, for occupations: the respondents were predominantly white collar and highly educated (90 percent of those who gave their occupation have education beyond high school), well above the metropolitan rate of 44 percent, and therefore likely to exceed the median metropolitan income. This should not surprise us: participation in processes that give attention to civic issues, the future, and the quality of life can be more readily expected from those whose current needs are more amply satisfied and whose socioeconomic status affords enhanced access to information.

What They Said: Responses to Three Questions

Question: *What is your vision for the future of the city and the region?*

The first question asked respondents to imagine conditions fifty years ahead. The nonrestrictive wording of the question allowed respondents to

Table 12.2

Respondent occupations

Occupation	Number
Student	11
Architect/planner	5
Bureaucrat	2
Elected official	2
Attorney	3
Teacher	3
Other professional	5
Not-for-profit administrator	3
Business/corporate	4
Farmer	1
Retired	3

select the terms that define, for them, what is desirable with regard to a living environment. The words the respondents chose to describe Cleveland in 2046 reveal something about what they hold important and the values that shaped their responses, including justice, freedom, equality, sustainability, and the issues that prompted their most frequent concerns, including the economy, environmental quality, the size and type of settlement form, and current/future policies. From these vision statements, implied perceptions of processes and outcomes in the regional space were derived.

Answers implicitly contain individuals' perceptions of community and its physical and social boundaries. Therefore, the responses indicated whether respondents considered Cleveland mainly a physical space, a lifestyle, or a social environment. The visions could also reveal something about how people understand a span of fifty years: do they expect things to change as drastically, less, or more than in the past fifty years? Do they offer a vision that tinkers at the margin of the current situation, or do they take a flight of fancy? Do they perceive current societal ills to be stationary, to disappear on their own, or do they imagine some other new problems stemming from future science, technology, and societal changes?

These values are reflected in respondents' view of the present and future status of the region. A large measure of consensus was predicted, deriving not least from the broad terms the respondents were thought likely to use in formulating their visions. This expectation was based on an observed tendency for people to agree with positive and very general normative statements that provide for everyone without referring explicitly to any constraints or necessary tradeoffs and without implying any personal responsibility or requiring specific actions. This expectation was fulfilled to a large extent. Between one-quarter and almost one-half of the respondents mentioned three issues: social community, environment and its sustainability, and urban design or amenities (table 12.3). However, we found that overall responses fell into no fewer than nine broad categories of concerns.

Overall, while consensus may not be very apparent, there is not necessarily an incompatibility of values either. The pattern of responses merely suggests that respondents differed in their focus. Had they all been in one room working to hammer out a consensus, as is often the case in more traditional visioning, they would not necessarily have had substantive disagreements as much as differences over the salience of issues. Public participation efforts need awareness of such differences, which need to be reconciled if acute conflict over resources and their distribution is to be averted.

Surprisingly, eight of the fifty-five respondents offered negative visions of the Cleveland region in fifty years. Most often their pessimism stemmed from their belief that present-day trends and practices would continue. They clearly interpreted the question as an exercise in prediction (what will be) rather than wishful thinking (what should be).

Consensus among respondents was not as apparent as we predicted. The social community's well-being was the most frequently expressed value. Respondents mentioned the need for bonds between society members, for caring for those less fortunate, and for the building of a unified community despite present-day racial and economic disparities. One-sixth of the group mentioned race/ethnic relations. Healthy social bonds were often presented as a precondition for solving the economic and environmental ills of the region. One respondent believed the altruism Cleveland's residents have evinced in the past would also contribute to needed positive change in the future, saying:

Table 12.3

Expressed values

Issue	Number
Social community	21
Environment/sustainability	17
Urban design/amenities	14
Race/ethnic relations	9
Economic well-being	6
Political community	6
Personal qualities	5
Justice	2
Peace	1

Cleveland has always been a leader in many areas that have become models for our country. This has been possible because the city's residents have been able to resist the urge of being self-serving, and put the greater good of society before them.

Many of the respondents envisioned a society that, by 2046, will have resolved some of the racial discord they currently felt in Cleveland. One respondent stated:

The quality of life for the region will be determined by the quality of life in the urban Cleveland . . . and its neighborhoods. [In the future] Cleveland will be a vibrant city where people of diverse socioeconomic levels and ethnic backgrounds will appreciate each other.

Another respondent concurred :

For good or ill, my ideal Cleveland of the futures runs to the intangible qualities that, in my view, make a community great. Chief among these is, in fact, a real sense of community; a sufficiently shared spirit of appreciation and aspiration that enables forward progress . . . Such a sense of community demands celebration of our diversity without permitting it to be divisive. It requires a broadly based effort to maintain communication between all sectors of the community, for dialogue is the foundation for any form of partnership or common action.

One respondent envisioned a society that will have resolved some of the physical and psychological separation between the central city and suburbs:

Cleveland has the largest number of ethnic groups of a United States major city. Respect within a pluralistic society cannot be accomplished if each ethnic group lives in its own "ghetto" area and does not mix with others on the grounds of mutual respect. My vision for the future of the city and region is to accomplish interrelations of ethnic groups . . . The heart of Cleveland proper has overcome ethnic, economic and religious barriers, but not the suburbs.

Respondents' emphasis on ten categories of problematic areas that need resolution by 2046 differed somewhat from the values they said they held. Here consensus was more pronounced, with half of the categories mentioned by a third of more of the respondents (table 12.4). This suggests the respondent group could reach agreement about the priority ranking of a handful of issues.

Two-thirds of the respondents identified Cleveland's economy as a concern. Transportation, a distant second, was identified by half of the respondents. Quality of life, education and schools, and the environment got roughly equal billing from more than a third of respondents. Vision writers offered great detail, especially in their predictions, and that is where and why they diverged.

Many residents emphasized the need or hope for a fully integrated regional economy. They envisioned a high-tech revolution bringing jobs to Cleveland, a highly skilled labor force to work in new industries, and a stable economy that would bring jobs back into the city. A few respondents, on the contrary, anticipated a region that would fail to address poverty and jobs at its physical core, further exacerbating the region's "economic polarization." One respondent even predicted that a more regional economy would foster in the population an attitude "less oriented with neighborhoods, family, and culture."

Table 12.4

Expressed concerns

Issue	Number
Economy	38
Transportation	27
Amenities/quality of life	21
Education/schools	21
Environment	20
Social relations	16
Housing	12
Settlement/population location (sprawl)	11
Nontransportation infrastraucture	7
Government politics	5

What to make of the divergent views of the economic future of Cleveland? Although, in general, individuals have great difficulty deciding on the value of events and outcomes in the distant future, which they tend to overdiscount, economic concerns may be the easiest to project because they loom so large in the present. And since a discussion of the present, including causes and solutions, can get quite heated in any group, these differences persist with regard to the year 2046. Moreover, since people tend to view the current economic system as near-immutable, they may not consider it as open to questions or to change, even over fifty years. Not so technology, which many expect to change rapidly and to amaze them at every turn. So while people might readily agree that technology will make great strides in the next fifty years, they tend to expect more of the same from the workings of the economy, over which they tend to disagree in the future, as in the present.

The spreading of settlements into the countryside was a concern—in terms of consequences for both the transportation system and the environment. Respondents expressed the hope that a more useful public transit system would reduce the need for roads to be built into the country- side. However, many anticipated a continuation of the outward pattern of set- tlements due to economic development in the suburbs and were concerned over the ensuing expansion of the road network away from the city center. Here is how one resident expressed this:

> It still all comes down to urban sprawl. I visualize this present- day amorphous blob that's existed for a long time, but which is lately being brought a little more under control. The energy which drives this blob is a combination of all human beings going about their daily routines: people are working and play- ing, they are going to and from their homes, and they are mov- ing to new homes . . . this blob gobbles up undeveloped rural areas.

Amenities and a good quality of life ranked high with the respon- dents. Clevelanders wished for better and more green space, better hous- ing, bicycle lands and paths, walkable streets, and good schools. One rather disheartened resident stated:

> I see the city of Cleveland and possibly the majority of Cuyahoga County experiencing a long, slow, expensive death, unless these communities bring the quality of life up to a livable standard.

Derived Perceptions

The intent was to derive from the vision statements the respondents' implicit sense of community. This task was quite difficult, because respon- dents were not asked to be specific about what they meant by community. Respondents conceptualized their community and its geographic extent in a variety of ways. Some constituted their "community" in terms of neigh- borhoods, but they meant mostly someone else's, not their own. Others identified it with the city of Cleveland, the inner city, downtown, the sub- urbs, the inner-ring suburbs, the region, the bioregion, the metropolitan region, the six-county region, or Northeast Ohio. Several respondents focused on small-scale geographies, such as their neighborhood. Such a wide variety of scales and locations might indicate a fragmented sense of community space among residents. More often, however, respondents linked their welfare, and that of their neighborhood or municipality, with the welfare of the region as a whole.

These perceptions matter in several ways. They help explain people's individual choices of place and lifestyle. They also help understand when, why, and to what extent people can be expected to participate in decisions affecting their physical space.

Question: *What are the most critical actions that could be taken now to bring your vision to life?*

Answers to the second question can tell us more about the respondents' awareness of Cleveland's current problems and assets, although these were not far from people's minds even as they answered Question 1, which looked to the future. On the other hand, here too there was still room for dreaming, since the question did not restrict respondents to any particular realm, whether social, political, economic, or technological. Therefore respondents' choices reflect either their faith in various instruments of change or their perception of how reality operates.

Wide variation was expected in response to this question, not necessarily reflecting lack of consensus but rather a differential salience of issues among individuals. Variety is actually desirable in this case, since it is likely that solutions to the problems of a region should be responsive to a wide variety of specific conditions: the more, the better. The narratives themselves converged much more than might be inferred from table 12.5, which lists key suggestions covering a wide range. Respondents reiterated values, yet it was difficult to separate issues from values, the present from the future, and solutions from those who should implement them. This may be related to the overwhelming complexity of problems posed by a relatively large region.

The most frequently offered prescription for improving the region was enhanced access to education, both for adults and school-age children (see table 12.5). Many saw a good education as one of the essential components of a "good quality of life." Respondents advocated "raising the standards of education" as a vehicle for transforming the region from a member of the Rust Belt to a high-tech economy requiring a highly skilled workforce. In one respondent's words:

Education has to be addressed. The future is determined by the seeds we plant today. In this regard the Cleveland city schools

(and many suburban districts) are a complete and total failure . . .
a school system in collapse. If Cleveland is to succeed in the
future, the school system has to be made to be effective. A more
educated work force is what is required for the jobs in the next
century . . . The days of the mindless assembly job are fast coming to a close.

Respondents advocated reforming the school system and offering
parents greater choice of schools. Some wished for "completely new"
approaches to education, such as privatization of the school system or
strong participation by Cleveland's business community. One respondent
stressed the relationship between schools and family:

> The schools will have to be restructured to provide schooling
> for those that value education. Society must stop imposing fam-
> ily responsibilities on the school system. Let schools dedicate
> themselves to teaching academic subjects and not burden them
> with trying to correct the social ills of society.

Some respondents proposed stronger ties between city and suburban
schools. Others linked the decline of the city's schools to urban sprawl,
which caused property tax revenues to fall as the middle class moved out of
the city. To these respondents, preventing urban sprawl is key to the revitalization of the city's school systems and of the metropolitan region's core.

Many respondents observed that the region's residents themselves
could use more education about the region's problems. They hoped the
electronic media, including the rapidly expanding Internet, would become
a vehicle for adult education.

In connection with the next three most frequent responses—public
transit, sprawl, and land use—respondents emphasized the need for greater
efficiency in the use of such resources as energy and land, which are believed
to be negatively affected by the expanding physical extent of the city.

It is noteworthy that this question brought out not only a variety of
issues but also a wide range of levels of detail, including some broad suggestions for improvement as well as references to specific systems believed
to be key in bringing about the desired future. While education, transportation, urban sprawl, affordable housing, and governance top the list, some
of these are problems and others are solutions; some look to the commu-

nity to pull itself together, while others reflect a belief in government intervention; some are microlevel wishes for bike paths, while others are general
exhortations to public participation or the use of political measures.

Table 12.5

Actions needed

Proposed actions	Number
Stress education/improve schools	15
Provide public transportation/cut down on roads	9
Curtail sprawl	8
Support sustainable land uses/zoning	8
Provide affordable housing	7
Engage in cooperation/collaboration	7
Institute regional government	6
Use fiscal measures	5
Encourage economic development	5
Provide recreation/bike paths	3
Encourage regional planning	3
Encourage public participation	3
Protect the environment	2
Be judicious with infrastructure building/maintenance	2
Use political measures	1
Form public-private partnerships	1

A more directive formulation of Question 2 would undoubtedly have
elicited responses at a more even level of specificity. However, any insight
into the degree of salience of the issues to the respondents would have
been lost. For example, as expected, the frequently invisible infrastructure
got two mentions, although it is arguably central to any calls for curtail-
ing urban sprawl, enhancing environmental quality, and using resources
judiciously. In contrast, since education woes have dominated the local
news for some time, it turned out to be the most salient to respondents,

suggesting that media could play an important role in people's awareness of issues, problems, processes, and solutions. So, for example, if urban sprawl or infrastructure issues had had press exposure comparable to the coverage of Cleveland schools, respondents might have recognized them, too, as playing an important role in the region's future.

This finding suggests the media bears a measure of responsibility for the degree of salience of regional issues in the minds of citizens. Therefore, it is incumbent on key regional media to keep the public informed of issues and initiatives, even if such topics are not considered "newsworthy." The reverse of this coin is that individuals and organizations who engage in activities with consequences for the future of the regional space should be proactive in recruiting and using the media to inform the public.

Question: *Who must act and how?*

Answers to this question reveal something about what Clevelanders think shapes the environment and the urban community in which they live. Responses, derived from mental models of how the decision systems work and how long it takes to accomplish changes, reflect perceptions of power (who is responsible) and of the power to make changes: How do they perceive that decisions are made? Who has the power and authority to effect change?

Not surprisingly, this question elicited the most variety of responses (table 12.6). Quite a few respondents emphasized individuals taking responsibility for decisions and actions, as, for example, in this response:

> Democracy is only possible and effective on the neighborhood level. We all need to help coordinate individual neighborhoods efforts to create regional policies. We all need to act.

Or:

> There is a role to play for all of us—non-profits, churches, governments, civic organizations, and the business community . . . Each one of us can be a leader for a greater Cleveland.

At times, the individual's task seems imposed from above by institutional failure. As one respondent said:

Government, corporations, and labor all have powerful roles; but only many private citizens with the courage to support "community" can overcome the hatreds and greeds that arise from economic polarization.

Table 12.6

Who needs to act?

Category	Decision makers
Individuals	Citizens Families/parents
Communal entities	Neighborhoods Local communities
Private sector	Corporations/businesses Labor
Public sector	Schools Political leaders Local government Regional government/NOACA County government State government Federal government
Nonprofit sector	Nongovernmental organizations Churches Universities/colleges

To some extent, respondents put the burden of action largely on the shoulders of various government levels, and they have high expectations for governmental processes. One respondent advised:

The government should remove all special privileges of race. If we can look past the past to the future we will all be better off. We should all do our part to end all racism be it black or white, white to black, red to yellow, or purple to plaid.

Another declared:

The government should reward accomplishment.

And, covering the whole spectrum:

> The governor, to declare an immediate moratorium on building
> in rural areas, to contain urban sprawl; regulators to establish
> zero-discharge criteria; colleges, universities and research facili-
> ties to research and develop sustainable methods to meet zero-
> discharge standards; solid waste specialists to turn "waste" into
> resources, composting (including sewage) and recycling; faith
> leaders to call their communities to active witness in the daily
> liturgy of the world; individuals to be willing to charge artists
> and poets to help us to create visions and dreams, to articulate
> them, and to energize their realization.

Some pointed out the difficulty for individuals in making the changes
they desired. One respondent explained:

> Individuals must act, but when their most precious resource,
> time, is being utilized by driving, it's difficult. Make a 1 mile
> buffer zone around the Emerald Necklace [Metroparks system]
> and create an urban growth boundary. Create communal com-
> munities where DINKS [double-income, no kids] and people with
> children and single individuals with no kids can live together
> and provide communal nurturing.

The frequently proposed loci of responsibility for change seem predominantly institutional, mostly vague but sometimes quite precise. For
example:

> [T]here should be a comprehensive plan, or some kind of
> public plan, that is done every five years. All five counties [in
> greater Cleveland] should be working together to improve
> this area. The planners and the government should cut out
> some of the red tape to help to improve the bad areas of the
> city in a more timely manner. The business community should
> have to allocate some of their money toward residential com-
> munity improvement. With Gateway, The Rock 'n Roll Hall
> of Fame, The Science Museum, and the rest of the newly built
> businesses, some allotment of monies should go the less fortu-

nate, like the city schools, the homeless, the lower income people, etc.

And:

> In order to put this in place, a group has to be formed compara-
> ble to the Cleveland Civic Vision 2000 Group. This group has
> to consist of the leaders of the political parties, of the Greater
> Cleveland Growth Association, of NOACA, of Citizens League
> Research Institute, of the Levin College of Urban Affairs, and of
> representatives from the mayors and managers. This should be
> at least a five-county group.

Another suggestion was that letting things happen will result in desirable change: "Let sprawl choke itself off." Or, "Hope: the highest degree of well-founded expectations of good."

Such perceptions have important consequences for the nature and level of public participation one can expect. Citizens who feel powerless to bring about a desired future may become embittered or complacent, while those whose understanding of decision processes is deeper might perceive opportunities for partnership and might also take more personal responsibility for reaching their vision.

Others mistrust government and expect leadership for change to come from the grassroots:

> We not only have rights, but we have responsibilities. If our
> political process is jeopardizing our future, then we have a right
> to change it. Similarly, if apathy is allowing corrupt politicians
> to "have their way," we have a responsibility to vote, write,
> visit, protest, prosecute, or do almost whatever it takes to man-
> date change.

And:

> While my eco-city proposals are legislative, I do not trust legisla-
> tors to act upon them. Government today seems incapable of
> judging the cost-effectiveness of public spending or appreciating
> the natural forces such spending tries to influence. As a result, any

problem government touches—the economy, education, health care, poverty or land use—only gets worse. I don't think this happens because people in government are bad. Rather, I believe that the political process itself, despite even the best intentions, simply cannot make good decisions as individual adults. Therefore, it is up to the citizens of Cleveland and Northeast Ohio to build an eco-city.

What stands out in this collection of responses is their diversity. One cannot help but wonder how difficult it would be to get this group of only fifty-five citizens to agree on a plan of action. How much more difficult would it be to rally a region around a set of leaders and actions? What should be the vehicles for enabling consensus? We believe one key to regional consensus and resolve to act is an accessible, common base of shared information about problems, needs, innovative solutions, and successful practices, as well as about the decision processes themselves. Since there is sufficient room for disagreement over goals and means to reach them, we propose that, in order to avoid action paralysis, we need a regional information base and a set of innovative dissemination vehicles to draw the citizenry into informed action.[12]

Concluding Remarks

What We Can Learn

Visioning outcomes are instructive in several ways. The community at large and its decision makers obtain a snapshot of current thought on issues about which people care. Some of the strategies proposed reflect fresh thinking and ideas worthy of consideration. Everyone can gain some understanding about how empowered people feel to shape their living environment. One added goal of the exercise was to assess areas in which greater Cleveland residents might need information in order to become effective at participating and guiding political action. It was seen as a first step in a long-range project of tall order: providing the Cleveland citizenry with the access to information and the level of education necessary to become effective decision partners in bringing about the city of their dreams in 2046.

Information in a broad range of categories relevant to planning and decision making is accruing at a rapid pace, compared to even the recent past. However, this does not mean that the information is easily accessible or immediately useful to citizens, even to those highly motivated to participate and shoulder their responsibilities for the future. Access to information requires resources that are not always available to the citizenry, whether for purposes of acquiring data, computer hardware and software, or the training necessary to understand raw data and processed information. Information producers also face a dearth of resources for data collection and analysis. Therefore, the area of intelligent information dissemination, the key link between producers and users of information, is often neglected.

Intelligent information dissemination should become a tautology, but is still rather far from this target. Information that is produced with great effort but does not reach those who can benefit from it has not been intelligently disseminated. It would seem, therefore, that intelligent dissemination is all in the hands of information producers. This is partially correct: producers should indeed make greater efforts in several areas that would drastically improve the quality of dissemination. They should develop sufficient interaction with their peer community and with lay users to understand their needs and incorporate their knowledge in new developments. They should also explore new means of expressing their findings in ways that make the best of new technologies of visualization and interactive computer software, to increase the lay public's accessibility to information with high technical content.

The producer-user link is not unidirectional, however. Users, too, need to increase their effort to access information and incorporate it into their decisions. They can demand that public resources be allocated to education, to the acquisition of publicly accessible computer hardware and software, and even to the development of technical interpreters who could assist citizens in accessing information relevant to their problems. Information users can also cultivate relationships with information producers that enable them to communicate their knowledge and needs, actively helping the goal of intelligent dissemination.

The visioning exercise was expected to yield some useful knowledge regarding the need to foster intelligent information dissemination. A more extensive exercise of this kind, reaching a larger number of respondents, might not only improve the assessment in that regard but also serve the purpose of alerting the respondents themselves to the need for access to information.

What Next?

Atypical as this exercise was, it shared one characteristic with the more usual visioning processes: it was a learning experience both for those who asked and for those who responded. Those who asked learned about some dreams, some images, and some special knowledge of Cleveland. Those who responded may have learned that the future begins now, so that in order to reach a vision one has to know how public decisions are made, how to influence them, and how to do one's part in shouldering the responsibility for the future. While it would be difficult to claim that in the absence of this project respondents would not have reflected on these issues, it seems likely that they took this opportunity to focus on Cleveland's future and to express in a wide forum ideas they might otherwise never have shared.

Notes

1. W. Hansell, "A Common Vision for the Future: The Role of Local Government and Citizens in a Democratic Process," *National Civic Review* 85, no 3 (fall 1996): 5-13.

2. Steven C. Ames, ed., *A Guide to Community Visioning: Hands-On Information for Local Communities* (Portland, Oreg.: American Planning Association, 1993).

3. W. Potapchuk, "Building Sustainable Community Politics: Synergizing Participatory, Institutional and Representative Democracy," *National Civic Review* 85, no 3 (fall 1996): 54-59.

4. S. Kaufman and K. Snape, "Public Attitudes toward Urban Infrastructure: The Northeast Ohio Experience," *Public Works Management and Policy* 1, no. 3 (1997): 224-44.

5. W. Klein, "Visions of Things to Come," *APA Planning Magazine* 59 (May 1993): 11.

6. Hansell, "A Common Vision for the Future."

7. W. Kellogg, "Ecology and Community in the Great Lakes Basin: The Role of Citizen Advisory Committees in Environmental Planning Processes" (Ph.D. diss., Cornell University, 1993).

8. Hansell, "A Common Vision for the Future," 9.

9. Kellogg, "Ecology and Community in the Great Lakes Basin."

10. U.S. Bureau of the Census, 1990. Census of Population and Housing (Washington, D.C.: U.S. Department of Commerce).

11. Chi square tests of respondents' occupations and locations frequencies show consistence with a uniform distribution in both cases. The chi square test was performed with the list of occupations found in the sample, which are evenly represented but do not span the breadth of metropolitan occupations.

12. L. Susskind and J. Cruikshank, *Breaking the Impasse* (New York: Basic Books, 1987).

Conclusion

A Regional Civic Vision

David C. Sweet

This book emerged from a conference celebrating the bicentennial of Cleveland. It reflects on Cleveland's past, its dramatic attempt to recover from the decline experienced in the 1960s and 1970s, and the comeback it achieved in the 1980s and 1990s. However, as documented, the city continues to confront major challenges as it enters the new millennium. The question raised is, "What are the major challenges and how best to address them?"

In 1982 the Levin College convened the "Cities Congress on Roads to Recovery," where major cities in the United States that had lost population in the prior decade came together to share success stories for addressing this urban decline. The city of Cleveland followed the advice of the conference's keynote speaker, James Rouse, and developed a civic vision. The vision was a plan for the city's downtown and neighborhoods. As one drives through the city, now entering its third century, evidence abounds of the success of the vision and plan. There is new investment, vitality, and activity in the downtown, new housing in the neighborhoods, and yet problems remain.

The comeback of Cleveland has been held out as a model of an older, mature, industrial city successfully transforming itself through public/private partnerships into a "new" city. A city has "recovered," to restate Paul Porter's definition, when it is able to compete with the suburbs as a place to live, to reestablish a favorable climate for investment and the resulting growth of jobs, and to regain independence from massive external subsidies.

But as the New American City looks to the future, it finds that many of the problems that remain are the result of forces that lie outside of its municipal boundary. David Rusk describes the challenge of trying to confront the local problems with local solutions as running up an increasingly faster-moving down escalator. In other words, for the New American Cities such as Cleveland to effectively confront the future, they must look beyond their political boundaries and engage the region of which they are a part.

While the economic importance of the metropolitan region and the interdependence of the central city and suburbs have been well established in the academic literature, it is only recently that this message has been communicated to a broader audience through the writings of authors such as Neal Peirce, David Rusk, and David Beach, as well as through research by Tom Bier and others.

Academics and planners have long held that at the heart of the decline of many mature cities has been the ever-increasing sprawl of population across the metropolitan region's landscape. Those that can, move out. The result is an ever-increasing concentration of low income and minorities in the core city and declining tax base. For example, in the last three decades Ohio's urban land use increased at five times the rate of the state's population growth.

In the early 1970s, a series of reports was prepared by the state development department entitled "Ohio 2000: Choices for Today" that focused on land use development trends and called for more effective regional planning to offset the problems associated with urban sprawl. As in many states, these recommendations lacked broad support or a political constituency and little was done. Now, twenty-five years later, as illustrated in the chapters of this book, new constituencies have emerged.

To quote Neal Peirce, "the sprawl issue is in." Richard Moe, president of the National Trust for Historic Preservation, optimistically suggests that "sprawl is about to explode onto the American scene—moving up on the political agenda." Vice President Gore, in remarks delivered at the Brookings Institution on September 2, 1998, demonstrated a keen awareness of the policies and programs of the federal government that reinforced sprawl and called for a series of actions to foster smarter growth. A growing number of state governors are taking on the issue. Neal Peirce reports that eleven governors made a point of land use issues in their 1998 state of the state addresses.

What then of Cleveland and Ohio? As the New American City faces its regional future, what steps must be taken? Is anything different from a quarter century ago when similar calls were made to address the sprawl issue in Ohio? The answer is "yes." There is a growing and diverse set of constituencies that is calling for action. The emergence of Bishop Anthony M. Pilla leading the discussions surrounding "The Church in the City" is most encouraging. The report by the Ohio Farmland Preservation Task Force appointed by Gov. George Voinovich documents the concerns and offers recommendations of "voluntary" policies and programs to preserve farmland and open space, which is the flip side of the coin of urban sprawl. For the first time, there is a potential alliance between the central city and the rural areas in putting forth an agenda that addresses their common concerns. Another constituency that is becoming vocal is elected officials representing the mature suburbs adjacent to the core city, who have developed a smart growth agenda. The First Suburbs Consortium of Ohio has recently been established and represents twenty-six fully developed communities across Ohio with a combined population of nearly seven hundred thousand.

Co-editor David Beach has developed, in conjunction with the American Planning Association, a smart growth agenda for Ohio. The agenda is being circulated widely and seeks to gain leadership from Ohio's newly elected Gov. Bob Taft to address the critical role the state must play in addressing the sprawl issue.

Therefore as Cleveland enters its third century, there are continuing forces at work that can undermine the comeback. But there are also actions being proposed at the federal and state levels and alliances being formed to assist major cities of the state in addressing their futures.

The central city, first-ring suburbs, and the rural areas of the region must come together to form new partnerships and develop a plan for growth that seeks to further rebuild the core city, maintain the older suburbs, and preserve rural areas. If Jim Rouse were to return he most likely would suggest the time is now right for government, business, and neighborhood leaders, as well as elected representatives of the suburban and rural areas of the region, to come together and develop a vision of their future, a regional civic vision. It worked in the past; it can work in the future.

About the Editors

DAVID C. SWEET has gained national recognition for his work in economic development and building university-community partnerships, with a career that spans leadership roles in higher education, government, and research. Dr. Sweet currently serves as dean and professor of the Levin College of Urban Affairs at Cleveland State University. The College serves as a nationally ranked model for linking the resources of an urban university to the problems and opportunities confronting major urban centers. Dr. Sweet also serves as chair of the Ohio Board of Regents' Urban University Program. Previously, Dr. Sweet served as Director of the Ohio Department of Development and Commissioner of the Ohio Public Utilities Commission.

Dr. Sweet was recently recognized by his peers with his election as a Fellow of the National Academy of Public Administration. He holds a Ph.D. from The Ohio State University, an M.A. from the University of North Carolina–Chapel Hill, and a B.A. from the University of Rochester.

KATHRYN WERTHEIM HEXTER is director of the Ohio Urban University Program (UUP) at the Levin College of Urban Affairs, Cleveland State University. The UUP is a statewide network linking the resources of Ohio's eight urban universities to improve the state's urban regions. She joined the College in 1989 as project manager in The Urban Center. A public policy analyst, Hexter has managed program evaluations and projects on low-income energy assistance, housing policy, and neighborhood development. She has worked with governmental, philanthropic, and nonprofit organizations. With David C. Sweet, she is co-author of the book *Public Utilities and the Poor: Rights and Responsibilities*.

Prior to joining Cleveland State, Hexter worked in corporate giving, community and governmental relations at the East Ohio Gas Company. She has a bachelor's degree from Washington University in St. Louis and a master's in city and regional planning from Harvard University.

DAVID BEACH is the founder and director of EcoCity Cleveland, a non-profit environmental planning organization that promotes a regional vision of ecological cities existing in balance with their surrounding countryside. He edits the organization's award-winning *EcoCity Cleveland Journal*, which provides coverage of land use trends, transportation planning, and environmental issues in Northeast Ohio. In 1996, Beach edited EcoCity's book, *Moving to Corn Fields: A Reader on Urban Sprawl and the Regional Future of Northeast Ohio*. And, in 1998, he collected his writings about environmental and urban issues, along with selections from other environmental experts, in a comprehensive guidebook, *The Greater Cleveland Environment Book*.

Beach has been a prominent writer, editor, and community activist in Cleveland for the past twenty years. He speaks frequently on bioregional sustainability, urban sprawl, and transportation planning to community groups and university classes. He has a bachelor's degree from Harvard University.

Index

X0122471 2